MW01625938

July 11, 2007

Dear Holly,

It's with sincere pleasure that I give to you one of my favorite books. Every time I use it, I can't help but think of you as you think and live its philosophy.

Happy, Happy Birthday, dear astrology sister!

May we always be in touch in at least one realm at all times.

Love,

Eileen

Evolutionary Astrology

The Journey of the Soul Through States of Consciousness

This is a special
Limited Edition

Number____________

Evolutionary Astrology

The Journey of the Soul Through States of Consciousness

Raymond A. Merriman

Seek-It Publications W. Bloomfield, MI

Published in the United States by Seek-It Publications/MMA Inc.,
W. Bloomfield, Michigan

ISBN 0-930706-18-8

Manufactured in The United States of America

Cover design by Howard Weingarden

Charts provided by Astro Communications Services, San Diego,
CA.

Dedication

This book is dedicated to those
who love astrology,
who stand in awe
at the power and beauty which its symbolism imparts,
who seek insight
with an open mind and compassionate heart.

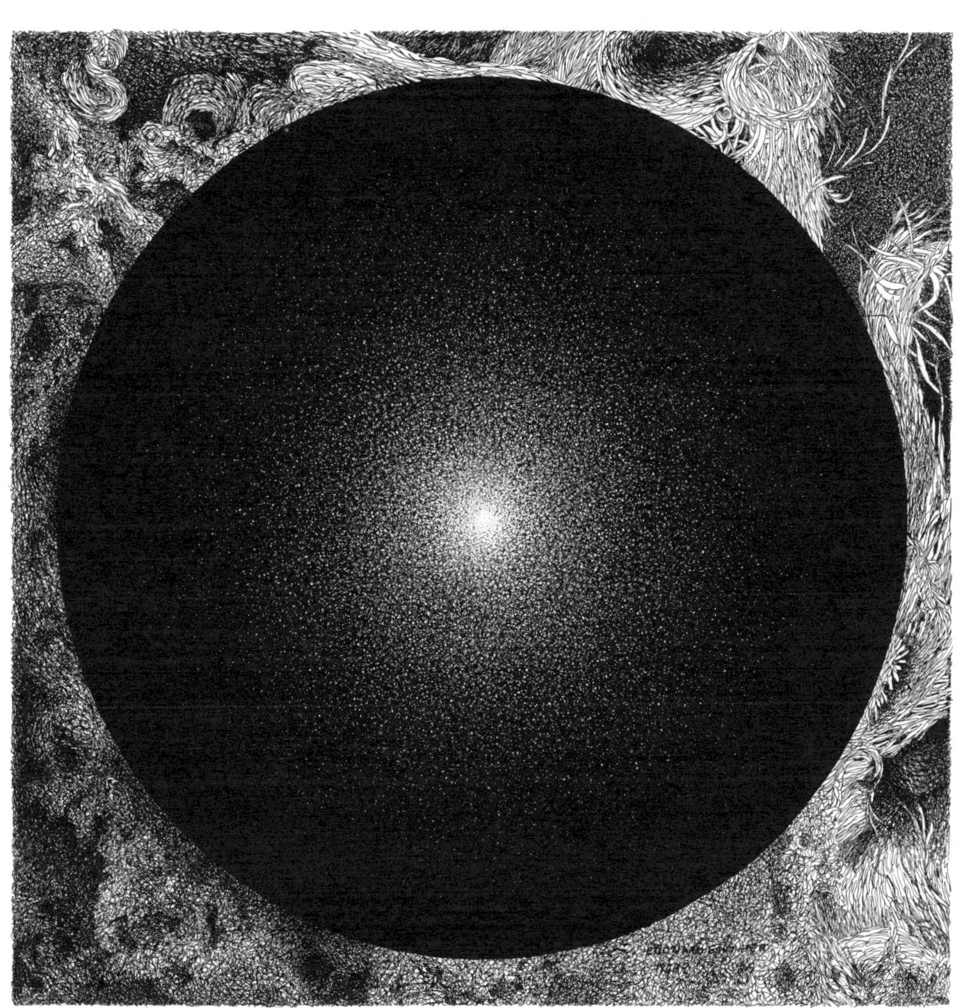

"The distinctive question for man is:
Is he related to something infinite or not?
That is the telling question of his life."

– Carl Jung (1875–1961)

Acknowledgments

I would like to acknowledge the following people for their help in the creation of this book.

The first is John and Gayle MacNair of Malibu, California. In 1974, when I sought a place of inspiration to write my first ideas on Evolutionary Astrology, they were generous enough to extend to me the use of their home. With a great deal of kindness and compassion, they allowed me to become a member of their family. In addition, they were always receptive to listening and commenting on the ideas I was in process of developing. This helped me to formulate these ideas in a clearer manner. For this, I will always be greatful.

I would also like to acknowledge the 50 students who participated in the special six-week class on Evolutionary Astrology, which was conducted Thursday evenings between March 21–April 25, 1991. It was the first class I had presented in several years, and their support and feedback played a very helpful and inspiring role in the completion of this work. The nature of their questions helped shape new ideas presented herein.

And finally I would like to thank Joan Nardi, one of the students in that class who is also a school teacher, for her help in editing this book. Her task was not easy, yet her skills are considerable, and for this I am also grateful.

Table of Contents

PART ONE
Principles and Models of Evolutionary Astrology

PART TWO
The Nature of the Incarnating Soul

PART THREE
The Potential Blossoming of the Incarnating Soul

PART FOUR
Evolutionary Phases of the Collective

Artists and Plates

Cover Design:	Series: *Time and the Eternal Now* Opus 7 "A Matter of Priorities"...	Howard Weingarden
Frontpiece:	"The Continuum of Infinite Origins"...	Edouard Gauthier
Part One:	Series: *Time and the Eternal Now* Opus 2 "The Path Through The Worlds"...	Howard Weingarden
Part Two:	"Reverence and the Illusion of Caprice"...	Howard Weingarden
Part Three:	Series: *Time and the Eternal Now* Opus 2 "Reawakening the Future"...	Howard Weingarden
Part Four:	Series: *Time and the Eternal Now* Opus 7 "Dance of the Stars"...	Howard Weingarden

A Note About This Book

In December, 1977, 1440 copies of *Evolutionary Astrology: The Journey of the Soul Through the Horoscope* were printed. The book was entirely handwritten and contained some of the plates that appear in the hardbound edition of this printing.

That first book on Evolutionary Astrology sold out within two years. Requests for a reprinting have been numerous throughout the years. I always knew that if it was reprinted, it would have to be typeset so as to preserve the uniqueness of the first edition, which has since become a valuable collector's item.

Reading through the original work, I realized what an enormous editing task would be required. Nevertheless, knowing that nothing gets accomplished unless it is first started, I measured up to the task. In the process of editing, however, a flood of new ideas began to take form. After weeks of working on the "old" version, I began to visualize a "new" version of the book. Now I was truly trapped: how could *Evolutionary Astrology: The Journey of the Soul Through the Horoscope* be made available for print again, when the ideas expressed in the original work had been expanded after nearly twenty years? (Even though the book was not published until late, 1977, it had been written in 1973–74).

The only rational solution seemed to be the creation of a book which contained the vital parts of the first writing, combined with new concepts generated in the intervening years. In this manner, the reader who wished the information contained in the earlier work would not be deprived. On the other hand, one who wished to see a progression of those original ideas would also be accomodated. The result is this book, *Evolutionary Astrology: The Journey of the Soul Through States of Consciousness*. As the new title suggests, the material in this latest book has a great deal to do with understanding the changing states of one's consciousness, an ultimate consequence for one who embarks upon a spiritual journey.

Several chapters of the original book have been left basically intact, except for minor editing. These include chapters 1–3, 6, 9, and 12–13. Chapters 4–5, 7, and 14 were also part of the original book on Evolutionary Astrology. However, the changes in these chapters are more considerable than just minor. All other chapters represent entirely new material, the result of half a lifetime of new experiences.

Due to this unorthodox approach to publishing, the reader may very well note a marked difference in style throughout the work. Some of the ideas and styles may seem "younger" than other parts of the book. This may be due to the fact that the chapters carried over from the original book were written when I was in my mid-twenties. The newer material was written as I entered my mid-forties. A man of forty-four years of experience thinks and writes differently than one who is nearly half that age.

In a sense, the decision to publish the book in this manner shows the effect of my own evolution in action. I hope the reader appreciates this effort to combine the "old" with the "new".

Raymond A. Merriman
August 24, 1991

Preface to Second Edition

It is nearly twenty years since I first wrote *Evolutionary Astrology: The Journey Of The Soul Through The Horoscope.* The same feelings and longings I experienced in 1973–1974, which seemed to have vanished in the interim, have returned. As in the early 1970's, I once again recognize that I – and the world – am experiencing a crisis in faith. The source of this crisis, and certainly the resolution of it, is a vast and unknown mystery. Yet the mystery has a warm and special magnetic effect upon me. I am compelled to search and explore, and I feel a great adventure awaits. If I embark upon this journey, I know that a special outpouring of love, compassion and understanding will unfold. The love and compassion will be first of all for other people, and especially for the children of this planet, for ultimately it is the child (within us) that truly is pure and innocent. I had already begun to experience this phenomenon when I contemplated the rewriting of this book.

But enough about me. This book is not really about me. I am simply a messenger, and whether or not the message which comes through this book is valuable depends upon the effect it might (or might not) have upon each person who reads it. In one sense this book is for the individual who seeks understanding of him or herself, as I do.

Yet understanding does not come in an isolated vacuum, and its presence is not without influence in the outer world. To understand one's Self is to begin a quest for freedom and liberation – freedom and liberation from loneliness and emotional or mental suffering. As one makes progress on this journey, others will do likewise through example, for everyone is pulled like a magnet to this same Mecca, even on a subconscious level. It is like the flower or plant which leans naturally towards the Sun. In its cycle other obstructions may arise which block out the Sun, and the flower temporarily loses its natural direction. It copes unnaturally with stress the best it can. Yet it longs for the warmth and comfort of the light of the Sun, and when the obstructions are removed it recovers with full splendor. As humans, we do the same. In a very subtle fashion, obstructions enter our path. So subtle are they that we do not take notice in many cases, until a certain amount of stress can no longer be ignored. We set about to remove these obstructions, to correct the injustices, and when we succeed there is a burst of renewed vigor and radiance.

I mentioned that once again I see myself undergoing a crisis in faith, and the world too appears to be undergoing the same. As I write this, it is the early 1990's. In the last section of the original text on *Evolutionary Astrology*, titled "The Hope", I referred to this period of the early 1990's, as a time of spiritual and psychical revolution, a time of new awareness. The affairs of humankind are quite remarkable now: on the one hand we see the incredible act of peace and cooperation as the U.S.S.R. grants freedom to the Eastern European bloc countries, thus appearing to end the long, cold war between the free countries of the world and those which adhered to hard line Communist doctrines. What a great gift for humankind as it entered the last decade of the Millenium!

One year later, however, the ugly face of war and conflict arose again as Iraq invaded Kuwait and the Soviet military shot and killed demonstrators in Lithuania. Instead of basking in the glow of a long-term peaceful world, humanity once more found itself having to face naked aggression and coercion amongst many of its brethren. On the positive side, nearly all the nations of the world have cooperatively come together to take a firm stand against the aggressors, or rather in support of a peaceful, war-free, world. Never before in the history of humankind have so many come together in a mutual mission whose goal was peace. Yet the leaders of the world are confronted with a difficult issue: if we want peace, must we again fall into the pattern of having to wage war to attain it? Are we really making progress by doing this? And will we regress, or continue our progress, towards attaining a world of peaceful cooperation?

Yes, I am at a crossroads, and before me lies a choice. I am facing a crisis in faith. I wish to plunge headlong into this vast mystery which is myself. I know that incredible revelations in the form of inspiration and discovery await. And yet I am afraid. Afraid of what I might lose, what I must sacrifice. Do I have the faith that these losses or sacrifices are worth it?

The events and conditions facing the world are in many respects similar to the events and conditions facing each of us in our own individual, outer world. For every effort we make to change these, there are known and unknown consequences. These two qualities–choice and consequence–require a great deal of mental and emotional energy. Within every choice there is a "right action", and the heart knows it. However the mind has created or accepted many obstacles that give doubt to that choice. A great deal of responsibility and self-imposed obligations to others have taken the form of obstruction to the sunlight. Or so we chose to believe. Perhaps these responsibilities and obligations are themselves part of the natural path. Perhaps they too serve the purpose of self understanding. Perhaps instead of feeling the need to remove and overcome them, they might better be viewed as something to be accepted and worked with, appreciated and cherished.

The physical body is a privilege and a gift. Souls long for physical embodiment, for experience and sensation, for a means to express their visions and dreams. Yet it does present interesting dilemmas: in the pursuit of taking care of the body, the being takes on many responsibilities and obligations which appear to obstruct the path towards liberation and freedom. This path is a spiritual one, and it comes about from "inner work." The needs of the physical require "outer work." The challenge is simple: how to integrate the two. The solution requires the resolution to a crisis in faith, a crisis which each one of us individually, and collectively as a nation and a planet, experience on this plane.

Let me suggest that you cannot change the world, its destiny or its karma. Let me also suggest that you cannot change the events or conditions in your own life, at least not outwardly by an act of will. You can however seek understanding of your Self, and in doing so, discover the beauty and wonder of who you are. As your understanding unfolds, the capacity to experience and express compassion and love will grow, and like the warm light of the Sun itself, others will "lean" towards you and grow. Events and conditions in your life will undergo a process of evolution; movement will begin. The life which you live will begin to look different; more alive, more beautiful, more exciting. Once more you will begin to view the world from the eyes of a child, and with the experience and wisdom of a loving parent.

It is with great joy that this book becomes available again. It is an opportunity for me to commune with others, to experience an outpouring of the little pieces of insight that I have experienced on my journey as I explore my own crisis in faith. I will leave you with one final understanding: my crisis in faith is an essential illusion on my inner path towards liberation.

Ray Merriman
January, 1991

Terminology

The following is a definition and explanation of terms as they are used throughout this book:

Conscious Mind: The active mind which makes choices leading to the initiation of behavior. Behind these choices of behavior is an *intent.* The nature of the intent, as well as the nature of the activity initiated, sets into motion a cycle. The results or consequences of this behavior is known as *karma,* and so long as the dynamics of that cycle are still in motion, the cycle continues. The repetitive nature of this cycle is known as a "karmic script", or "karmic pattern."

The conscious mind is comprised of three parts: Spirit, the soul, and ego. The relationship of the conscious mind to these three concepts determines the degree, or level, of one's "consciousness."

Spirit: Life force. All living beings share a common quality of life. Without this life force, or Spirit, there is no living being. It is the source of life, or the dynamic energy that is known as life.

In astrology, the **Sun** symbolizes Spirit. The Sun is the source of life on Earth. Without it, life does not exist. All living organisms "lean" towards the Sun. The daily activity of human beings rotates around the Sun. The annual activity of human beings rotates around the Sun. The same is true in nature. The daily and annual cycles of nature are related to the Sun (seasonal).

Every soul is becoming the Sun. Every soul seeks to be life force itself.

In this book, Spirit is sometimes referred to as God-force, Oneness, Higher Self, or creative life force.

Soul: Every living human being has a soul. The soul existed prior to physical birth and will exist after the physical body ceases to exist (i.e. after death). The soul has one primary urge: union with Spirit.

This is the basic "inner longing" of all human beings: to experience union with Spirit, which is to say, to experience unconditional love. The deepest and fondest memory of the soul is of its union with Spirit.

However, it is the soul of the individual which ultimately is the recipient of karmic cycles. When an individual consciously sets into motion a behavior that becomes governed by cyclic law, it is the soul that must undergo these consequences. The soul cannot experience this union with Spirit if cycles related to the world of phenomena are still operative. The cycles are not yet complete.

Prior to embodiment, the soul contracts to undergo conditions, or experiences, in a lifetime which are consistent with the cycles of that soul. The soul's purpose is to guide the incarnated being through these experiences in a manner that produces a "shift in consciousness." In this way, the cycle may be completed, or terminated, or transcended. Once the "blockage" is transcended, the soul continues upon its journey back to the home it longs for.

Once a karmic script is understood, and the individual begins to respond to the dynamics of the cycle with a greater degree of consciousness, there is a "breakthrough". There is a shift in consciousness. The cycle is transcended and the individual experiences an "outpouring of compassion." At that moment, the soul experiences union with Spirit. At that moment, the soul experiences unconditional love, and will from that point onward, continue to seek this experience. How successful the conscious mind will be in this quest is another matter.

Soul is sometimes referred to as the *being* of the individual.

Ego: The part of the conscious mind which makes the decisions and choices which are centered upon the "self first". In many cases, such a choice is at the expense of another, or others. An example is littering, or polluting the environment. Such an activity is expedient for the self, but harmful to the community, if not the planet.

Choices and decisions made from this part of the mind are oftentimes in violation of one's deeper understanding. They are oftentimes in conflict with the counsel of the soul. Choices of behavior that are dictated by the ego give rise to cyclic patterns and scripts.

Once these choices are initiated, the ego (an aspect of the personality) is truly born. Its purpose is to rationalize, justify, and explain to the conscious mind that such behavior is acceptable and even desirable. Every time an issue arises related to this cycle, the ego seeks to defend the original decision and behavior. Its survival depends upon it. Hence the individual will respond with definite emotional sets regarding certain issues in life. As a result, these themes or scripts reoccur time and time again.

The ego's purpose is to protect the individual from physical, or emotional, or mental pain. It also seeks pleasure. By itself these things are neither good nor bad. However when such motivation leads to behavior at the expense of another's well-being, then it is in violation of natural law. At this point the ego is in conflict with the soul. At this point, the results of the ego's influence become detrimental to the journey of the soul.

The conscious mind has two advisors: the ego and the soul. The soul's purpose is to guide the conscious mind with wise counsel, in such a way that one's karmic cycles are completed. In this manner the soul experiences union with the Spirit. However in the course of a lifetime (or many), the ego is born. Its advice to the conscious mind is totally self-centered. The more influence it has, the less able (or willing) is the conscious mind to receive input from the soul. A personality that is primarily "self-centered" has a consciousness dominated by the ego, and not at all in communion with its soul. This individual may thus be "egotistical", and not of a very high degree of consciousness, and does not likely experience any sense of real union with anyone. It is likely that all relationships in this person's life exhibit a similar theme, because this individual is a product of a very fixed karmic script (i.e. fixation).

Individual: Also referred to as the **person**; the physical embodiment of the soul.

Shift In Consciousness: This occurs when the counsel of the soul "breaks through" the defenses of the ego, and thus reaches the conscious mind. When the script is identified and then consciously changed, the ego dissolves. Its existence, like physical life itself, is transitory. It is impermanent. The ego is an illusion whose apparent reality is based upon things that are impermenent.

A shift in consciousness will likely unfold as major planets transit or progress over natal angles or their midpoints, or the rulers of the meridian axis.

PART ONE

Principles and Models of Evolutionary Astrology

CHAPTER ONE

An Allegory

Long ago, in an area extending from the Dead Sea southward through the Nile River Valley in Egypt, a community of individuals once gathered. They were highly skilled and talented individuals as far as the affairs of the world were concerned. But one day each made a commitment – a commitment that not only affected the rest of their lives, but also the lives of many people for many centuries to come. Each member of this community decided to give up mundane skills and talents for personal ends only, and to come together with a unified purpose in a band which has come to be known as the Essenes.

The time began around 500 B.C. The planet Earth was entering a critical cycle. The Age of Aries was drawing to a close and the Age of Pisces was fast approaching. A change – nay, a great change – could be felt in the air. People were confused and frightened, for things which they could not understand were happening so fast. All the prophecies of old seemed to be manifesting at once, with one exception: the birth of a great savior.

"Where is our Savior?" was a cry heard across the lands.

Then, one by one, the saviors began arriving: Bodhidharma in the Far East, Siddartha Gautama (the Buddah) and Mahavira in India, Lao Tzo and Confucius in China, Zoroaster in the Middle East.

But the Essenes were looking for another yet, one who would appear according to the prophecies of the Old Testament, and according to the prophecies of their own wise men known as the Magi.

They knew the time was upon them to prepare for the advent of this new age, for the arrival of a Great One. They knew that a new age of devotion, self-sacrifice and love for all people was necessary for the Earth's evolution – in fact, it was necessary in order for the planet to remain in balance with the universe itself.

So they made the commitment. They would band together and be the examples of the new age. They would give up their selfish pursuits and begin using their skills and talents for the good of the community which they would form. They would become love and devotion in action. *And they promised to devote their lives to successfully usher in the new age and a new savior for humankind.*

For a few centuries their community prospered and grew. It grew in the bond of the commitment, in the faith of a promise they made and kept to one another. And then one day the prophecies of the Magi came to be. The bright star, the conjunction of Jupiter and Saturn in the sign of the Fish, hovered above in the evening skies. A sign, an omen, long awaited signaled not only the end of waiting and preparation, but the beginning of the great task which now lay before them. The Essenes were to be the teachers for Jesus of Nazareth. An age had come to an end, and a new age had finally arrived.

The Essenes carried out the task they had chosen, and had been chosen, to do. They successfully ushered in a new age based upon the principles of love and devotion, largely through the teachings of one great master: Jesus of Nazareth. Within two centuries after the birth of Jesus, their purpose at this point completed, the Essenes vanished from the face of the Earth.

Nearly two millenia have passed. The age which the Essenes ushered in is now drawing to a close. Again the planet Earth is in the midst of a crisis. Great changes are rapidly taking place and a new age is fast approaching. Humankind is again in the precarious position of seeking – no, needing – to balance itself with the natural order and flow of the universe. The process of the evolution of this planet is once more unfolding in a dramatic fashion. Once again the call for preparation for such a change is being sounded.

The Essenes made a promise: A promise to commit themselves as workers for a universe of love, peace and harmony. They promised to work against all the forces of negativity by concentrating their efforts totally toward the creative and positive forces within the universe. And this promise was made for eternity.

This book is dedicated to the Essenes who have come once again to fulfill their promise to humankind.

****

It begins with a "you" and a "me". We look at one another and notice differences. You don't look like me and I don't look like you. We don't always think alike either. In my thoughts, I form judgments about you, and you do the same about me. I define who and what you are all about by constructing forms and limits. I look at you as I look at life: you have a birth, a life of events such as marriage and children, occupations and avocations, awards, honors, set-backs and disappointments. Like life itself, you seem to have a beginning and an end.

And I function as if these things are real. But are they?

Does life consist of a beginning and an end? Is reality based only upon the physical appearance of things? Is it possible that there is something beyond the appearance, that there is something beyond the birth and death moments?

I look about and I notice things. I notice that everything is in movement – however slow – and that everything changes over a period of time. In the world in which I function, nothing remains constant forever.

"Why do things change?" I ask myself. "Are these changes without a purpose, are they aimless and coincidental?"

In this lifetime I have chosen – or been chosen – to be an astrologer. I am proud of this position. I dearly love my art, for it gives me a sense of the nature of the universe which no other intellectual endeavor has ever afforded. There is one thing in particular that I (and other astrologers) have discovered in my studies: there is an order to life. There is a timing function operating in the universe, one which affects every living organism. As an astrologer, I see that one's marriage, one's job, illness, even death, all seem timed in accordance with astrological cycles.

Seeing correlations which occur between the celestial bodies and the events in one's life, another question arises: "Is not the moment of birth itself also well-timed? Is not the birth also an event just as important as the others? Might not one's birth moment constitute a major event in a cycle which is greater than (and includes) this single lifetime?" And I can see how I may have fallen into the fallacy of looking upon life in terms of limitations and restrictions, as if there is a birth and events and a death, and no more.

But now I begin to see life a little differently. I see there is a reason, a purpose, for the moment of birth. I see that every moment has a quality to it, and that one's birth is in harmony with the quality of that moment. I see that there is something beyond the appearance, beyond the physical, beyond the "reality" which tells me that I am different than you. I see that there is something which I will refer to as the "soul" of each individual. And that part of the individual – the "soul" – lives before the birth moment and after the death moment.

I understand now, that to study astrology from the point of view of just a single lifetime is like trying to understand a period in history by examining the prevailing conditions of *only* that time period. Conditions existed prior to the moment of each phenomenon on this plane, including the moment of one's birth.

I also understand now, as an astrologer, that one earns the right to reincarnate at any given specific moment, a moment in which *the quality of the universe is in harmony with the prior actions of that soul.*

This allegory is a dedication to the Essene souls. One might ask why the above thoughts are brought out in reference to the Essenes. It is because of the nature of the Essene mind. The Essenes did not see life in terms of a beginning and an end; they did not see reality in terms of limitations and definitions; they did not see the self – the Spirit – of each individual as alienated and apart from the rest of the universe.

The Essenes made a commitment for *eternity*. They did not expect to fulfill this commitment in one lifetime, in the course of only sixty or seventy years. That would be a very short eternity.

No, the Essenes had a sense of the soul's immortality, a sense of the everlasting relationship of each soul with the Spirit of life, the Spirit of the universe, the Spirit of a God-force which created and sustains order in the universe.

At present there is a school of thought emerging known as "Evolution." This school assumes all of the universe, including humankind, is in a constant state of change, or evolution. It furthermore assumes that there are *levels* of evolution – everyone is not on the same level. Some souls are more evolved than others, just as some species of animals are, biologically speaking, more evolved than other species. Applied to humankind, the concept of evolution helps to explain the world of phenomena, a world in which exist apparent differences between individuals.

As long as we act as if we are separated and alienated from life and one another, we are going to attract conditions which support this illusion. Each condition in life is one which we have attracted, according to what we have projected into life (at some point in time). And at the same time, each condition attracted potentially becomes a lesson through which each of us might evolve. This is a universal law, present in every major religion, and applicable to every condition in the phenomenal world. It is known as the Law of Retribution, or karma: what you sow, so shall ye reap; as one thinketh, so he or she is. If we think of ourselves as limited and separated, then we are going to act as such. If we act as if we are limited and alienated, then we are going to attract situations which enhance this illusion. This is the nature of the physical Earth plane.

The Earth plane, like every other sphere, is like a school. There are lessons to learn and these come from situations we experience. The purpose of these experiences and lessons is to understand the self more deeply, to liberate the being from isolation and loneliness, and to become whole. This happens when the soul of an individual merges with Spirit, which is the same Spirit that created and sustains this universe. Until this point is attained, every action continues to create a reaction. Every cause continues to have an effect, and the existence of the "I" as well as the "not-I" seems real.

Each of us, because we have the energy of life, the consciousness of being, are of Spirit. In this higher awareness we are a part of a universe which is in balance, in harmony. This is why every action performed has a reaction – the universe always seeks to maintain balance. That is why every soul which reincarnates *must* reincarnate – its prior actions have set up conditions which must be re-balanced. And until the soul is balanced, it will reincarnate time and time again, and experience various versions of the same patterns, or scripts.

This was a concern of the Essenes. What if a number of souls became out of balance to an extreme? What if a group of souls occupying the planet at once continued in a direction contrary and out of synch with natural order and natural law? What if the planet Earth became greatly out of balance with the rest of the universe? Would Earth, like some stars and like the planet once existing between Mars and Jupiter, have to "burn itself out," or explode in order to maintain a balance in this universe?

One wonders. Here we are, approaching a new age, the Age of Aquarius. This is to be the Age of the Humanitarian, of Enlightenment, Truth, and greater awareness. The Earth is to be making strides in higher consciousness, strides toward the realization of a true brotherhood, a planetary identity.

And what do we see happening? We see violations of natural law all about us. We see innocent citizens slaughtered in wars. We see young people throughout the world murdered for expressing outwardly their beliefs and ideologies. We see dishonesty and corruption in governments and the business community. It crushes our very Spirit to see man fighting against man, exploiting one another, looking for ways to take advantage of each other.

Yet we know, because of the Law of Retribution, that one cannot really gain at the expense of another, that a balance must and will be achieved. But we wonder "how" it will be achieved, given the nature of what we are suppose to be learning as we progress into the new age.

Many of you reading this book see these things happening. You know how frustrating life can seem to be at times. We are a people with a hope, a dream, an ideal. Many of us are seekers, seeking some peace, some love, some truth. From this seeking, many of us have already begun to discover. We are discovering that we are not alone, that there are others like us – compatriots of the universe – who are on the same journey. We are beginning to discover that life is not meaningless, not purposeless, and that we are not helpless. We are beginning to realize that there is a reason for being born now, into this time of great change and flux.

It is the dawning of a new age. Changes are rapidly taking place. The consciousness of the people upon this Earth is beginning to transform. It is no coincidence that you are here now. It was no coincidence that you were here 2000 years ago.

You made a commitment for eternity. And your time has come again.

CHAPTER TWO

Astrology and the Evolution of the Soul

This book begins with, and is based upon, one primary thought: humankind, and the individuals which comprise humankind, constantly evolve. Limits to this evolvement – a beginning and an end, a birth and a death – are nonexistent. In one sense, such phenomena are not real. In another sense, they are the same thing: a beginning is an end, and an end is also a beginning. Only the body – the physical, the apparent – is born and dies; the soul within that body exists before the physical birth and will continue beyond the physical death. Consequently there is no real birth or death. These are merely phenomena which occur in a physical world, a world of appearances which operates accordingly in a realm of limitations, dualities and other apparent realities which might rightfully be considered as "illusions." That which appears as limits, or opposite ends of some spectrum, turns out to be related to the very same thing, like birth and death.

This is not really a new thought nor a difficult one to comprehend. But it is here that this book commences because so many students of astrology accept this thought once they begin to question why astrology works. Several metaphysicians and philosophers have written discourses on the logic of this thought, and several scientists have conducted studies which demonstrate the plausibility of "soul survival," or the continuation of the soul after physical cessation. Therefore, instead of proving the soul exists – rather, evolves – and repeating the efforts of others, this book will start from that premise.

The attempt to relate astrology to an individual soul's growth, rather than to the individual's condition during a single lifetime alone, is a somewhat recent pursuit in the Western World. In fact such attempts have led to the development of many new astrological schools, such as: Esoteric Astrology, Cosmic or Spiritual Astrology and Karmic Astrology, to name a few. Each of these schools attempt to convey the understanding that astrology is more than just an empirical science, that it is instead a most valuable tool in deciphering the very mysteries of life itself.

The only reason why the title of this book does not coincide with one of the above mentioned schools is because it encompasses all of them. Inasmuch as a great deal of the information contained herein will appeal only to a few–perhaps initiates of some sort or another–the subject matter may be considered "Esoteric Astrology." The crux of the book is based upon the supposition that there is indeed an order to this universe which affects everyone, according to the movements of the celestial bodies. Therefore this book may be considered in the category of "Cosmic" or "Spiritual Astrology", which assumes a "Divine Plan" is in operation. And finally, as this work conveys the presence of universal laws like cause and effect upon the individuals functioning in this universe, it may also be considered "Karmic Astrology".

Evolutionary Astrology is thus inclusive of all the abovementioned schools. It deals with an evolving soul, one which is constantly changing, prior to and during this lifetime, as depicted in one's natal horoscope. It furthermore deals with the individual soul's evolvement in relationship to humankind's evolvement–how the individual plays a role in the "Cosmic Drama" unfolding upon the planet Earth at any given point in time.

Everything living goes through changes and transformations. Nothing remains constant over a period of *time* in the phenomenal world. Is it to be assumed that these changes are purposeless, that there is no reason or meaning behind these changes? Why, for instance, do human beings make changes in their lives? Certainly it is not to go backwards, to regress (although this sometimes appears to happen). These changes are purposeful, even if the individual involved is unaware of that purpose at the time. On a physical level, the purpose might be for *perfection*; on a mental level, it might be for *understanding*; on a spiritual level, it might be for *fulfillment* and *harmony*. In any event, every living thing is changing, moving toward some-thing, is going some-where, even though it is not always clearly defined nor understood by that which is undergoing the change.

Evolutionary Astrology seeks to answer these questions. This search, however, is not limited to the confines of an individual's single lifetime, nor to a single period in the history of humankind. The horoscope, the basic tool of mapping out changes in the celestial spheres, is a key in this search. The arrangement of the planets, in relationship to the axes of the Earth, is not just a clue to the potentials which lie ahead, but also a clue to what has already happened. It is through understanding the causes and nature of one's life patterns – however long ago these causes may have been initiated – that one can begin to understand the conditions existing in the present.

The evolution of a soul is basically a concept. It is a concept founded upon many assumptions, which when added together develops into a school of thought. This school of thought applies the principle that there are *levels* and *cycles* of evolution. Individuals are at different points along the evolutionary scale, just as some species of animals are more or less evolved than others (biologically speaking). It is a model that can be used to explain the world of phenomena, the apparent reality. It is a means to determine the various differences which seem to exist among individuals – why some are leaders and others followers, why some have great personal appeal and others are dull, why some have strong self-control and others have little. It does not negate the effects of heritage, environment, education or other cultural influences upon the individual. It merely provides a metaphysical philosophy for explaining the conditions of the soul as it enters this lifetime. And that includes *all* of the forces (such as those just mentioned) operating upon that individual. This school of thought, for instance, assumes one's education is *not only* a result of one's environment and family upbringing in this lifetime; it assumes one's position in life is *not only* a result of one's education and mental capabilities. Instead, it assumes that all of these things – the environment, the family, the education, the mental development, the cultural influences – are *effects*, or *results*, of causes laid down prior to and within this lifetime. Furthermore, these effects serve specific purposes in the course of this lifetime, purposes which may be assets for the further evolution of that soul within this lifetime. These conditions have been earned, and they serve to facilitate the individual's further evolvement.

At one point, all souls were created equal. At one point, all souls were one with the creative Spirit. But as souls became *apart* from the Spirit as well as *a part of* the Spirit, differences manifested between souls, between individuals, between personalities. All souls relate to the Spirit, but in different and varying degrees. Some souls identify more closely than others, and some see themselves as "apart from" rather than "a part of", more than others. This then is the basis for an evolutionary school of thought, whereby there exists an equality of the Spirit, but a difference in the karma of the souls, and whereby some souls are more evolved and other souls less evolved, but whereby all souls *do* evolve.

Many of the ideas presented herein will be found operative, given certain metaphysical assumptions. They make astrological sense. The application of these ideas to individuals, to world conditions, will yield correlations which can be observed, even if they cannot be inductively explained (yet). Astrology, even in its mundane application, is still essentially a deductive study – changes in the celestial sphere may be correlated to changes on the Earth plane. But *why* this is so has not been (and may never be) properly explained, except through metaphysical principles. Yet humankind continues to use deductive knowledge such as astrology (and various fields of science) and builds more and more upon it in an attempt to know, to understand, to perfect, even to evolve.

CHAPTER THREE

Basic Spiritual-Astrological Laws

For everything there is a season
and a time for every matter under heaven:
a time to be born, and a time to die;
a time to plant, and a time to pluck up what is planted;
a time to kill, and a time to heal;
a time to break down, and a time to build up;
a time to weep, and a time to laugh;
a time to mourn, and a time to dance;
a time to cast away stones, and time to gather stones together;
a time to embrace, and a time to refrain from embracing;
a time to seek, a time to lose;
a time to keep, a time to cast away;
a time to rend, a time to sew;
a time to keep silence, and a time to speak
a time to love, and a time to hate;
a time for war, and a time for peace.

Ecclesiastes 3, verses 1–8

"A time to be born, and a time to die." As the Bible and so many other great spiritual works point out, there is a "season and a time for every matter under heaven." Every matter in the phenomenal world (under heaven) occurs in cycles, cycles that are well-timed, well-ordered, and not "coincidental." There are reasons and there are seasons, and each according to a cyclical rhythm in the universe.

This law of the universe, wherein all worldly phenomena is well-timed and well-earned, is known as the Law of Retribution, or karma.

The above quote from the Book of Ecclesiastes demonstrates the existence of this law in the Judeo-Christian religions. It is a universal law prevalent in all major religions—"You reap what you sow." In another sense one is responsible—at root, the very cause—for everything that happens to oneself.

Literally translated from its Hindu origin, the word karma means *motion*. Anything put into motion on this phenomenal plane becomes subject to natural laws which exist upon, and govern, this plane. From that motion initiated follows a cycle whose duration and quality is in direct response to all the energies present at that moment of initiation. Included in that cycle are reactions, responses and consequences to the initial motion put into effect.

According to the American College Dictionary, karma is "the cosmic operation of retributive justice, according to which one's status in life is determined by his deeds in a previous incarnation . . . the doctrine of inevitable consequence."[1] Thus it can be seen that karma is a concept of reactions and consequences applied to the human condition. For every motion put into play on this plane (whether thought, action or deed), the law of karma states that an inevitable consequence will follow for which the initiator will bear responsibility.

From this philosophy many adjuncts have evolved. One is the belief that each person is wholly responsible for every experience he or she encounters in a lifetime. At the root of every experience is something which the individual did, or caused, and thus each experience is actually the result of that individual's choice of action (or motion). Because human experience consists of a wide range of emotional reactions, and these reactions are judged favorable or unfavorable, desirable or undesirable, the concept of karma too has come to be judged in terms of "good" or "bad". In truth karma is neither good nor bad. It is simply consequence. If the Law of Karma does indeed operate in this world, then all experience is karmic, for all experience is a consequence of prior initiated motions. Along this same line of thought, every reaction to experience (or, action which follows from the experience) becomes an initiation point for subsequent inevitable cycles or consequences.

It is human judgment that gives birth to "good" and "bad" karma concepts. In cases where the experience is judged to be fruitful, beneficial, fortunate, or eliciting emotions of happiness, it is said to be "good karma", or "karmic merit." In those instances where the experience is

[1]*American College Dictionary* (New York, Random House, 1970).

accompanied with feelings of suffering, pain, or a sense of misfortune, it is judged as "bad karma", or "karmic debt." In either case, it is assumed that the individual earned, or created, these conditions – even "chose" them.

Yet this line of thought seems only partially complete if a total picture of karma is to be accepted as operative. Why would an individual "chose" an experience of suffering and pain? To say that he or she earned it is not enough; that assumes that the experience of suffering brings it all to an end. The idea of closure at this point is premature. To judge it as "karmic debt" might explain the experience itself occurring as it does, but does not imply the dynamic quality of the *motion* continually in effect, constantly at work in this ever-changing physical reality.

This is the danger of applying judgments like "good" and "bad", "merit" and "debt" to universal and natural law. It limits. It stops short. It fails to see the whole picture, to understand the entire process, because of its focus upon material result. Material result, or manifestation of an emotional reaction to an experience, is not an end, not a completion point. *It cannot be truly completed until this very point – the reaction – is understood, and then integrated constructively into the essence of that being who initiated the motion.* Without the understanding and integration of the reaction to the consequence (i.e. experience), the motion is still in effect. Thus the experience, or rather similar experiences eliciting similar emotional reactions and judgments, will repeat; a *pattern* or *script* of experience is created.

Inherent in all of this is the idea of *purpose* within experience. Yes, experience is consequence, or karmic. But also experience is purposeful. When viewed in this light, experience becomes the basis for personal challenge, rather than personal tragedy, catastrophe, good fortune, or whatever other judgement can be made from an emotionally reactive position. The challenge of the experience is to understand the self more completely, particularly in its relationship to the set of circumstances it is going through. If the individual puts a judgment upon the experience as "good" or "bad", then that individual has at once separated itself from the experience (or wishes to). The experience becomes something the individual no longer wants to be with (why?), for it elicits reactions (usually emotional) which he or she is not prepared to experience, or willing to accept. Everyone has their "ring-pass-not" limit, but this limit can be challenged and expanded through a relationship to experience.

When that relationship is terminated, as in the case of judging it "good" or "bad", it is only temporary. The motion which created the experience is still operative. The decision to terminate only ends the "apparent reality" of the motion. The decision to terminate one's relationship to experience (any experience, which is done by judgement) actually becomes another motion initiated to bring forth similar experiences. The pattern, or script, is still operative unless a deeper understanding of the self is effected. Change only takes place as a natural consequence of understanding. The being will evolve to a new level when understanding of the pattern unfolds, and then this understanding is integrated into one's consciousness.

This brings forth The Law of Relationships (sometimes known as the Law of Right Relations). *One cannot terminate a relationship; one can only and ultimately integrate a relationship* into his or her essence through understanding of the self. Again, the motion is not completed when a judgement to terminate, or separate from, the experience is made. That itself is only a point on a continuum of the cyclical consequence of motion. For the consequence or cycle to be complete, for karma to run its full course, an understanding and integration of that motion and its consequences must occur. Thus the experience (or experiences, depending upon the individual's willingness) is potentially always a learning one. With that learning (or understanding) comes growth, or personal evolvement. At the moment of understanding comes an intense *outpouring* of love and compassion, sometimes referred to as *bliss*. This ecstatic sensation may be quite profound, signalling that the soul is ready for "motion" (or karma) of another level than dictated by the previous script.

Without the learning, patterns of repetitive-types of experiences occur and emotional sets and blocks are created. These cause one to judge experiences as "good" and "bad" and relate to life in terms of tragedy, catastrophe, suffering and pain, instead of challenge and purpose. Ultimately, in the former case, the patterns are not simply emotional ones, for they tend to translate to all areas of the individual experience, including health, love, work, etc.

One's experiences in life are thus karmic. They are the result of motions put into effect which have not been completed or not understood and integrated into the essence of the being who initiated them. Through every choice made in this lifetime, the individual is initiating motions for which there will be consequences – consequences for which the individual is ultimately responsible. One's circumstances in life are the responsibilities of that soul. They are the consequences of that being's former choices. If one choses not to relate to a particular experience, that very choice suggests the creation of a new experience that is very similar to the script, or pattern, still in effect. This brings to light the Law of Creation.

The Law of Creation states that the ultimate force in the universe is a creative one. It is not destructive, nor negative, and that in truth these are aspects of creativity. To terminate and bring to an end a matter is impossible (except in the "apparent reality"). Therefore one's decision to separate from an experience (as in judging it) does not in reality succeed. One cannot negate an experience; it only serves to create the same experience again (though it "appears" different). At work here is the Law of Creation with the Law of Retribution (or, karma). Something is put into motion, a consequence results in the form of experience. Now at this point the initiator of that experience, the one who is responsible to and for the consequence, has a choice. This choice determines the duration of the cycle of this karmic action. In the first instance, the individual does not actually choose anything, but rather views the experience as a challenge – a challenge to *understand* his or her relationship to the experience. This involves a "going through" of the experience, and transcending or expanding one's own "ring-pass-not" of emotional reaction. Up until this experience, the individual typically is "fixated", or stuck at a certain level of expression relating to the nature of this experience. This point of "fixation", which the native has never passed, is known as the "ring-pass-not" for him or her. It limits his or her level of expression.

Now by going beyond that point through this experience, a whole new level of expression is achieved. One "knows" when this is happening – there is that "outpouring" of love, of compassion, which is the result of self discovery and understanding. That experience has now been integrated into the essence of that being, and itself becomes a creative force for whole new expressions which will then result in a whole new set of experiences in that individual's life. In this manner, the cycle of that karma which resulted in that experience (consequence) is completed. *Completion involves understanding and results in integration, not termination.* Evolution, or the appearance of change then takes place. Integration is consistent with creative force; willful termination is a negation of creative force, and therefore does not really exist (only "appears" to).

Going back to the model and the point of individual choice, there is another "drama" that could (and usually does) unfold. After the motion has resulted in an experience (consequence), the individual can instead chose NOT to experience it (i.e. not experience the experience, or consequence). This typically happens when the native reacts emotionally to it, and sees fit to judge it good or bad, great or terrible. The act of judgment is a separation from the experience. It need not be final, but usually is. It is as if to say: "I have done this (thing), and now this thing has resulted from it. This result is wonderful (or terrible). And that is that." In other words, the manifestation of the result is not only judged as good or bad, but also as the end of the matter (i.e. "Our relationship is obviously a bad one, so why don't we call it quits.").

When a judgment is made and a termination assumed, the cycle is not in reality completed. It is stuck, or fixated at a point equivalent to the individual's own "ring-pass-not" level of expression. The motion (cycle) thus stays in effect, and actually serves to *create* other experiences (consequences) that are a result of the same initial motion. So the decision to negate did not in actuality negate at all; the decision to end or terminate the experience did not end or terminate the "real" experience at all. It (the motion, which is creative) created another experience that, from an evolutionary viewpoint, is really the same experience. And it will continue creating the same experience (i.e. a "pattern", or "script") until the whole cycle of that initial motion finally results in an understanding of self. When that happens, the meaning of the cycle is integrated into the being's consciousness, and one transcends the "ring-pass-not" to new levels of expression. The soul has thus evolved. A *change* has unfolded. A cycle has been completed and the being has been liberated from a karmic condition.

So experiences, being the consequences or results of the Law of Karma, are purposeful. They are the challenges through which individuals evolve. They are the means by which individuals are able to integrate circumstance with meaning, and thus transcend self-imposed limitations. They are the means by which individuals may become whole, and realize their relationship to Spirit. They are the means by which one becomes One.

The World of Appearance

The world of phenomena or physical world, is basically a dualistic reality, based upon the self and others, or not-self. This is largely so because of the physical – the body of the being, the objects which the body uses, the different parts of nature, and so on. In a manner of speaking, the world is thus made of two facets of reality: the self, and everything that is not-self. The matter is further brought into focus by the fact that the self must function most of its conscious life *among* that which is (or appears to be) not-self.

This is the nature of the Earth realm for souls. It is a realm where the soul may have a physical body, and at that a body which appears different than the physical bodies of other souls. It is a realm wherein that body survives only according to its functioning with and among these other bodies. The Earth is a realm of interdependency among souls – souls which have different bodies, different skills, different levels of functioning. It is thus a dualistic realm between the self and not-self.

But the basis for this dualism is on *appearances*. Underneath the body, the physical, even the mind, there is *consciousness*, the life or essence of the being. There is no difference here, no levels where one can be compared to another. For beyond the physical, the realm of appearance, there is that constant flow within each, the very "audible life current" itself. This is where the self of one is the self of the other, for there is not the realm of "other-than-self." This consciousness might be called the Higher Self, or Spirit, which is present within each individual.

It is this Spirit which permeates the entire universe. It gives life, it gives light, motion, and movement within the universe. Every living thing in the universe has at root the presence of Spirit. Every thing – living or not – in the universe is affected by this Spirit.

Each one of us, because we have the energy of life, the consciousness of being, are of Spirit. This is why we can make things happen, why we can "materialize" things. For within Spirit there is power – the power to create. There are many kinds of power because there are many applications of power. Once power is applied by the Spirit, laws of the universe are put into motion, for the universe is *balanced*, it is in *harmony*. Astrology, astronomy, physics, and various sciences, acknowledge that there is an *order* to the universe.

The original application of power by the Spirit was creative. Within each living being lies the power to create. Essentially it was – is – the application of this power itself, by Spirit, that set into motion the Law of Karma, of action-reaction, of cause-effect, which seeks a "balance" at all times within the universe.

It is not the intent of this book to theorize as to how everything came to be. This will be left to those who study religion, and perhaps sciences such as anthropology. It is hoped though, that one can see the basis for karma, for cycles, that operate in the lives of humans; that there is indeed an *order* to the universe upon which these cycles are based, upon which the Law of Retribution is operative.

Without speculating upon such questions as to why self (Spirit) applied power to create not-self, or an image of self, or a physical embodiment for self and consequently many expressions of self, this study begins with the understanding that these now exist. There is

Spirit, life force and consciousness within every living being. There is a soul which is an expression of this Spirit, and which continues before and beyond the life and death concepts of the physical world. And there is the physical body which houses the soul and accounts for the differences in appearance between souls, between self and not-self, or the world of "maya," the illusion. All souls long for embodiment. The body is a divine privilege, and not all souls are given this privilege until it is their "time." One's "time" is measured by the cycles of planetary bodies. At the time of a soul's embodiment (i.e. incarnation), all the celestial spheres are in harmony with the karma of that soul.

The Earth is a sphere where maya exists. It is a sphere where reality is based upon the appearances of the physical, for here it is necessary to relate to – and function with – others who are also "in the body," and at that, bodies which appear to be different from one another. The means by which humans relate to one another is greatly based upon language, which along with the body is another limitation which necessitates individuals to function interdependently. Obviously this serves to make the distinction between self and other-than-self even greater, for language becomes a convenient means to define reality (what is real, what makes sense) for the collective whole. Language serves as a useful vehicle for humans to function with one another, which is one of the purposes for reincarnation on Earth (to cooperate, interrelate with one another). In another sense though it is a trap, for it fosters the reality of the dualistic (not-self) "maya". It does so because through language, through the existence of the physical differences, through the fact that humans must be interdependent in order to survive, one easily falls into the illusion that the world of "other-than-self" is the *only* reality. Early in life an individual's activities and thinking processes become based only in the world of the physical, of the appearances, and never upon self as it relates to the world of non-physical, non-appearances, non-limitations. The trap is to become caught in this duality and in so doing become alienated from the Spirit. One begins to function as if apart-from, rather than a part-of an interdependent universe, for one sees self as apart from (different than) others. This in turn gives rise to actions which are designed to also make one appear different than (usually better than) others. Oftentimes this is at the expense of others.

The entire process of acting or functioning in *comparison* to others, when in essence one and others are of the same Spirit, makes up the cosmic drama. It is the world of illusion, where exists the "good" and the "bad," the "birth" and the "death." It is here, perhaps more than anywhere else, that the universal Law of Retribution (karma) is constantly in motion.

The Earth, like every other sphere, is like a school. It is a realm where it is possible to learn lessons. It is often said that life is a continual learning process. But what is the lesson to be learned on Earth, or any sphere for that matter?

The goal is to become *whole*, for one's consciousness to become aware of its soul and the soul's needs. The basic need of the soul is to commune and integrate as *one* with the Spirit. Until that is realized one's consciousness will always be caught in the realm of duality, of illusion, in which it is never wholly integrated. The individual will continue to initiate actions for which there will be more and more reactions and consequences to experience.

The Earth is a school in which the soul is honored with a physical vehicle. That physical vehicle can survive only as it learns to relate with others in the same predicament. Through such practices as the golden rule—"do unto others as you would have them do unto you"—and learning to function cooperatively *with* one another, is the individual soul able to *realize* that "The Christ within me (Spirit) is the same as the Christ within you." In other words, the Earth is a realm in which evolution is not only possible, but potentially occurs at all times; a realm in which souls are able to gather together and act as One ("Wherever two or more are gathered. . . ."), where there can be wholeness or unity, even in the illusion of diversity.

Astrology is the map of the soul. It is the reflection, in the mirror of the heavens, of an individual's past and future experiences, or scripts. The horoscope, the tool by which astrology is actualized, is itself a product of the Law of Karma. Just as every individual is different in some degree to every other individual, so too is the horoscope of every individual different in some degree to every other horoscope. This is because all individuals (with some exceptions) are born at different times and at different places. As each point in time has its own unique quality, so too does each horoscope have its own unique quality, and each individual soul has its own unique quality.

Essentially astrology is the study of cycles. On one level these cycles are of celestial bodies; on another level, they correlate with cycles upon the Earth sphere, such as the cycles of individual experience. Again one is reminded of the verse from the Book of Ecclesiastes quoted at the beginning of this chapter, which states there is a season for *every* matter under heaven. Astrology is the key to understanding these cycles—cycles which are in accordance with the Law of Karma. Astrology is one of the keys in the quest for understanding karma because astrology itself (the horoscope, the moment of birth) is the result of this universal Law of Retribution.

Yet astrology is not everything in the understanding of this law. It is just a great part of the understanding. If it were the entirety of the understanding, then in those rare instances where two individuals are born in the same place and at he same time (in other words, have *identical* horoscopes) one would expect the Law of Karma to manifest identically in both cases. But it does not. The individuals, for instance, may not be born of the same parents (even if the parents seem similar in nature), they do not marry the same mate (even if the mates seem similar), they do not have the same occupations, go to the same places for vacations, and so on. In other words, the fine details of karma which manifest in the lives of each cannot be pinpointed through astrology alone.

There are, however, a remarkable number of similarities in the lives of these persons to indicate that astrology, or birth moment, does have an effect. For instance there will be similar types of physical ailments, similarities in relationships to spouses, parents, children, and most importantly of all perhaps is that their *cycles* throughout life will be similar. From this it may be deduced that they are working on similar "lessons" in this lifetime.

What are those "lessons" one is to "learn" in a lifetime upon Earth? Well there are many roads to the same destination, many means to one end, many paths to the same Spirit, many faces of the same Creator. When one reaches the destination, arrives at the end, becomes the Spirit and of the Creator, then one is no longer affected by these universal laws, for one is One with the creative Spirit of life. One no longer has lessons to learn, for all lessons are for this very purpose – to become whole, to be at one with one's Self, or God. But there are many ways in which one may realize this, become this Higher Self. These are through certain experiences which the soul undertakes in the reality of "maya," in the realm where universal laws are operative. Earth, the realm of the physical, is one of them.

Lessons are like virtues. They are qualities which one may develop and express in dealings with other people; they uplift others as well as oneself. Consequently the understanding of these lessons, the development of these qualities, facilitates one's functioning in an interdependent realm and enhances not only one's own evolutionary state, but others as well.

Astrology offers a tool in understanding the soul's development. Each planet represents a certain lesson and its relationship to other factors in the horoscope (which will be discussed in this book) describes the soul's relationship to each of these lessons. The following is a list of the planets and their corresponding evolutionary lessons.

Sun: Unity
Moon: Unconditional Love
Mercury: Service
Venus: Forgiveness
Earth: Reverence
Mars: Right Action
Jupiter: Wisdom
Saturn: Faith
Uranus: Freedom
Neptune: Compassion
Pluto: Self-Understanding

During the course of a lifetime, each of these "lessons" comes to one's attention through a variety of astrological cycles, such as transits and progressions. Yet it is also the case that in each lifetime, which itself is like a cycle within a greater cycle of many lifetimes, certain and particular "lessons" present themselves time and time again for that soul's unique development. The qualities of development which the soul concentrates upon in a particular lifetime are outlined in the natal horoscope. The evolution of the soul depends upon the individual's *response* (free will) to these cycles (measured through astrology) of experience. Evolution occurs when the "lesson is learned" or the liberating quality "developed," according to the karma of that soul.

What is the karma of a soul? Basically it is the consequences a soul is confronted with in any given lifetime, resulting from actions initiated by that soul in prior lifetimes. It is the result of responses by the individual, in former incarnations, to situations in a phenomenal realm, usually involving the well-being of other individuals or its self. For instance if a situation occurred in which someone was mistreated by another, the former may *respond* with hate, anger, or vengeance. Or that person might instead forgive and express compassion, if there is understanding. Assuming the individual responded with hate and anger, then the karma of that soul would reap similar circumstances time and time again until the individual developed enough understanding to respond with compassion and forgiveness (Venus or Neptune). As a point of interest, the individual who *initiated* the mistreatment would also set up a karmic circumstance whereby that soul might be placed in similar situations, with the roles now reversed, in order to develop the same quality of compassion. In both cases the Law of

Retribution has been put into motion, consequently bringing forth new situations and new opportunities. By this process the soul may yet achieve understanding and thus evolve to the wholeness of Spirit, depending upon how the individual responds to these apparently new karmic situations. In reality these situations are not new at all. They are simply part of the same pattern that will exist until an "outpouring" is experienced through a deeper understanding of self regarding this pattern, or karmic condition.

This is the nature of the order in the universe. Everything happens for a reason. All predicaments are earned, even if not in this very lifetime, and from all predicaments one may learn and hence the soul may evolve. The timing of these predicaments, or cycles, is shown by astrology. Changes which occur within an individual's life coincide with an astrological cycle in that individual's life and may also coincide with an event in that person's life.

However it must be pointed out that it is not the true nature of astrology to predict "events," for too often individuals respond in different ways (or different events "happen") under the same aspects. As astrologers, it is helpful to understand that there are basically two types of "events" which may lead to major inner changes: events which seem to "happen to me," and those events "I make happen." Astrology cannot in all cases distinguish between the two, only that the timing is such that either type of event may happen. It is either through the free will of the individual to act or respond *in this lifetime* (which determines future situations for that soul), or through the consequences of that free will's actions or responses in a *former lifetime* that determine which of the two types of events are likely to happen under a given aspect. If the latter is the case, then it is a result of the individual's karma. If the former is the case, then new karmic conditions will result. In both cases, the event will affect one's evolution, and hence future experiences.

Astrologers can and do see these correlations which exist between the cycles of an individual's horoscope and the cycles occurring in the phenomenal realm of the individual's life. In light of astrology, events are not coincidences or happenstances; they are "timed" *in accordance with* the movements of the heavenly bodies. Yet, strangely enough, it has been the rule of astrologers – particularly those in the Western World – to apply this thought *only* to the events which occur *after* the birth moment. Why should events like marriage, personal accidents and tragedies, divorce, even death, be timed in accordance with the position of the planets, while an event like birth is not? Is the moment of one's birth to be considered a coincidence? Is the fact that one individual is born on Tuesday and another on Wednesday just a happenstance of no significant importance?

Over Memorial Day weekend in 1972, this writer had the opportunity to observe a demonstration in regression hypnosis, conducted by Philip Chase, an Educational Psychologist from Toledo, Ohio. Whether the reader accepts the validity of regression hypnosis or not is unimportant regarding the contents of this book, but this particular experience serves a point in explanation. During this demonstration the subject was regressed, through hypnosis, to a point in time "before birth" (this followed a gradual process of regression through this lifetime, even back to the period of infancy, which the subject was in many ways able to recount). The subject at this time suddenly took on an accent to his voice, a noticeably British accent. He began to describe a setting somewhere along the coast of England, the nature of the times he was living in (late 19th century), and the ways of the people about him. He answered questions from Chase concerning his marital status (a sad tale in which a fiance had died very young in his life), his occupation (a ship builder), and his familiarity with psychical matters (he knew nothing about them – did not even know what Chase was talking about). When Chase elaborated on the last point, the subject became very irate and blasted those who undertook an interest in psychical pursuits as "working for the devil!"

Chase next asked the subject to progress to the point of physical death in that lifetime, and describe the experience. The subject died of natural causes, apparently a saddened, forlorn man. At first he did not accept death, for at that point he described several attempts to communicate with those few persons he knew, but with no response. Some time after he actually died, he finally accepted his "death" state.

At this point in the regression, the subject (upon inquiry from Chase) described levels of experience on "the other side." Although this writer does not remember all the details, each level seemed very much like a "school," a place of learning. It seemed as if he was being "prepared" for another incarnation. The description implied he was with "very great persons," and they were in fact preparing him for another lifetime. To the question as to whether or not these "very great persons" were known as the *Lords of Karma*, the subject replied, "They say they are sometimes called that."

Chase then asked those observing if there were any questions they would like him to ask the subject. As several astrologers were present, this writer asked, "Is there any correlation between the *time* you will again enter the physical body, and astrology?" Chase repeated the question to the subject whose reply was a stern "No!" Apparently astrology was also lumped into the category of the work of the devil.

A voice in the back of the room spoke up after a couple of minutes of silence. "Ask him to ask that question to the Lords of Karma." Chase consented and asked the subject if he would mind asking these "very great persons" if there was any correlation between the moment of entering into a physical body, and astrology.

What next transpired was almost frightening. The subject did not respond for a long time. He began to undergo extreme physical changes, from calm and assurance to great discomfort, loss of color and heavy perspiring. The reply, spoken with a noticeable tremor and very slowly, was, "They-say-yes."

When asked by Chase if this was "something new, something you yourself did not know?", the subject responded in the affirmative.

The symbolic implication of this experience is that the moment of birth is not a matter of coincidence. The birth moment is as well timed by the cycles of astrology as are all the other important events in a lifetime. This idea is perhaps most effectively conveyed by Sri Yuktishwar, teacher of Paramahansa Yogananda, in Yogananda's *Autobiography of a Yogi*, wherein he states, "a child is born on that day and at that hour when the celestial rays are in mathematical harmony with his individual karma."[2] Thus one may conclude there is a different harmony with each passing moment of time, and that there is a relationship between the harmony of the universe and the soul of each individual as it is being born. That may be why the soul could not be born 15 minutes earlier – the harmony of the universe was no longer consistent with the nature of the soul to be reincarnated – or any time other than the actual moment of birth. For this reason, even Ceasarian operations, premature births or delayed births make sense: only at those times would the arrangement of the heavenly bodies be mathematically consistent with that soul's karma, and not at the times of expected birth.

In the natal horoscope, then, lies a story. It is a story of the soul. Through the arrangement of planets in the sky, the relationship of the planets to the zodiac, of the zodiac's and planets' relationship to the axis of the planet Earth, dwells a key that begins to unravel the mysteries of life. It is a key that begins to answer the question: "Why am I here? For what purpose?" At the moment of birth there is a mathemati-

[2]Paramahansa Yogananda, *Autobiography of A Yogi* (Los Angeles, Self Realization Fellowship, 1971).

cal harmony, a particular quality in the universe that is *of that soul.* The horoscope for that moment, showing the mathematical arrangement of the universe, describes the journey of that soul up to the point of birth, and a path of evolvement for that soul after the moment of birth. It describes the strengths and the weaknesses, the lessons learned and those yet to be learned, the nature of responses in prior lifetimes and the potential of liberating responses in this lifetime.

The natal horoscope is the result of the soul's karma. The situations to be experienced in this lifetime are a result of the soul's karma. One's responses to those situations in this lifetime will determine the nature of one's future karma, one's future horoscope. It is through the natal horoscope, the point of the soul's harmony in and of the universe, that a path to wholeness is given to humankind.

CHAPTER FOUR

The Natural Path of Self-Unfoldment: Sun-Earth Relationship at Birth

Time is a measurement of individualization.

In 1949, in the forward to the Wilhelm/Baynes rendition of the now-classic *I-Ching: Or Book Of Changes*, the great Swiss psychoanalyst Carl G. Jung writes a most-thought-inspiring idea, totally foreign to the Western philosophical schools at the time: "... whatever happens in a given moment possesses inevitably the quality peculiar to that moment."[3] The beginning of the statement suggests Jung's awareness that such a thought would not be easily accepted by the Western, Judeo-Christian intellectualism of his time. For those who are interested in his preface, it begins, "With us (Western minds) it would be a banal and almost meaningless statement (at least on the face of it) to say that whatever happens in a given moment possesses inevitably the quality of that moment."

If the author may be allowed to take liberties to expound on this thought, it seems that Jung is suggesting that there is a quality always present, a quality which is always changing, and only time (or at least time) measured by "moments" has a direct relationship on that which happens. Every moment is different – time is constantly moving and changing. Everything that "happens" is different from everything else that happens – at least in details – because the two things happen at

[3]Wilhelm/Baynes with introduction by Carl G. Jung, *I Ching: Or Book Of Changes* (Princeton, Princeton University Press, 1950).

different times. Along the same line, then, anything that happens at the same moment (two or more things) will be of a similar quality.

Besides a clock and calendar, one of the only tools that records *time* is a horoscope. The horoscope, the primary tool in the subject of astrology, takes into account an additional matter in its measurement of individualization: *space*. With astrology it is possible to have two things happen at the same time, but in different places, and thereby have different qualities (though many qualities of the two events will be quite similar). Thus Jung, from an astrologer's perspective, is giving credence to the idea that no two horoscopes are the same, unless they relate to births taking place at the same moment; thus, no two people are alike unless they are born at the same moment. Actually, though, no two people will be alike unless they are born not only at the same moment, but also in the same space. And what is alike, as most people realize, are principles, or qualities, and not necessarily physical appearance.

This difference, the subtle, physical difference in manifestation, cannot be measured in time *alone*, as Jung's thought suggests. But that concept of time ("moments") is certainly a most significant variable in the attempt to understand the existence of individualization (an obvious reality). Astrologers know this, particularly those who have examined the horoscopes and lives of identical twins. Here it is frequently in evidence that two people born in the same moment, same locale, and thus with identical horoscopes, still exhibit differences. Physically they may appear different. Many times the sex is different. The personality is not exactly the same: where one is joyous and kind, the other seems serious and cold. And events do not always happen at the same moment for each. For example, marriage may occur years apart, job changes at different times, children born at different times. What does seem to happen though, as Jung's statement would suggest, is that the two beings of identical horoscopes respond to the same principles in effect, both inwardly from birth as in personality expression, or outwardly in terms of what principles are being worked on at the same time. For example, when one astro-twin marries, the other is working on a principle of relating to others, perhaps in love, maybe business, maybe family.

But why the difference? Why are not the details the same, given the event of birth occurred at the same moment? For this one might ponder upon the thought of Sri Yukteswar as mentioned in the last chapter. Yukteswar was the guru of Paramahansa Yogananda, founder of the well-known Self Realization Fellowship (SRF). He was also a great philosopher in his own right. One day, Yukteswar indicated that

Yogananda should get an astrological amulet. Upon questioning his Master's reasons for suggesting such a thing, Yogananda was told: "Astrology is the study of man's response to planetary stimuli. Of themselves, (the stars) do not help or harm humanity, but offer a lawful channel for the outward operation of cause-effect equilibriums that each man has set into motion in the past.

"A child is born on that day and at that hour when the celestial rays are in mathematical harmony with his individual karma. His horoscope is a challenging portrait, revealing his unalterable past and its probable future results."[4]

From Yukteswar's concepts, one can expand upon the statement given at the beginning of this chapter: **Individualization is a product of karma.** And since the earlier idea stated that **"time is a measurement of individualization"**, it may be further deduced that **through the analysis of time, one can begin to understand the characteristics of one's karma, and hence the individualization process.**

The only study that provides meaning to this concept of "time-related-to-individualization" is astrology. The primary tool used for this measurement and analysis is known as the **horoscope.**

The horoscope is a circular representation of the heavens as seen from a particular point (space) upon Earth at a particular point in time. This horoscope can be divided into many sections, the most common of which are 12 parts known as the "houses" of the horoscope. It can also be divided into 360°, representing the size of a circle, or every degree of the band of 12 constellations known as the "zodiac", which acts as the backdrop against planets orbiting the Sun.

The horoscope can also be divided into four points known as the "angles," or sometimes referred to as the "cardinal points" (see Figure 1). The point rising in the East at any time is known as the "Ascendant", while the opposite point setting in the West is referred to as the "Descendant." The plane on the Earth connecting the Ascendant to the Descendant is called the "horizon", and separates that which is "above" (i.e. in view) from that which is "below" (i.e. not in view). For example, during daylight hours the Sun is "above" the horizon (i.e. in view), while at night time the Sun is "below" the horizon (i.e. not in view). In the horoscope of one born during the daylight hours, the natal Sun will be in the top half of the horoscope (i.e. above the horizon), while the natal

[4]Paramahansa Yogananda, *The Autobiography Of A Yogi* (Los Angeles, Self Realization Fellowship, 1971).

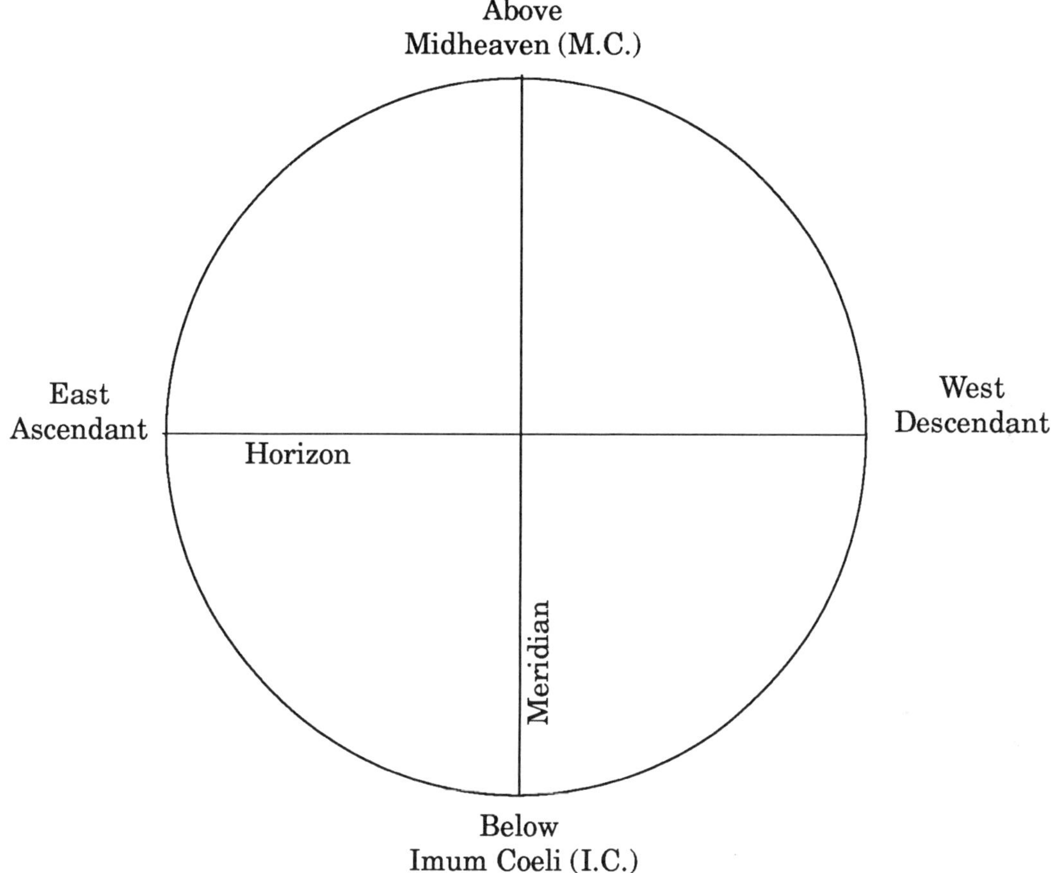

Figure 1
The four angles bordered by the horizon and meridian

Sun position of one born at night will be posited in the lower half of the horoscope (i.e. below the horizon).

As one can see, the horizon (or Ascendant-Descendant axis) is a function of the Earth's rotation on its own axis. As the Earth rotates constantly on its axis, each area upon Earth goes through a daily process of day and night. In other words, in a 24-hour day (actually slightly less), the Eastern and Western horizons (Ascendant and Descendant) will find each degree of the 360° zodiac circle rising and setting once. The orbit of the Earth on its own axis is thus the basis for a measurement of time, known as the seconds, minutes, and hours of a day. Modern clocks are based upon this measurement of time.

In contrast to the clock, there is another measurement of time utilized by man. It is the **calendar**, and it measures in terms of planetary orbits around the Sun. Several centuries ago a very intelligent civilization known as the Mayans used to measure time based upon the orbit of Venus around the Sun. Very accurate records were kept, and on the basis of these calculations the Mayans had a frame of reference by which they conducted their mundane affairs (i.e. planting, harvesting, etc.). Today modern man's calendar is based upon the orbit of the Earth around the Sun. By means of this measurement, man has conveniently been able to divide the days into weeks, months, seasons, years, and centuries.

Obviously the calendar measures durations of time which are greater and longer than that measured by the clock. Put in another way, time as measured by the orbit of the Earth around the Sun is of a longer or greater duration than that measured by the orbit of the Earth on its own axis. Both are important in the functioning of human affairs upon Earth. Yet it appears that the calendar time (i.e. Earth in orbit around the Sun) is more significant to the **"collective" or "group"**, while the **clock time** is more significant to the organization and functioning of the **individual**.

If time is a measurement of individualization, then it seems that the finer details of individuality will be signified by those parts of the horoscope which are most sensitive to changes in time. Thus the "angles" of the horoscope, which change as the Earth rotates on its own axis, may offer more insight into the karma, or nature of a soul being born, than the positions of the planets relative to the zodiac. The latter change slowly in relation to the movement of the angles of the chart. Their relationship to one's natal angles, and perhaps to each other, may describe the individual's relationship to (or functioning within) the collective, or group. The relationship of the planets to the angles and to one another, even to the zodiac constellations, may provide insight to the experiences each soul has had (and may yet have) "in the world."

For purposes which will become known later in this book, we will consider the planets like "messengers", or "servants" to the soul being born. We will consider the angles the key as to "who" this soul really is. In other words, the "angles" are the essence of the soul now incarnating; the planets are the experiences, talents, powers, conditions and even behaviors that one not only brings into this lifetime, but potentially will come into contact with during this period known as a lifetime.

The division of the horoscope by the horizon (i.e. above and below) has already been introduced. Another division may be made by the **"meridian."** The **meridian** divides the heavens into East and West by a vertical line in the horoscope. The uppermost point in the heavens at any given time (i.e. about 12:00 o'clock on a watch) is known as the Medium Coeli, or **Midheaven**. This is where the Sun is at approximately noon every day. A person born near noon will find the Sun posited near the natal Midheaven, or uppermost point in the horoscope (i.e. above the horizon). The lowermost point at any given time is known as the **Imum Coeli**. It is the point furthest **below** the horizon. It is not visible. The Sun is at the Imum Coeli near midnight, which is the time of day furthest from daylight. A person born at midnight will find the Sun posited near the Imum Coeli in the natal horoscope, or very close to the bottom of the chart. The line connecting the Imum Coeli to the Midheaven (also respectively referred to as the Nadir, or I. C., and Media Coeli or M.C.) is known as the **meridian**. All points to the left of the meridian in the horoscope are referred to as the **Eastern** portion of the chart, the center of which is the Ascendant. All points to the right of the meridian are known as the **Western** portion of the horoscope, of which the Descendant is the center. For purposes of this book the upper point of the meridian will be referred to as the Midheaven, the lower point as the I. C.

These four points then – the Ascendant, Midheaven, Descendant and I. C. – are known as the four "angles" of time, or the four angles of the horoscope. Like the minute hand on the clock, they too constantly change as the Earth makes one complete revolution on its axis every day. And like the clock, the "angles" of the horoscope separate the quality of the individual from the quality of the individual as he/she relates to the collective. The uniqueness of each individual soul begins in astrology with an analysis and understanding of the angles of the natal horoscope.

Models

Life processes are frequently explained by four-fold models. This is true in almost all aspects of study, from science to religion to economics. Many of these models cannot be tested by the rigorous tools of science because they are primarily logical in their nature. The test of the validity of these models is whether or not they are workable, which in many cases may simply mean: do they make sense? Given certain premises, or assumptions, do these models follow a logical progression? If so, they work, and hence they are useable.

If the models are truly exceptional, they do more than simply explain reality, or processes of life. They also inspire. A greater purpose of a workable model is to yield understanding, or illumination, in an area where there may have been no prior thought, explanation, or understanding.

Why are most models of explanation presented in the "four-fold" manner? The reason may lie in the nature of cycles, and the structure of time. For example, during the course of the Earth's orbit around the Sun, the Earth undergoes four seasons of change: winter, spring, summer, and fall. In most of the world's growing regions (i.e. Northern Hemisphere), the cycle of growing food (i.e. grains) follows the four-fold cycle of seasons. During the spring season, the seed is planted and shortly after it germinates. As summer unfolds, the plant or grain blossoms and eventually bears fruit. As autumn approaches, the growth cycle ends and the grain is harvested. The tree or soil then goes into a state of rest and/or replenishment as it prepares for the next planting season again. The season of rest and replenishment of the soil takes place in the winter season.

The natural order of the day is also based upon a four-fold cycle, which correlates closely with the individual's own body cycle. At sunrise, the Earth "awakens," and so too do many members of the human race (or shortly thereafter). The light of the day increases until noon. In like manner the most productive part of an individual's day is generally the quarter of the day that follows awakening. The day is completed at sunset, and likewise is the day of the individual completed thereabouts. Shortly after sunset the individual goes into a state of sleep, or rest, the deepest of which is usually around midnight. In "military time", these four quadrants of the time equate to the four cardinal points of the clock: 00:00, 6:00, 12:00, and 18:00.

Four-fold models are used in many of life's studies. According to Joseph A. Schumpeter, *business cycles* can be explained in a four-fold cycle model. A period of **innovation** starts each new business cycle. This is soon followed by a period of **prosperity**, when the economy would experience consistent growth. After the business cycle peaks, it is usually followed by a period of **recession**, or pause. Finally, when the value of the original invention has outworn its usefulness to the society, the economy enters a final cycle of **depression.**[5] A new innovation is then necessary to bring the economy out of depression and into a new, grand four-fold cycle.

In literature and drama there is also the four-fold pattern of unfoldment. The story begins with an introduction. The characters and setting are introduced to the reader or spectator. Following this the story evolves into a **plot**, in which a series of events **grow** into a **climax**. After the climax, there is a **resolution, or ending** to the entire story.

Evolutionary Astrology utilizes a four-fold model of explanation. The model is based upon the cyclic nature of life, and finds its roots in the four-fold cyclic nature of the Earth – with regard to the order of its natural day, and as well to the order of its annual cyclic orbit around the Sun. Time, like life, can be conveniently divided into four phases of a cycle. The beauty of this model, like most four-fold models, is that it is workable.

The four angles – the I. C., Ascendant, Midheaven and Descendant – are the basis from which an evolutionary approach to the study of astrology begins. Their relationship to the Sun in the natural order of the day provides symbolism that yields a deeper understanding of each soul as it incarnates into the physical body at a given moment of time.

Earlier it was stated that the planets are like "messengers", or "servants" to the soul. In this analogy, the Sun is the "master" within the soul. The planets represent specific evolutionary lessons each soul works upon in any given lifetime. The Sun represents the potential of integrating all of those lessons into one overview, one higher consciousness. When the individual is operating along the current of the Sun principle, then he or she is radiant, energetic, and creative. It is as if the soul has achieved a level of self-mastery. There is a sense of wholeness and completion within that individual. Hence the lesson ascribed to the Sun earlier was that of unity.

In its simplest terms, a basic principle of Evolutionary Astrology is that all souls seek to express themselves from the principle of the Sun. The Sun is the master, the planets are the servants. When the master is in charge, the expression of the individual flows without obstruction. One's consciousness is fully in alignment with the needs of its soul, which itself is fully in alignment with its very Spirit, or life force. These concepts, and the potential expression of one in alignment

[5]Joseph A. Schumpeter, *Business Cycles* (New York and London, McGraw-Hill Book Company, Inc., 1939).

with this energy, is symbolized by the position of one's natal Sun. It is denoted to some extent by the constellation in which the natal Sun is posited (calendar), but more so by the relationship of the natal Sun to the angles of the horoscope (clock). That is, the time of day when one is born is important. The time of day denotes the relationship of the Sun to the Earth. It denotes the path of self-unfoldment for each individual being born. It denotes the path of integration between the needs of the soul and the experience of communion with Spirit.

The Earth-Sun relationship is very special to all living beings. As the Earth rotates on its axis once every 24-hour day, individual's organize their daily activities, from sleeping patterns to eating, working and even mating routines. In astrology this is denoted by the relationship of the Sun to the angles of the horoscope. If an individual is born during the daylight hours, the Sun will be positioned *above* the horizon. Likewise if the individual is born during the hours of darkness, the Sun will be posited *below* the horizon.

The symbolism of **light** is the **outer, physical, world**. In light, one functions with and amongst other people. The individual learns about its self through interaction with others. The reality of this realm is based upon the relationship of the self to everything that is "not-self." It governs the world of duality, appearances, or maya. Reality is defined by the consensus, and the individual learns through dealings with, and feedback from, others. One who is born between sunrise and sunset will have the natal Sun **above** the horizon. Generally speaking this will suggest a soul whose sense of identity and natural path of evolution is most easily actualized through interaction with others, through activity in the **outer world**. In terms of Oriental philosophy, this section of a chart is "yang", or active.

Those born between sunset and sunrise are born during the **dark** part of the day. The symbology of **darkness** is that of the **inner world**, or unity. This part of the day (i.e. below the horizon) is "yin", or reflective. In darkness there is no relationship to that which is outside of the self, only to that which is "of the self." It is the self relating to the self. One's sense of identity and path of evolution is **innately** known, and it comes about most naturally through **contemplation**, or **interpretation** of one's experiences, not through the activity itself or the learning from others, which is more consistent with the person born during daylight. For the soul who is born during the dark part of the day, life is more of an initiation process, the self is more of a mystery. When the individual receives feedback from others as to what he or she is like, there is generally a sense of surprise and interest. The "real me" is something that is known primarily from a subjective viewpoint.

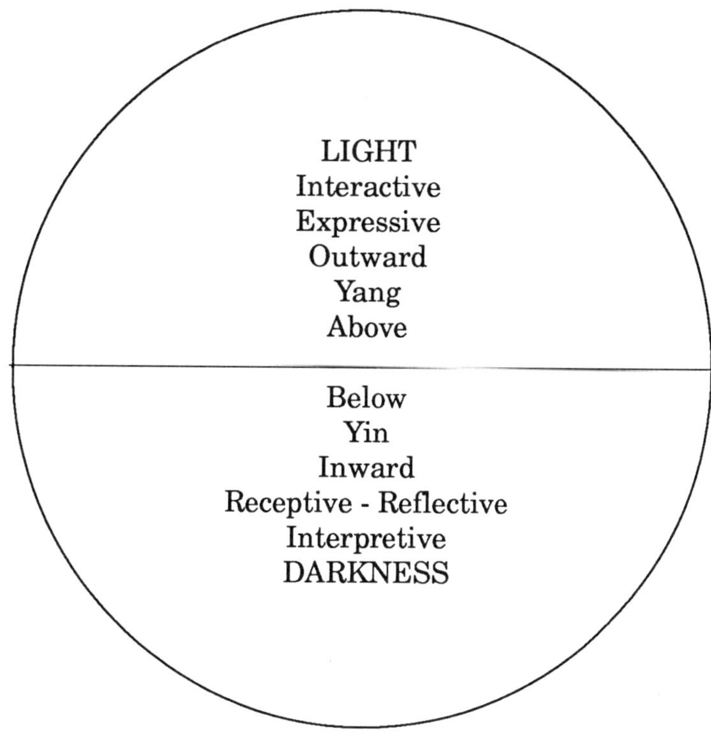

Figure 2
Division of the day; above and below the horizon.

For one whose natal Sun is below the horizon, evolution most naturally unfolds when time is spent in reflection, as in meditation or contemplation. For one whose natal Sun is above the horizon, evolution most naturally unfolds when activity and experience take place with and amongst other people. There may appear to be exceptions to this general thought: an individual with a natal Sun above the horizon may appear very reflective and contemplative, while one with a natal Sun below the horizon may show a disdain for reflection and time by oneself. This would suggest an individual whose natal Sun is not dominant. In the analogy given previously, the Sun is like the master of the household and the planets are like the servants. As long as the master is at home directing the servants in the proper expression of their roles, the household runs smoothly. However there are instances of unsuccessful households where the master is not home, or "out" temporarily, or even "weak". In these instances the servants run the household, and as a result certain areas receive more attention than "normal", while others less. The development is not whole, but rather imbalanced. Where some areas are very strong, others are very weak. In time such an imbalance will lead to problems.

In astrology a weak Sun denotes an individual who is likely "blocked," or "blocking" in some way their natural unfoldment. That individual is not "becoming" their Sun, and is likely showing great strength in some other planetary expression through a process known to psychologists as "over-compensation." A consequence of this may be a very complex karmic pattern and script, and an inability to experience any meaningful outpouring of love and compassion. It may also indicate a tendency to deny any opportunity to learn more deeply about the self through the difficult experiences that life brings forth. Several other consequences are likely as well which will not be discussed deeply at this point, except to say that one's relationships of intimacy may experience a certain amount of unusual stress through repetitive patterns that may be obvious to everyone but the individual him/herself.

In addition to the "outer world" (above the horizon) and "inner world" (below the horizon) division of the horoscope, there is likewise another two-fold division based upon that which is **East** of the meridian and that which is **West**. In the analogy of the natural order of the day, the Eastern part of the horoscope is that section wherein the Sun is located between midnight and noon (houses 3, 2, 1, 12, 11 and 10). This is that half of the day when the Earth is coming from darkness into greater light. This symbolizes awakening and growth, the urge to create and to move from the formless to the world of form. In terms of yin and yang, this part of the chart is also "yang".

As the light of the Sun steadily increases in this hemisphere, the power (or strength) of the individual to effect his/her environment also increases. The soul now moves into the world and into the field of activity. There is a sense of one's power and ability to make things happen. In this awareness of creative power, one discovers that he/she is the **cause** behind life's experiences, that he or she can make things

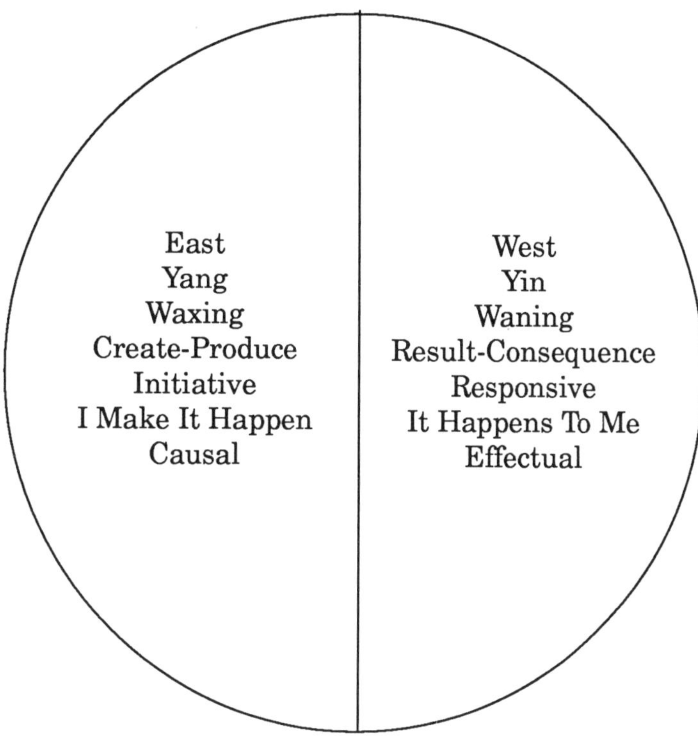

Figure 3
Division of the day; East and West of the meridian

happen and thereby affect external conditions. Generally speaking, one who is born between midnight and noon (with the natal Sun in the Eastern Hemisphere) finds the self through acts of creativity, and by means of an understanding that he/she is the *cause* behind what one experiences in life. The process of evolution unfolds most naturally when this individual willingly assumes those roles of "making things happen" in life, and undertaking projects and activities that require creative thinking.

In the natural order of the day, the period of time between midnight and noon is when the Earth is "waxing" in relationship to the Sun. The terms "waxing" and "waning" are usually applied to the relationship of the Moon in its phases to the Sun. When going from a new Moon (no visible Moon in the skies, or the "dark Moon") to the full Moon, the Moon is in its waxing stage. This is considered a period of increasing energy, and a favorable time to initiate new activities. Likewise between midnight and noon the Earth is increasing in light in reference to the Sun. As such the same principle applies: energy increases and the symbolism is that of initiating action. **In a spiritual sense, this waxing phase (new Moon to full Moon, or midnight to noon) represents the principle of *karmic* conditions being created.** An individual born during the waxing phase of the Moon (new Moon to full Moon) or the waxing phase of the Earth (natal Sun in the Eastern portion of the horoscope) may have a lifetime filled with opportunities to create karmic conditions, for better or worse. It may seem as if consequences unfold rather quickly for the actions initiated in this lifetime.

Given these principles it is easy to see the importance of creative activities and leadership roles in the lives of these souls. They are the means by which these souls most naturally evolve. Of course not all individuals with the natal Sun in the Eastern portion of the horoscope will seem to be leaders or the creative types. Again this implies an individual whose Sun is not dominant, that the path of natural evolvement may be blocked. In these cases there may be an over-emphasis (over-compensation) on some other planetary function. In childhood there may have been circumstances in which these behaviors were suppressed; the environment may not have been conducive to the natural evolution of the individual as implied by the horoscope. This does not mean that the individual will never develop in these ways. Remember the analogy of the plant or flower, which always leans toward the warmth and light of the Sun. Sometimes in its life cycle the light of the Sun is blocked from view and the plant's growth is stunted. It still grows, but in a rather twisted and perhaps painful manner. However when the obstructions are removed, the plant's natural growth cycle is rekindled, and in time its health (spiritual as well as physical) may be restored. In the same manner, once the individual understands and corrects any blockage to the natural self-expression, an abundance of energy is released, and the psychological, spiritual as well as physical growth process is renewed. It is as if the individual is "reborn." The key word is *understanding* of the self. Once that is transmitted (and that may be the role of the astrologer), the risks will usually be taken and the soul will seek an environment which supports this natural urge.

The Western section of the horoscope represents that part of the day in which the Sun (Earth) moves from noon to midnight. It is the waning phase of the day, when the light of the Sun decreases and darkness increases. It is again "yin", or receptive. When the phase of the Moon shifts to the waning stage it is said that one receives the consequences of those actions initiated under the waxing phase. The same symbolism applies to the waning phase of the day, or Western part of the horoscope. This is the realm in which the individual experiences the consequences of its prior actions. Reality appears to be one in which "things happen to me". One's life may appear to be a series of events brought on by external circumstances outside of the individual's control.

Generally speaking, individual's born during the waning Moon or waning Earth phase (natal Sun in houses 9–4 clockwise) may experience a lifetime filled with karmic circumstances, the consequences of actions put into effect in prior lifetimes, for better or worse. One's scripts are well-defined; one's patterns in life may be repetitive. In this case the individual has the opportunity to understand the needs of the soul through examination of these life experiences. If indeed there is a pattern to the experience(s), then these events serve as a lesson. One's responses are extremely important, for they will determine the quality of (attitude toward) all future experiences. The key word for these individuals may be *acceptance*. Understanding comes through acceptance, and vice-versa. The opposite behavior may simply deepen the pattern or script, making life seem more complex and perhaps difficult, depending upon the nature of those patterns.

In this cycle of one's evolution, the soul has choices of responses. The events or circumstances that confront the individual in this lifetime may be out of one's hands, so to speak. The people one meets may appear to happen by chance or coincidence, as if the individual just happened to be in the right or wrong place at the right time. Even one's parents or siblings or children may seem to be more by happenstance than by choice. These "happenstances" may even generalize to one's friends ("we just happened to grow up in the same neighborhood"), or teachers and even spouse. Everything may just "happen" to fall into place, and the individual was simply the recipient of these forces. Yet there are *choices* of responses to these conditions, and these *choices* will ultimately determine whether or not new patterns will emerge this lifetime. The control over one's *choices* and hence life's scripts, will come about when one 1) undergoes the consequences of prior actions set into motion and 2) understands the lessons inherent in those experiences which have a repetitive theme. In this segment, then, one ultimately becomes aware of his/her actions upon others as well as understands the effect of other's actions upon him/her.

An individual born with the Sun in the Western part of the horoscope will evolve most naturally by taking the time to examine "why" things happen in life. Giving and receiving feedback to and from others is very important in understanding who one is. By studying the nature of events, and the meanings behind their symbology, one gains a greater understanding. One is thereby able to give of him/herself to others and thus experience wholeness and joy, a communion of one's soul with its very life force, or Spirit.

This is but one way of using the angles of the horoscope to describe a four-fold model of experience. There are others, and each may be just as insightful as the first, just as workable and poetic in its symbolism as the one just set forth.

As mentioned earlier, the I. C. represents the darkest part of the day, the point where the Sun would be located at approximately midnight, local mean time. It is the part of the day furthest from light, and the part of the chart furthest from the horizon (lowest point in the horoscope). In another model of Evolutionary Astrology, the I. C. may symbolize the moment of **conception** in the life cycle, that point in time when the soul becomes **aware** that it will soon be given the privilege of expression in a bodily form. At the moment of conception, the arrangement of the heavens is in precise mathematical harmony with the quality (karma) of that soul. Its time has come. A process of preparation for the physical experience upon Earth begins. The period of time between conception and birth itself is known as the **gestation** phase. According to Roget's International Thesaurus, "gestation" is a synonym for "preparation." Regarding "preparation", Roget quotes Confucius: "In all things, success depends upon previous preparation, and without such preparation there is sure to be failure."[6]

At the point of the I. C. is the sum total of all prior preparation of this soul. It is the essence of the soul being reincarnated. The area of the horoscope between the I. C. and the Ascendant, usually referred to as quadrant one, is the "gestation", or preparation phase, the period of time in which the soul prepares (or is prepared) for this lifetime. As it is **below** the horizon, humankind's knowledge of this developmental phase

[6]*Roget's International Thesaurus*, 15th printing (New York, Thomas Y. Crowell Co., 1958).

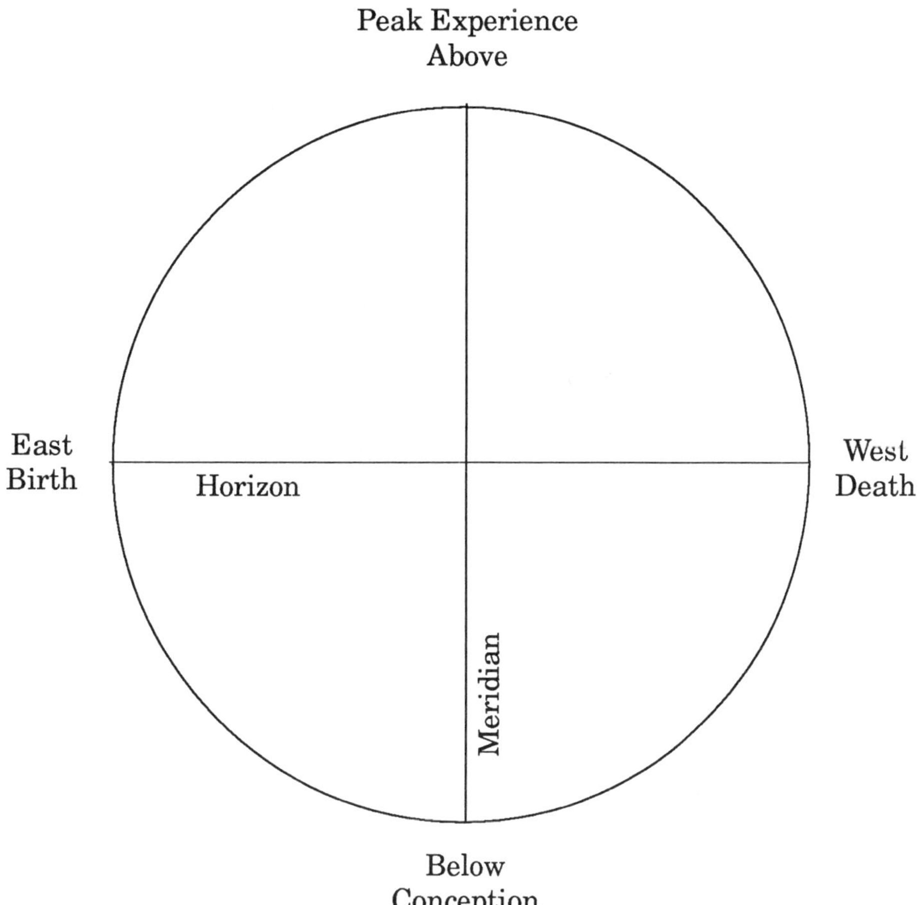

Figure 4
The four angles and their correspondence to the cycle of life.

is limited. It does not fall into the area of "outer" knowledge (above the horizon), the area which is readily available for humankind to explore, test, and become masterful over.

The second phase of the life experience comes about at delivery, the moment of **birth**, which is symbolized by the Ascendant. As the Sun rises in the East every day (Ascendant), Earth moves from darkness into light. Likewise when the baby is delivered at birth, the soul moves from the dark, comfortable world of oneness to the world of form and external stimuli. The transition may be shocking. Suddenly one's destiny "seems" to be in the hands of others and indeed this is literally true. The doctor or birthing facilitator actually puts his or her hands onto the baby as it comes out of the womb and into the phenomenal world. A multitude of new and perhaps surprising sensations are introduced all at once.

The birthing moment is a critical point in one's life. How one adjusts to outer conditions will greatly determine the quality of experience which lies ahead. The ability of the soul to achieve its life purpose depends to a larger extent on the segment of the horoscope known as the second quadrant in Evolutionary Astrology (houses 10–12), which symbolizes that period of life from birth to mature adulthood. Note that this is not the second quadrant of traditional astrology (houses 4–6). This second quadrant is based upon the natural order of the day, beginning at midnight. The second quadrant is thus that part of the day from sunrise to noon, and symbolizes the segment of life that unfolds from birth to the zenith in one's life.

At noon (local mean time) the Sun is posited in the highest point of the horoscope, the Midheaven. In the natural order of the day, this represents the period of greatest light. This symbolizes the **"peak life experience"** of this incarnation. Of the four cardinal points in the chart (I. C., Ascendant, Midheaven, and Descendant) and their corresponding symbolic representations of the life cycle, this point alone is the most difficult to measure. If the I. C. represents *conception*, the Ascendant *birth*, and the Descendant *death*, then what is that nexus point between birth and death? What is the height of that span of time in which the soul takes on the physical vehicle and functions in the phenomenal world of maya? Somewhere between birth and death is a moment just as significant to the soul's development as birth and death itself, and even as significant as conception. This moment of truth, this special experience that "changed the course of one's lifetime", is just as meaningful as the other three moments, and the consequence (karma) that is created or derived is just as significant.

But what is that moment? For each individual it will be different, but there are some guidelines that may help in identifying it. For example, everything in life appears to be a process of growth that builds up to this event, or moment. Furthermore, from the moment of that event onwards, 1) the effort, or act, or accomplishment coinciding with this event takes on a momentum of its own, and 2) the individual makes a psychological determination that the physical and mundane aspects of life "peak out", or enters a stage of decline in terms of life's own momentum. It will seem at that point as if one's life effort has made a transition from "being a challenge", in which everything was a challenge to be met and mastered, to one of either acceptance or struggle to maintain.

This is the point in life in which the individual comes "closest" to overcoming all fear, to feeling "mastery" and "fulfillment" of one's destiny. It is the point of attaining that which one strives for and desires in life. It is, on some level, rewarding. It is a moment of great happiness.

Obviously not everyone will experience the same degree of "rewarding experience" from this moment. This is where it becomes apparent that souls are on different levels of the evolutionary scale. Perhaps a general form of measurement of one's evolutionary state may be the *time* of this "peak life experience." The later in life it occurs may indicate a more evolved soul. For those whose peak life experience is death (in the physical) itself, for whom the entire life was a growing challenge, and for whom the event of death was something fully accepted before and during the experience, it is possible that a level which seekers refer to as "mastery" was present.

Another level of one's evolutionary state may be ascertained by the *nature* of the event that correlates with the Midheaven, or "peak life experience." For some it may be the moment of attaining fame, title, or acceptance. For others it may be the manifestation of an artistic or creative effort, like the publishing of a book, the exhibition of one's art project, the building of a house, or the birthing of a child (this latter creative effort is very often the peak life experience for many souls). For some it may be as simple (or complex) as one's first sexual experience, or even an early marriage. For them the growth process stopped relatively early in life, and life may have become quite a struggle from that point onwards.

At the moment of "peak experience", it is possible for one's creative efforts to take on a life and momentum of their own. The manifestation, or form of this effort may even live beyond the individual's own life, carry the "essence" of the individual soul onwards, as in the case of giving birth to a child, publishing a book, or completing an art project. It is the manifestation of one's essence, the "putting into form" the greatest expression of one's life energy, of what one is capable of achieving in the course of this lifetime.

Does one know when this "peak life" experience is happening? As a rule, no . . . no more than one is conscious of the conception, birth and death moment as they are happening (except possibly in the case of masters, those who are supposedly fully aware and conscious at all moments). However there is often a point in time (afterwards) when one becomes aware that this "peak" has unfolded, but by that time the Sun is usually in the "setting" phase. One may recognize that he/she has left the stage of the *warrior* and entered the stage of *sacrifice* (sometimes householder) in order to perpetuate the momentum of what has now been put into form (i.e. one's child, or project). Astrologically this is the point of moving from quadrant two (houses 12–10) to quadrant three (houses 9–7). At the point of "crossover", the individual begins doing things more out of responsibility to others rather than to itself. At the point of "crossover", the soul has met its primary challenge of this lifetime, the purpose for which it reincarnated and took on the bodily form. How it handled this challenge determines the next stage of evolution.

It bears reminding that there are many cycles within larger cycles. Up to this point great emphasis has been placed upon one single event, represented by the Midheaven, that overshadows all other experiences in life. Such a single event may be hard to define. It may appear that there are many such "peak experiences" in life. One may have many children, many books, many art works, many instances of fame and reward, which seemed to "change" one's life. Each one of these events takes on a momentum of its own, creates a "script" or "pattern" of a karmic nature in the individual's life. For each effort there is a cycle created, a series of consequences that follow, and a period of sacrifice and responsibilities that ensue. So long as one continually views life as a "challenge", continually meets "peak life experiences", then it may seem as if this lifetime is comprised of several lifetimes. The child within is forever growing – conceiving, giving birth and reaching a peak life experience and then taking a momentum of its own. Such may be the quality of a masterful soul and very aware individual.

The symbology of the Midheaven is **"peak life experience"**, an event of great fulfillment and meaning to the individual. For those souls who continually test the potential of their capacity to experience greater and greater dimensions of the human, or perhaps divine, experience, these "peaks" may be innumerable. Furthermore each "peak life experience" may in itself become a conception for the whole process to renew itself. In this sense the process becomes like a spiral. That is, the "peak life experience" is a moment of fulfillment and personal completion. Yet from it is born (conceived) another script, or another level of a similar life script. It is as if the one "peak" experience liberated the being from a certain confining pattern (karmic). The cycle was completed. In its completion, though, was born the beginning of a new cycle (or perhaps another layer of the old cycle). In this sense, rather than one

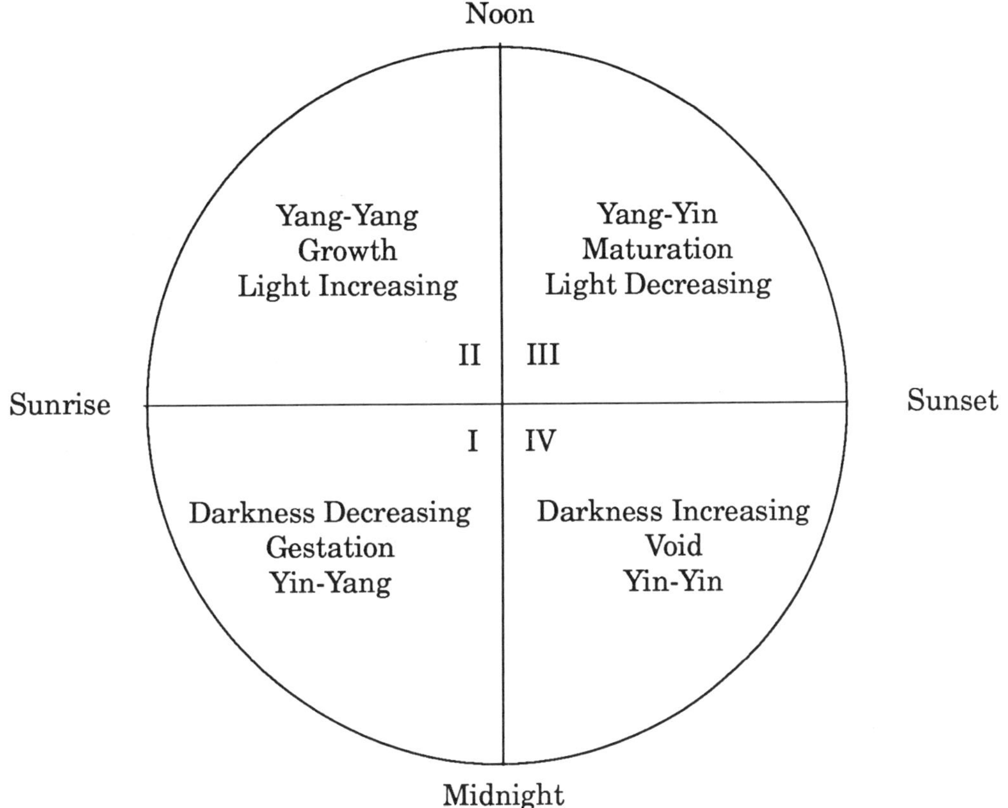

Figure 5
The four cardinal sections of the day and their correspondence to yin-yang and four-fold journey of the soul from one life to the next.

single **"peak life experience"** between birth and death in the physical, there may be a series, or spiral, of such fulfilling events in which each leads into the other. Perhaps one indication of evolution may be the number of times an individual has such a "peak" life experience in this life cycle. One's capacity to experience such intense events and consequent transformations suggests a soul who is moving quickly to liberate his or her being from the confines of karmic patterns that continually result in suffering of one kind or another.

The final point of the four-fold natural day model is the sunset. This is the point in the day when the Sun crosses the Descendant. This is the moment of *death*. This is the point in which the soul leaves the realm of light (maya) for the world of darkness (the inner plane). Because the cycle now enters the area below the horoscope (dark part of the day), it represents the "unknown" to our outward and collective mind. Again humankind is limited in its use of physical skills and knowledge to test and explore this realm. It is not part of the outer world where science reigns. More of this area will be discussed in the next chapter, but for now suffice it to say that like sunset itself, wherein the Earth graciously accepts the night without struggle or fear, so too does the evolved soul accept the end of its bodily life experience. All life form dies and regenerates. It is part of the larger cycle. In the world of appearances (maya), it "appears" to be the end. But it is only an appearance. Even in life itself, many cycles may appear to come to an end, but later it is seen that the same patterns and scripts return, just in different forms.

In the case of the soul, in reference to the archetype of the horoscope being a map of the soul's journey, the soul is leaving (death) its physical form (Descendant) and returning back to its essence (I. C.).

The response of the soul to its death in the physical body may determine the quality of the experience symbolized by the fourth quadrant (houses 6–4). Many souls fear and resist physical death. Unlike the Sun which graciously accepts the dark, the soul may find it difficult to accept the dark after a lifetime of light. Without going into states of consciousness which may exist "on the other side", like ghosts and spirits, suffice it to say that all souls eventually accept darkness. As in life itself, when one is in a lighted area, it may take awhile to adjust when entering a room of darkness. But eventually the eyes do adjust, and even in darkness one begins to see. In fact after awhile, one sees quite clearly, perhaps more clearly (in a spiritual sense) than one saw in light, because now the individual is no longer distracted by all of the stimuli of the outer world. There is more necessity for thought, contemplation and reflection. One is no longer in the world where the responsive and reactive mind are so dominant.

The key word for the Descendant is *acceptance*. The more able the soul is to accept death in life, the more one is able to understand the meaning and purpose of that life (or cycle). The same holds true with all cycles in life, from one's work to one's relationships. Once the termination phase of the cycle is accepted, the purpose of the cycle becomes clear. It works in opposite too: the more one understands the purpose and meaning of the cycle, the more easily the ending of it will be accepted. For this reason the deeper understanding of oneself is the foundation upon which Evolutionary Astrology is based. As understanding unfolds, meaningful movement along the evolutionary path proceeds. With each understanding comes a release: a release from past karmic conditions, and a psycho-emotional release of energy that can be described as the sweet outpouring of compassion. The experience is a spiritual one, but comes only when the soul registers that understanding. It is free to evolve to the next level, to meet the next challenge. It recognizes and accepts the end of a karmic script. One is released.

CHAPTER FIVE

The Natal Sun in the Quadrants of the Horoscope

The Sun is the center of our solar system. It is the source of energy that creates and sustains all life forms on Earth, our realm of physical existence. Without the Sun there is no physical life as we know it. Time, as measured by the rotation of the Earth on its axis (hours, minutes or seconds), or the orbit of the Earth through the skies (days, months, seasons) is a relationship of our planet Earth to the Sun. All major life activities are dependent upon the Sun. In our universe, the most important celestial body is the Sun.

In astrology the Sun represents energy, life force, and creative expression. In Evolutionary Astrology the Sun represents the natural path of the soul towards wholeness and fulfillment of purpose (destiny). The position of the Sun in the natal horoscope represents the natural path of evolution, or personal unfoldment for each individual. When this path is pursued, the soul becomes more radiant, more energized, in a manner similar to a plant as the Earth moves from darkness to daylight. Once the Sun rises, the plant seems to come to life again; it becomes strong and firm during the day (and during the spring and summer seasons), whereas after daylight (and seasonally after summer) it appears to retreat and go within itself.

The principles of the horoscope as an archetype of the natural day presented in the last chapter may now be applied to four quadrants of the chart. In so doing a deeper understanding of one's natural path may unfold, a path which potentially energizes and illuminates that soul. It is a path in which the individual becomes aware of the needs of its soul. It is a path by which the soul communes with its Spirit, it's very creative life force.

In Evolutionary Astrology, as in traditional practices of astrology, **quadrant one** is that section of the horoscope covered by houses 3, 2 and 1. In the natural order of the day, it is the time between midnight and sunrise (local mean time). The Sun is below the horizon (yin) and East of the meridian (yang). Hence it rules the "inner world" and the reality wherein the individual is able to "make things happen." During this period of the day, **darkness decreases**. In the Far East, the word *guru* means "one who dispels darkness."

As the Earth moves from greater darkness to lesser darkness, the kingdom of living organisms is (for the most part) ending its resting state. During the final stages of rest, it is preparing itself for activities which will soon begin in the outer world. In the previous chapter we referred to this segment of the life cycle as the "gestation" phase, and gestation was another word for *preparation*. As darkness decreases, *awareness* begins. In the natural order of the day, one becomes aware of the world of form that lies ahead; one becomes aware of a part or role it will play, of a dynamic interaction with others that will soon begin.

This is the state of preparation. It is like the time the actor takes before the curtain rises, or the athlete takes before the contest begins. In this state one requires a certain amount of peace and quiet to garner all of his/her strength, and to focus his/her attention. This is thus the quadrant of *meditation* and *focus*, of *preparation* and *awareness*. It is the area in which one is gathering strength, drawing in power and force that is to be released after birth (or commencement of the activity). The more time and care given to this process of preparation by those who are born with the Sun in this quadrant, the stronger and more confident this individual will become.

As this quadrant symbolizes that of "darkness decreasing", it is thus the area of *intuition*. As one becomes more and more aware, one senses things before they take form. Furthermore it represents a path of **self-mastery**. As it is the area below the chart (darkness), the soul is in a self-Self relationship for evolvement. As the Sun is in the Eastern portion of the skies (waxing), the soul's natural expression is to "create", to "make things happen". The soul therefore most naturally evolves in life through first-hand experiences. He or she has to experience it alone, has to find one's own path in life. Ultimately one is one's own best teacher. It is likely that efforts to find a "master" or "guru" prove disappointing, and deep self understanding comes more from creative initiation of activity. However this self-understanding itself is enhanced through effective preparation, like meditation and contemplation, before action is undertaken. In this manner, a natural path of evolution for the soul unfolds and in so doing the individual becomes an

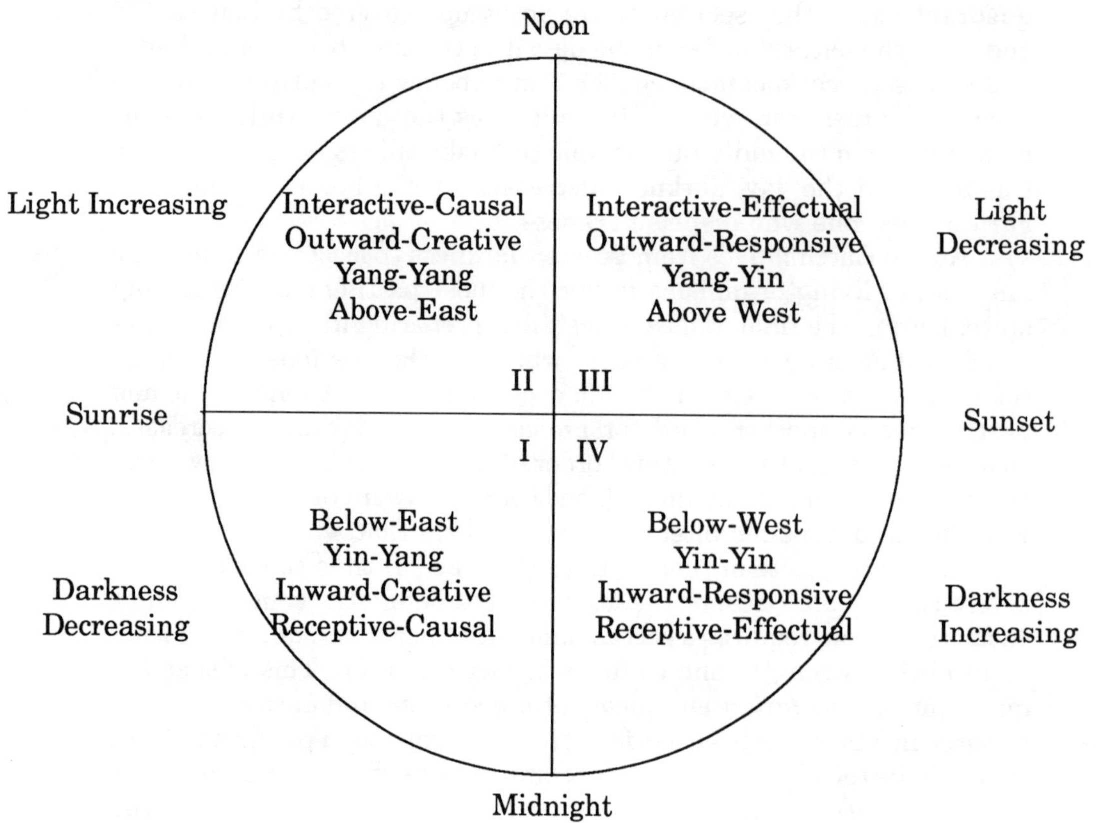

Figure 6
The four cardinal sectors of the day and their correspondence to the Law of Karma.

example for others. Though this soul may be awkward or uncomfortable as a leader, he or she may be one nonetheless, more through example than through intent. In fact this soul may have no need to be a visible leader, for having followers could very well hamper its activities. Responsibilities for others, which is required of leaders, may in time distract this soul from its primary objective. At the very least this soul is not a follower by nature, and to be in such roles would suggest a spiritual and/or psychological blockage wherein the personality developed resultant reaction formations which have weakened the will.

The **second quadrant** in Evolutionary Astrology covers houses 12, 11 and 10 (this is quadrant four in traditional schools of astrology). During this period of the day (when the Sun is in these houses) the Sun moves from sunrise to noon (local mean time). Thus **light increases**.

As the Sun is above the horizon there is an awakening. Living organisms generally "wake up" at this point, and leave the state of rest. This is yang. It represents entrance into the **outer world**, of the self relating to not-self. It is the individual functioning in the world of maya, or appearances, the outer, dualistic world. The Sun is also East of the meridian, also yang, and thus the soul can creatively initiate activity. He/she "makes things happen."

This is the empowerment quadrant (yang-yang). Moving from darkness (quadrant one) to light (quadrant two), awareness gives way to form. Creative urges in the outer world result in manifestation. To manifest an idea means something has been put into action; to creatively put forth effort and commitment to a project yields something of form and substance. There is power here – the power to manifest form or activity. This requires a certain amount of skill, or talent, or at least knowledge. It is therefore the quadrant of **skill, drive, and talent**, and the path of one with a Sun in this quadrant (born between sunrise and local noon) is that of a **warrior or magician**. It is not a magician in the classical sense of casting spells and incantations, but rather in terms of a soul who can transmute the formless into form, who can take the idea and manifest it into something of substance.

The natural path for a soul born during this segment of the day (natal Sun in houses 12, 11, or 10) is to develop and express some natural and creative skill. Unlike the soul born at night though, this soul does not function to the best of its potential when alone or in isolation. It is important to express its creative ideas in the outer world, whether through speaking, writing, or artistic expression. Communication with others is essential for self understanding. In many instances this individual may be viewed as an intellectual, or at least very skillful in some expression (i.e. geniusness or talented). An individual with natal Sun in this quadrant who does not express these qualities may exhibit some degree of psychological and/or spiritual blockage, particularly if not at all skilled or comfortable with other people. When the Sun's expression is blocked, regardless of which quadrant it is in, the individual will generally seem meek, tired and of low vitality. The individual is not in touch with, or conscious of, the needs of its soul. When the Sun is strong in expression, then the individual appears radiant and confident. That individual is in touch with the needs of its soul. The subject is of course more complex than this, but suffice it to say for now that many individuals do not follow their "Sun", and according to the principles of Evolutionary Astrology set forth herein, life for them is an emotionally reactive, separative, and possibly lonely experience. There is no connection between the ego (personality) and the soul. The Sun is the life-giver. Every soul is *becoming* their Sun. For some the path is pursued and rewarding; for others the path is avoided and the result is complex and repetitive patterns in life.

The natural evolutionary path then for a natal Sun in the second quadrant begins with knowledge. This knowledge is then to be applied towards a specific activity and requires **commitment** to purpose. Such a knowledge and commitment results in the development of a **skill or talent**. The individual thus has the potential to turn the idea or dream into form. It is therefore the quadrant of **manifestation**. The commitment to purpose is symbolic of the **warrior**, and the talent to transform the formless into form is symbolic of the **magician**.

The **third quadrant** spans houses 9, 8, and 7. In the natural order of the day it is the time between noon and sunset. Light is decreasing. The Sun is still above the horizon (light and yang) so it still pertains to activity in the outer world (self to not-self). Now however the Sun is West of the meridian (yin), so it is the reality wherein the individual bears the consequences of prior actions (receptive). In this segment, things seem to "happen to me", as opposed to me "making them happen." Like quadrant one, this too is a balance of yin and yang principles (active-receptive).

This is the realm of **socialization**. One now bears the consequences of his/her actions upon others. One now becomes the recipient of cycles previously put into motion. Experiences arise in the individual's life over which it appears there is no control. The individual has no choice but to go through these experiences. Yet there is choice within the experience itself. One may choose how to respond, and what to learn. Such choices depend upon the individual's awareness of its soul, and the needs of its soul.

From every major life experience that appears out of one's control, there is something to be learned. First of all, one must understand what can be changed and what cannot. That which cannot be changed must ultimately be accepted. The process of coming to acceptance of something involves a deeper understanding of oneself, and this is where the learning comes in.

Fortunately (in most cases) this quadrant not only brings events in the life that serve a learning purpose, but it also brings into the life path other significant individuals who likewise facilitate the learning (and accepting) process. It is from these people that one learns. Hence this is the quadrant of the **student, or apprentice, or disciple**. Once one learns, though, the script is not complete. Remember this segment is above the horizon, so the individual stays "in the world." Once the student learns or the disciple masters, then he or she must become the **teacher,** or **master,** or **mentor** (or even **guru**). In this process the **exchange of understanding** continues.

For lack of a better word, this quadrant represents **assimilation and understanding** that comes through **experience**. The lifetime may appear to be filled with crises, but as the individual realizes these are opportunities for the soul to learn and understand life in a more complete fashion, he or she will then begin to understand the deeper meanings of his or her life. In this way that soul will achieve its destiny of teaching others, for this is the quadrant of the **teacher**. One who develops the soul as a teacher by learning from life's experiences will express the radiant and confident qualities of the Sun. Those that resist learning from these experiences, and persist in seeing life as a miserable series of helpless crises, will find it difficult to transmit understanding to others (let alone learn understanding from others). Their Sun may not shine, and their vitality and confidence may be low.

The natural evolutionary path for the individual with natal Sun in the third quadrant begins with **experience**. These experiences may seem (and perhaps be) **crises** compared to the lives of others. Yet these experiences, or crises, serve a definite purpose (i.e. completion of karmic cycles as well as deeper self understanding in order to transcend these cycles). Therefore it is essential that the individual **learn** from these critical experiences. This is done through integration, or **assimilation** of these experiences (not denial). Once the experiences are assimilated and their deeper meanings understood, a **transformation** takes place. One either **accepts** him or herself at last, or else sees a way to change (transform) the script. Ultimately this involves a **sacrifice**, an understanding that one's life is to be used for the betterment of others. A strong sense of responsibility to others will likely emerge at this point in the evolution. If the evolution is "stuck", or the individual becomes fixated, then instead of a sense of responsibility to others and willingness to sacrifice, there is instead a **denial** of responsibility, either for things which happen to the individual, or to others. However with those souls who are evolving in their natural manner, there is first **learning (through experience) and then teaching to others**.

The final **fourth quadrant** covers houses 6, 5, and 4. In the natural order of the day this time corresponds to the period between sunset and midnight, local mean time. The Sun now travels below the horizon, so it is the realm of one having a dialogue with its self, of interpreting experience. It is the **inner world**, the world of unity (yin). It is also west of the meridian (yin), so it is still in the reality wherein "things seem to happen to me." The individual encounters events that appear non-causal.

This is a very subjective world (yin-yin). Events unfold in the individual's life, and he/she must interpret and find meaning in those events by him/herself. Outer stimuli having an inward effect is the basis for **inspiration**. As an example, one may be traveling down the highway some starry night, listening to a song on the radio. The words in the song catch the listener's attention and touch off a series of associations. Upon arriving home this individual may sit down and write a poem or a song. In this example, the individual was inspired by an event that happened to him/her, but internalized that event and then interpreted it subjectively according to his/her own life experience. In this quadrant, one is very susceptible to internalizing outer events. It is as if one is a **channel** to very subtle forces.

As the Sun goes from the world of light to darkness, the soul is going from the world of the known to that of the unknown. In the world of light, activity proceeded according to predictable and accepted consensus rules, or laws. In the world of darkness there are also laws in effect, natural laws, but these are not the same as those "of the world." Making this leap from light to darkness requires a high degree of **faith**, for it is like jumping into the void. Faith requires overcoming fear. There is a certain **risk** one must be willing to accept, for the result of one's actions is never known beforehand; the result of one's "leaps" cannot be known until after a commitment to action. Consequently this soul approaches life as a **mystery**. If the Sun is dominant and pursued naturally, this individual may appear to venture into unknown areas where the results and consequences are not determinable. Yet if one's faith is strong, there is an inner sense of confidence that each of those adventures will yield something of great value. Fear and risk are normal here, but to the individual who takes the risk (makes the leap into the void), fear is conquered, and a connection to the soul is formed. Great vitality and confidence results from meeting the challenge and emerging successfully. For the individual who does not wish the risk, who does not have the faith in him/herself, fear likely remains. Life becomes a series of repetitive and uninspiring routines, and/or compulsive adherence to schedules.

The natural path of the soul born between sunset and midnight

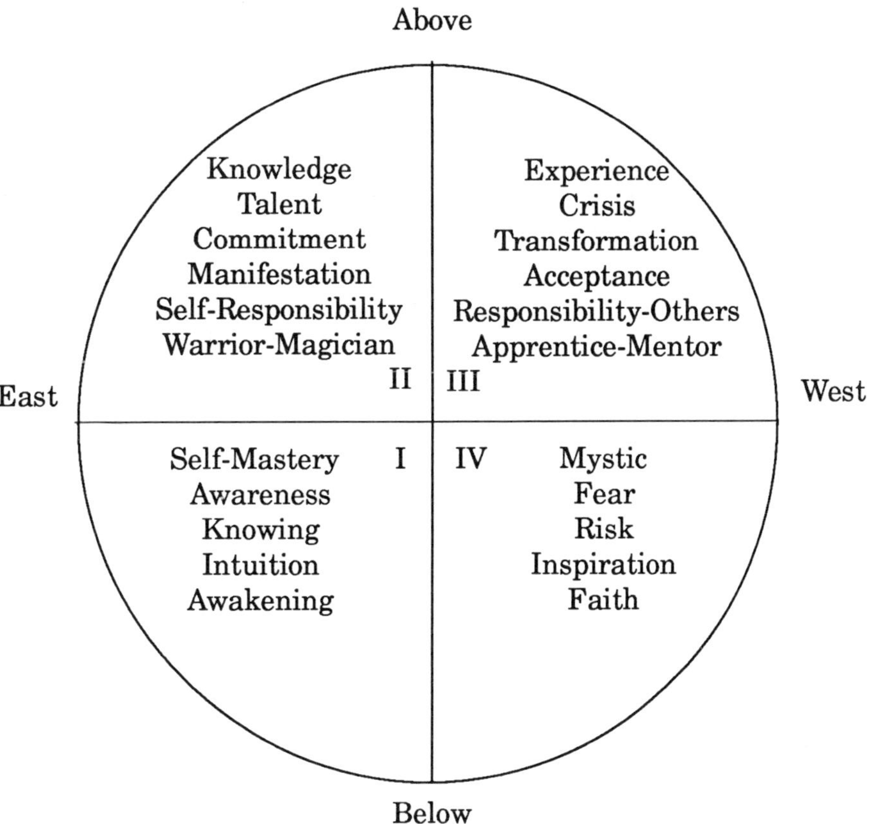

Figure 7
The four sectors of the universe
and their correspondence to paths of self-realization

(natal Sun in houses 6, 5, or 4) is that of the **mystic**. The soul does not try to control or manipulate events, but rather learns to accept them. There is a faith that everything is in divine order, and things do not have to be proven according to codes of the outer realm.

In summary, then, there are four quadrants of the horoscope (see Fig. 7). The Sun is in each quadrant at various parts of the day. The quadrant of the Sun at birth determines a natural path for that soul's evolution. There are certain qualities and processes that naturally unfold and enhance that soul's path, according to the quadrant of the natal Sun.

The Sun in quadrant one denotes *self-mastery*, a soul with a heightened sense of **awareness and intuition**. The Sun in quadrant two denotes the path of the *magician or warrior*, one who possesses a skill, drive, talent or knowledge to transform ideas into form. A quadrant three natal Sun indicates the path of the *student-teacher*, or *apprentice-master*. This soul develops a deep **understanding of life** through assimilating experiences, by seeing crisis as an opportunity to learn. The natal Sun in the fourth quadrant represents the path of the *mystic*, one whose faith in the divine order and balance of the universe allows receptivity to the phenomenon of **inspiration and channeling**.

By understanding this four-fold path of spiritual activity and personal growth, the soul's journey may be illumined.

PART TWO

The Nature of the Incarnating Soul

CHAPTER SIX

Imum Coeli

The Imum Coeli or I. C. represents the essence of the incarnating soul. It symbolizes the sum result of one's past experiences brought into this lifetime.

The journey of the soul through the horoscope begins with the I. C.. Traditionally the I. C. symbolizes the home of the individual and interestingly enough, there is an old Zen anecdote where the master welcomes the wanderer returning from a long journey "back to the home you have never left." In one sense, the universe itself is the home of every soul. Just as we look at one's home in a mundane perspective as the foundation for each individual in this life, so too is the I. C. viewed as the astrological foundation of the soul in this incarnation. It is the "roots" of each soul, for in that very degree (and minute) lies a quality which is the result of all past life experiences – even all experiences prior to the birth moment. In this single point – the I. C. – lies the essence of the question: "Who am I?"

Since the I. C. is an angle – and a most important one in Evolutionary Astrology – it too will change quite rapidly in time. In fact, it changes one whole degree approximately every four minutes. As previously mentioned, every degree (even every part of a degree) has a specific and unique quality. In terms of Evolutionary Astrology, the quality signified by the degree on the I. C. correlates with the basic nature of this soul. It describes traits – strengths – which the individual has developed and brings forth into this lifetime. It may be likened to "innate" qualities, rather than "learned" qualities (which is more the Midheaven function).

It is necessary to point out that individuals do not always express their "real self" as symbolized by the I. C.. More often than not most individuals express the social, or ego self symbolized by the Ascendant.

This is because of the illusion of the outer world we live in – the illusion that the *only* reality is that which is shared with others (the outer realm). When one is expressing from a foundation which is a result of experiences beyond this single lifetime and not solely in the context of the world of maya in this lifetime, then that expression is more likely according to the nature of the I. C. symbolism.

It is also important to note any planets located around the I. C., as well as the planet(s) ruling the I. C.. I. C.-related planets indicate particular lessons the soul has learned, particular abilities and powers the soul has developed, which it now carries into this incarnation. This will be discussed more in another chapter.

The method of analyzing the I. C. begins with a consideration of the sign itself. This sign describes the primary traits of the soul's nature. These are the strengths already developed, the expression of which comes easily in this lifetime (like "second-nature"). It describes a type of individual, molded as such through many, many experiences prior to this life.

Next, one may analyze both the decanate and the dwadashamsa of the I. C.'s sign and degree. These two factors describe secondary strengths, previously developed, which may now be used for the successful expression of the basic nature (I. C.'s sign). It describes how one integrates other factors into its greater, primary expression.

Finding the decanate, dwadashamsa, and individual degree for each I. C. is a somewhat detailed and complicated technique. Decanates consist of a three-fold division of each sign according to the elements. Therefore the explanation of this technique rightfully begins with a brief review of the elements in astrology.

The four elements are Fire, Earth, Air and Water. Each sign of the zodiac belongs to one of these elements and each element contains three signs of the zodiac.

Every fourth sign beginning with Aries belongs to the fire element. This includes Aries, Leo and Sagittarius. The quality implied by fire is one of involvement, desire, growth and action. Every fourth sign beginning with Taurus, which includes Virgo and Capricorn, belongs to the earth element. Present here are the qualities of analysis, practicality, achievement, and understanding. The air element includes every fourth sign beginning with Gemini; hence Libra and Aquarius fall into this triplicity. This quality is one of detachment, intellect, inspiration, and the expression of ideas. Finally, there is the water element which includes Cancer, Scorpio and Pisces. The quality of water is one of acceptance, but acceptance of one's own intuitions. Water also possesses a "feeling" or emotional quality, and tends toward attachment.

Table 1

Sign	1st decanate (0–10 degrees)	2nd decanate (10–20 degrees)	3rd decanate (20–30 degrees)
Aries	Sagittarius	Aries	Leo
Taurus	Capricorn	Taurus	Virgo
Gemini	Aquarius	Gemini	Libra
Cancer	Pisces	Cancer	Scorpio
Leo	Aries	Leo	Sagittarius
Virgo	Taurus	Virgo	Capricorn
Libra	Gemini	Libra	Aquarius
Scorpio	Cancer	Scorpio	Pisces
Sagittarius	Leo	Sagittarius	Aries
Capricorn	Virgo	Capricorn	Taurus
Aquarius	Libra	Aquarius	Gemini
Pisces	Scorpio	Pisces	Cancer

Every 10 degrees of any given sign is ruled by a specific decanate. Every decanate belongs to the same element as the sign itself. For example if the sign is Aries, then every decanate of Aries will be a fire sign, for Aries belongs to the element of fire. The first 10 degrees coincides with the sign of the same element *preceding* the sign being analyzed. Thus if we are concerned with the first 10 degrees of Aries, its decanate corresponds to Sagittarius, the sign of the fire element which precedes Aries. The last 10 degrees of a sign corresponds with the sign of the same element which *follows* the sign being analyzed. Therefore, the last 10 degrees of Aries would correspond to the Leo decanate, for Leo is the fire sign following Aries. The middle 10 degrees is the decanate ruled by the sign under examination itself. Thus, 10–20 degrees of Aries corresponds to the Aries decanate.

To use another illustration, let us consider the sign of Scorpio. The first ten degrees of Scorpio would correspond to the water sign preceding Scorpio, which is Cancer. The middle ten degrees would be Scorpio itself. The last ten degrees would correspond to Pisces, the water sign which follows Scorpio. Thus the first decanate of Scorpio is Cancer, the second decanate is Scorpio itself, and the third decanate of Scorpio corresponds to Pisces.

It is only important to realize that a decanate is like a sub-ruler of a sign. It gives an added dimension in understanding the qualities of that particular part of a sign. It is *not* stronger in influence than the sign itself, but does have a *modifying* influence on that segment of the sign, according to the nature of the decanate sign. In terms of Evolutionary Astrology, the decanate is like a secondary trait, aiding the expression of the individual's primary quality (signified by the sign on the I. C.).

The matter of dwadashamsas is a little more complex. Dwadashamsas are the twelve-fold division of each 30 degrees of a sign. Hence each dwad contains 2½ degrees. All 12 signs of the zodiac are contained within every single 30-degree sign through the application of dwads, beginning with the decanate ruling the first 2½ degrees of any sign. Every following 2½ degrees makes up another dwad, a dwad which corresponds to every sign following the first decanate sign. For example, if the first decanate of Aries is Sagittarius, then the first dwad of Aries (the first 2½ degrees) is also Sagittarius. The next 2½ degrees (from 2½–5 degrees) of Aries corresponds with the sign following Sagittarius, which is Capricorn. From 5–7½ Aries is the Aquarius dwad, and 7½–10 Aries is Pisces. The first 2½ degrees of the next decanate (which is the sign itself) is the same as the decanate, or in this case, it is Aries also. In fact, from 10–12½ degrees of any sign, will be the area in which the decanate and dwad are always the same as the sign itself. And so on it follows; every 2½ degrees makes up a new dwad corresponding to the following sign. In the end, every sign is assigned a dwadashamsa in any one given zodiac sign.

To use another example, consider the sign of Virgo (see table 2). The first decanate is ruled by Taurus; hence the first dwad of Virgo is also Taurus. Every dwad (2½ degree segment) which follows, does so in a fashion consistent with the order of the zodiac. Therefore, 2½–5 degrees corresponds to Gemini, 5–7½ to Cancer, 7½–10 to Leo, 10–12½ to Virgo itself, 12½–15 to Libra, and so on until the very last 2½ degrees, which correspond to Aries.

Like the decanates, the dwadashamsas are not as influential as the sign itself. In fact, dwadashamsas are not even as influential as decanates. But like decanates, they do have a modifying effect, both on the sign and the decanate of the sign. And in terms of analyzing the I. C., the dwad will also indicate secondary traits which have aided the expression of the soul's basic self (shown by the sign on the I. C.).

As each dwad corresponds to a sign, it too can be further broken down by a three-fold (sub-decanate) and a twelve-fold (sub-dwadashamsa) division in the same way each sign itself was broken down. For instance, the first third of any dwadashamsa (the first 50 minutes of its 2½ degrees) would correspond to the sign of the same element as the dwad, which precedes that sign in the zodiac. The second 50 minutes would correlate to the sign of the dwad itself, and the

Table 2: A breakdown of the dwadashamsas for the sign of Virgo.

Degree of Virgo	Dwadashamsa of That Degree	Decanate of These Degrees
0–2½	Taurus	Taurus
2½–5	Gemini	
5–7½	Cancer	
7½–10	Leo	
10–12½	Virgo	Virgo
12½–15	Libra	
15–17½	Scorpio	
17½–20	Sagittarius	
20–22½	Capricorn	Capricorn
22½–25	Aquarius	
25–27½	Pisces	
27½–30	Aries	

final third of the dwad would correspond to the sign of the same element which followed the dwad's sign.

To find the sub-dwad would then be a matter of breaking down each dwadashamsa into 12 equal parts, or 12½ minutes per sub-dwad. The first 12½ minutes of each dwad would correspond to the sub-decanate of the dwad. Every 12½ minutes following would be associated with the following sign, until all twelve signs had been assigned a sub-dwad rulership for every 12½ minutes of each dwadashamsa (see table 2 for proper order).

Although this seems a very detailed and perhaps tedious analysis of each sign, it does serve the purpose of explaining the uniqueness of each soul, even to the point of those born only one minute (or slightly less) apart from others. To analyze a sign only to the point of the dwadashamsa alone (to the nearest 2½ degrees) allows a margin of up to 10 minutes in time between the births of two or more individuals. To analyze a sign only to the point of one degree allows a margin of up to 4 minutes in time between births. To further extend the analysis to the sub-decanate of the dwad cuts the margin of similarity between individuals down to a three minute span, while the sub-dwad would further reduce the time difference to about 45 seconds of time.

One may question the necessity of going to this extreme in detail of analysis. The answer depends upon the nature of the astrologer doing the analysis, and how specific that astrologer wishes to get in the delineation of the chart being studied. It is obvious that the matters of sub-decanates and sub-dwadashamsas are comparatively weak influences to that of the sign itself on the I. C.. Although the smaller divisions such as the sub-decanates and sub-dwads do distinguish the individuality of one soul more finitely from another, the process may seem cumbersome. As such, the fine tuning of these sub-degrees will not be illustrated herein, but rather left to those who enjoy calculating such detail.

The analysis of the sign, its decanate and dwadashamsa, and perhaps the symbolism of the degree itself on the I. C., will likely prove illuminating enough to produce a deeper understanding of the essence of the incarnating soul. For our purposes we will consider first and foremost the sign itself on the I. C.. It is suggested that the meaning and symbolism of this sign be furthermore modified by the decanate and dwadashamsa of that sign's degree. Each sign has a unique and special quality; when combined with the decanate and dwad, the uniqueness becomes even more distinguished. Below are the descriptions and symbolisms inherent in each sign on the I. C.. Read and meditate upon them and their combinations (sign, decanate and dwad) to more deeply understand the answer to the question: "Who am I?"

Aries (The Explorer):

These souls are the pioneer types of the zodiac. The urge for adventure and action is very strong, because in past incarnations these individuals made up what might be described as a "new breed." The symbol of the explorer literally means this soul explored into new areas, whether physically or mentally or both. Therefore the desire to travel to new and uncultivated lands, or to explore areas of consciousness where few have tread, may be great in this lifetime. Souls with Aries on the I. C. are by nature not afraid of danger or pain; in fact, they take more risks than other souls, even where their own well-being is concerned. They are accustomed to being the first, having established and perfected themselves insofar as being the initiators of new activities from which others may benefit and grow. An urge for greatness, to do something entirely different yet never tried before, is also characteristic of these daring types as a carry-over from past life experiences. There is a need to express the self creatively and freely, and when this "natural expression" is blocked, the individual is apt to do something drastic (probably to itself).

Taurus (The Earth Magician):

Here we have souls who seek truth and purity. Extremely self-sufficient, due to previous lifetimes alone or with nature, the Taurus I. C. individuals still seek a life of simplistic purity. They are natural healers. The study of herbs and natural healing processes come quite easily in this lifetime. The symbol of the Earth Magician conveys the innate ability to sense what is ailing another, and to put together that which may heal the ailment. This is because they have the gift to be "in tune" with the properties of nature. Many of these individuals will gravitate toward a very natural living style (a "oneness" with nature) or spiritual subjects. They tend to form their own unique ideas and may develop a special relationship with a "higher force", again perhaps a result of lifetimes spent alone in deep contemplation. Since these souls have devoted much of their efforts toward studying the true nature of life, they are not likely to let the ideas of others influence them easily on this subject. Once they are re-acquainted with spiritual matters in this lifetime, they may find that they possess great inner powers and gifts. Taurus also rules bookkeeping and accounting, so there may also be a natural talent and trustworthiness in these roles.

Gemini (Akashic Record Keepers):

Over many, many lifetimes, these souls may have developed the gift of keeping records in order. On the higher planes, this could deal with the records of the soul's growth, known as Akashic records (hence the symbol). In this lifetime these souls may tend to keep notes, either for others or for themselves if they decide to pursue any particular area of self-development. For instance, if they choose to be chefs, somewhere in their files will be very orderly notes on recipes they might use. These souls are also developed in the art of communication, perhaps due to prior lifetimes as speakers, writers, journalists, humorists, or merchants. Consequently they do very well in the "marketplace" where others gather to exchange thoughts and ideas, for they are equally charming and refined in their manner. Because they have learned how to deal with people (what to say to others) in lifetimes past, they usually excel in business transactions in this incarnation. There is also a mental openness, a receptivity to discuss new ideas, for their minds have become very flexible and their interests greatly varied.

Cancer (The Romanticist):

The nature here is very sensitive, yet very maternal and protective. Over the course of many lifetimes, these souls have learned to "sense" what is going to happen, not only for themselves, but for those whom they love. Family loyalties may be strong. Love and devotion are qualities which are natural and yet necessary, for they believe in ideals as something that can and should be attained, but always with someone else (a mate, a family, or a community of compatriots). The symbol of the Romanticist depicts this love, this devotion, which they willingly give to another with whom they feel a strong bond. Through prior lifetimes of "watching and caring for the homefront," while others (usually loved ones) ventured out into the world of the unknown, these Cancer I. C. souls developed great and refined domestic talents. Consequently in this lifetime they may possess highly developed culinary tendencies, skills at making things in the home, and refined taste in both art and music. The need to share in experiences, ideals, and dreams as well as realities, is a necessary criterion for natural self-expression of these souls.

Leo (The King and the Queen):

Royalty and/or rulership abound in the backgrounds of these souls. Great power over others has been experienced, and from it comes a very strong will in this lifetime. These souls may have a strong magnetic nature which either attracts or repels others (and sometimes both) who now return into one's life to work out the karmic accruement from the past. Because power has been so strong in the past, and because influence has been over many, almost all of one's relationships in this lifetime will reflect repetitive karmic (psychological) scripts. Almost instinctively these souls expect others to be loyal to them now, and when this is not so, they may still tend to wield their power in some way. They are natural rulers, natural "kings and queens". For those who are loyal to them, these Leo I. C. souls can be very kind and generous in their rewards and affections. They understand power and they understand authority, and consequently they are very aware when others treat them unfairly (which they tend to despise). Another carry-over from the past may be the ability to be very dramatic when they wish to get a point across.

Virgo (The Apprentice):

Here we have the souls who know the true value of a cooperative effort in order to get things done effectively. These individuals are master planners, having developed the ability of putting things together, getting things in order, for the proper and perfect manifestation of any and all endeavors. They do not, as a rule, seek the limelight for themselves. They are more concerned with the effects or consequences of those activities with which they associate themselves. Therefore they tend to serve others – and very competently – who are "in the limelight." They may have been prepared for this role over many lifetimes wherein their service was necessary for the successful culmination of efforts on the part of others. The symbol of the apprentice implies that they are seekers of knowledge. For those bearers of truth, the Virgo-I. C. is ready to learn, serve, and advise. In effect they are gifted at preparing the scene in which others will interact in the "cosmic drama," then quietly removing themselves to observe. This they may have done so many times that they now possess an innate gift of foresight, of "knowing" what the results will be even before the drama begins.

Libra (The Refined, or the Artist)

Such a rich and illustrious tradition lies behind these souls. In civilizations gone by these individuals may have assumed the role of "the beautiful people", those high on the social spectrum. They may still possess grace, charm, and tact. As a result of past experiences these souls might now be born into families much lower on the social structure than they were used to before, but their inherent quality usually strives for the best in everything, from clothes and material possessions, to the "kind" of people they will associate with in this lifetime. Many of these souls may have been artists, in societies where art was held in high esteem. Even in this life they may retain a highly developed sense of beauty, both outer and inner. This sense of beauty is a cause of admiration toward them on the part of others – these souls attract others who put them on a pedestal where beauty is concerned. In all their affairs, these individuals may try to handle matters in a fair, just or proper way. They know there is great value in being "supportive" of the ideas and efforts of others. They value "relating". Many of these souls have also been associated with the courts, the law-making bodies of the land; consequently, they have a highly developed sense of justice in this lifetime. Another symbol here is the "grand ballroom dance", excitement signifying the physical grace and charm of the soul on one level but also the mental state of falling in love with one's "prince charming" – the fairest one in the land, (which this soul would usually get!). Many of these souls seem in constant search for the "soul mate", one who will compliment them perfectly, as if they remember such an experience in a past life.

Scorpio (Master of the Hidden Forces):

Great inner powers and control of outer forces characterize the history of souls with Scorpio on the I. C.. In past lives these individuals may have assumed roles as alchemists, magicians, mystics, healers and even rulers of great power. Their greatest developed gift may be that of transformation—the ability to go into any situation and change it to a more productive or useful one. In fact, every situation they enter into they may naturally attempt to re-mold. This is a part of their make-up from former lifetimes. As natural mystics they tend to see life as a mystery (and tend to think every one else does too). They sense the hidden, unknown, about themselves with respect and perhaps a certain amount of fear. Yet they know that therein lies a wealth of power if they would only tap it. Their feelings run very deep. This shows in their relationships which tend to be very strong "love-hate" types. In past lives they may have held power over the lives of others, and in this lifetime may do the same, or else they may attract others who now hold this same power over them (i.e. either as healers, or even to the opposite extremes as criminals and/or gangsters).

Sagittarius (The Wise Oracle):

Here dwell those souls who have developed wisdom in the affairs of humankind over several incarnations. Others naturally seek these souls out for advice, for they possess a natural understanding of life and all its verities. The symbol of the "wise oracle" suggests the prophetic nature of these types, for there is an innate sense of the future where others are concerned. In former lifetimes these souls may have been gurus, yogis, philosophers or teachers. Their minds may now be very highly developed and when they speak, others tend to pay attention. In fact, even though they may not acknowledge it, others may follow them in this lifetime as in the past. With some souls this may create a conflict because of their natural desire to be free of any binds whatsoever—free to pursue truth and understanding according to their own unique path. In former lifetimes they may have been wanderers and travelers. In this lifetime the urge to travel may still be strong, but travel not necessarily limited to physical movement, for they also yearn for the far corners of the mind and spirit as well. Sagittarius pertains to the Far Eastern cultures, so it is not surprising that these souls now have a natural attraction to the understanding of these philosophies.

Capricorn (A Powerful Sphinx):

These individuals are accustomed to positions of great power and authority – whether it be as the head of a clan (or family), a business, or an empire. No one knows what goes on in their minds, for they are very complex and have learned to think (analyze) things out very carefully. As a whole they make up a core of excellent strategists – and results are usually in their favor. As the symbol is a "powerful sphinx", there is also the quality of mystery and control of an unknown power associated with the Capricorn I. C.. Tremendously gifted as clairvoyants, this is just another remarkable power that may have been cultivated over several lifetimes. There is also a natural suspicion toward others here, for in the past these souls may have been betrayed and tend to fear the same in this lifetime. Because truth and sincerity are extremely important, and because they are so sensitive, these individuals may now be very selective in whom they choose to associate with. Generally speaking they have learned to associate only with those who support them and their ideas, and not those who tend to be critical. The assumption of responsibility for a group of people, to organize successful efforts, are other qualities developed in prior lifetimes wherein these souls enjoyed the privilege of leading others with a great amount of power.

Aquarius (An Inspired Master):

Great inventors, eclectics and remarkable personages describe the heritage of individuals with Aquarius on the I. C.. These souls may have had very unusual and uncanny past life experiences, and now bring with them an attraction toward the odd and bizarre. Usually a good deal ahead of times with their ideas, they are quite accustomed to being viewed as non-conformists, or eccentrics. They do not especially like to do things others have already done. The symbol of the "inspired master" implies that their ideas are highly unique and even unorthodox, but they work amazingly well. Where these ideas originate, no one knows (possibly from higher levels of consciousness). It might be that these souls are not as familiar with the Earth cycle of rebirths as are other souls – perhaps their background is from another dimension altogether. There is a very strong charisma present, which may lead to very erratic lives and relationships with others, oftentimes leading to a great sense of being misunderstood. When they "tune in" to higher levels of thought, (and very few can tune in like these souls), it is as if they have a direct channel to a universal knowledge. Oftentimes such inspiration becomes the basis for efforts which bring about sudden riches in this lifetime. It should also be pointed out that such remarkable natures as these types often feel "out of place," as if strangers on the planet Earth.

Pisces (The Wandering Minstrel):

The individuals with Pisces on the I. C. characterize a highly spiritual, mystical and yet emotional lot. Perhaps more than any other I. C. sign, this one contains psychics of all types. From former lives these souls may have developed the ability to see – to truly *see* – as if they are able to just float out of their bodies and view something they are interested in. Their past lives may have been as varied as their experiences in this life will prove to be. These may include such lifetimes as: seafarers, guides, mystics, spiritualists, poets, musicians, artists, actors, monks, nuns and romantics. They live for their dreams, and for them dreams may come true because of an indomitable faith in a Supreme Being. This is what the "wandering minstrel" symbol implies – an individual gliding happily along in life knowing that all will be taken care of. It should be mentioned that when this faith is dulled or not realized, then there is a very "sad minstrel". Pisces on the I. C. needs faith, and in the past may have developed faith to a degree beyond all other signs. They can provide excellent service to others, because in others they realize they are serving a "higher purpose" than just themselves. In fact they must serve others, without becoming attached in order to become liberated in this lifetime.

CHAPTER SEVEN

The Developed Powers and Abilities of the Soul

How can one discern the evolution of a soul?

As implied in Chapter Two, astrology offers but one of the keys in the understanding of an individual. Astrology is the study of cycles—cycles relating to time. In so much as each moment has a particular quality, and in so much as individuals born at the same time (and space) share the quality of that moment throughout their current Earth cycle, then it may be assumed that to a great extent these individuals will share similar lessons in the nature of events they experience in this lifetime. And yet it is also apparent that these "astrological twins" do not necessarily have the same specific phenomena occur within their lifetime, due to certain universal laws (karma) of which astrology is only a part.

With the understanding, then, that astrology may offer several clues (but not all) to an individual's evolvement, the next three chapters will examine these critical facets of Evolutionary Astrology: 1) the plantetary-angular relationships, 2) angular midpoints, and 3) the Evolutionary Moon.

Planetary-Angular Relationships: Powers and Abilities

The angles of the natal horoscope represent critical points of unique individual development and/or experience. They shape one's view of "reality." They lend insight into critical areas of self-understanding, as they shed light upon important questions about oneself. The **I. C.** deals with the question of "Who am I?" The I. C. is symbolic of the sum total of one's past experiences. In a sense it describes where one has been, at least spiritually, and how one has developed according to those experiences.

The opposite point to the I. C. is the Midheaven, where the Sun is located during the height of the daylight hours. The **Midheaven** deals with the question: "What am I here to do; what is my **purpose**?" Every soul has a "calling in life", a purpose for reincarnating. It is not necessarily one's career or vocation, for even these may be symbolic of the "real" calling or purpose in life. In a sense, it is the **destiny** of the incarnating soul to discover and actualize this purpose. Once this purpose is understood, and pursuit of it begins, the life may seem as if it is one of "destiny". It is as if that activity is what the soul was meant to do, for it comes naturally and brings a measure of success (not necessarily in material terms) to that soul.

These two points, the **I. C. and Midheaven**, represent the most "pure" points in the horoscope. At midnight there is the greatest darkness of day. It is thus the most mystical point in time. It is the horoscope point of the I. C.. In this point which is furthest removed from light, or most totally immersed in darkness, is the "real self", a point of **unity** within the self, the point wherein the self is most in communion with God, or at One with everything. There is just self, the Zen state of "nothingness", the Brahman state of "Oneness." Planets located near this point, the **I. C.**, describe unique personal development that comes from meditation, contemplation, and reflection.

At high noon there is greatest light of the day; there is no darkness, for it is furthest removed at this time. In the horoscope, this point in the day is representative of the **Midheaven**, for this is where the Sun is at noon. This is thus a point of **light**, or **illumination**. The path is most clear here, and the pursuit of this direction yields **clarity**. The light emanating from this point in one's life is to illuminate one's purpose for incarnating. It shows the path of destiny that this soul may embark upon, and in so doing discover the real meaning of one's incarnation. Planets located near the **Midheaven** describe special skills that enhance the fulfillment, or completion of one's destiny (or purpose) in life. The assumption here is that these skills have been cultivated over many, many lifetimes. Reality here is encountered not in the act of understanding, as in the I. C., but in the act of giving totally of oneself. What one may "give" to the world is shown at the Midheaven.

The **I. C.-Midheaven** axis, also known as the **Meridian**, thus contains the points of greatest light and darkness in the chart. They represent points of the absolute, the unadulterated. There is, symbolically, only self and not-self here. These are the points of total self-realization and understanding on the one hand, and total giving of oneself, or detachment from any sense of self whatsoever. All other parts of the chart, all other points in the natural day, have a mixture of light and dark, self with not-self. All other parts of the horoscope represent awareness of things other than the self, and the self in relationship to these other forces. In a sense, all parts of the horoscope outside of the **Meridian** represent various degrees of the ego.

Within the space of light and darkness are two points of equal balance: sunrise and sunset. Sunrise in the natural order of the day coincides with the **Ascendant** in the horoscope. Like the I. C. and Midheaven, the Ascendant likewise deals with a critical point in the evolution of a soul. It attempts to answer the question: **"How?"** "How am I to achieve my purpose in life, or understanding of my real Self?" What tools or skills or experiences must I initiate in order to achieve these enlightenments?" Any planets located near the Ascendant describe the potential experiences (their nature) and tools that the native may choose to initiate and cultivate, much as he or she may have in the past. But the real question now is: how will the native use these tools and experiences? As light and dark are critically balanced, so too is the *choice* in the use of these. Will they be used for self-centered ends even at the expense of others, or will they become means to accomplishing the real purpose in life, such as the liberation of one's (or others') being? Planets located near the Ascendant or Descendant represent tools and strengths, but the question is: does the soul center them upon itself, in a selfish manner, or upon the "higher" aspects of it's "real self"? The use of these powers determines the nature of karmic consequences forthcoming for this soul. The temptation (an appropriate word for the Ascendant) to misuse these qualities is great. Only by following one's heart (I. C.) or one's higher knowledge of what is right (Midheaven) will one make the choices consistent with the terms of the soul's evolutionary journey.

At sunset, light and dark are once again in critical balance. Choice is imminent. The **Descendant** is representative of this point in the natural order of the Earth's daily rotation on its axis. The **Descendant** copes with the question of **"Who and/or what conditions must I encounter in order to achieve my destiny or liberate my being?"** Again, does one utilize these people and conditions to focus upon the lower aspects of self, or upon God, the higher aspects of Self? These are the most critical of the repetitive scripts or patterns in one's life, particularly with regard to relationships. For each soul, the path to liberation and self-understanding is not achieved in a vacuum. There is a series of circumstances and a number of people one meets in life. These people, in one way or another, serve the purpose of helping to understand or come to the realization of what one is to do. They may do this with tenderness, or they may force one into this realization in a most difficult fashion. Sometimes one discovers what is right for him or herself only by first understanding what is **not right**.

It is also through undergoing the consequences of karmic experiences that one completes cycles initiated in prior lifetimes. In the process of "meeting up" with these circumstances, one has the opportunity to fully understand the dynamics (of one's self) which created these patterns. This is the first and most important step in completing these patterns and scripts, of completing these cycles, and thereby liberating one's being. The planets located near the Descendant describe the nature of these people who come into one's life to help achieve this critical understanding. But the choice one makes is also critical: does one attempt to see the purpose and rectify the pattern, or does one weakly fall into the same trap (i.e. pattern) again and again? When the soul is able to view these relationships and circumstances in terms of lessons instead of wondering "why do these things keep happening to me", then that soul may actually use the powers and abilities signified by these planets (i.e. people and conditions) for the attainment of its purpose or the deep understanding of its self.

In this manner, then, the planets near the horizon (Ascendant and Descendant) are also representative of powerful tools the soul brings into this lifetime. The tools become the means to attain the ends signified by the I. C. and Midheaven, which themselves symbolize the paths of liberation (absolute self and absolute not-self). Now let's examine these concepts in more detail.

The houses which border these angles, the first, fourth, seventh and tenth, are known as angular houses and are considered the most *powerful* of the houses. In Mundane Astrology, the succedent houses (second, fifth, eighth and eleventh) are considered next in power, while the cadent houses (third, sixth, ninth and twelfth) are assigned as the weakest.

If, in Evolutionary Astrology, one views the angles as points of unique individuality and development, then planets posited near the angles would imply the development of a particular *behavior* or *principle* according to the nature of the planet(s). In terms of houses, the angles are the borderlines separating the angular and cadent houses. Therefore to consider cadent houses, especially the area of a cadent house which is very close to an angle, as the weakest part of the horoscope, does not hold in Evolutionary Astrology. The closer a planet to an angle, the potentially more developed its qualities are in terms of the individual's expression in this life. Consequently the more powerful or able the individual might be in the use of the functions inherent in such planet(s).

The difference between an angular and cadent placement is one of an action or usage state compared to a mental or service state. This difference is also held in Mundane Astrology. Angular planets indicate an activity function; third and ninth house planets (cadent) signify a mental function while the other cadent houses (the sixth and twelfth) imply a service, devotional nature. Therefore the peaks of power are right on the angles, and as one moves further and further away from the angles this power may steadily decline. Thus cadent planets may be just as powerful as angular ones, though the power will be expressed in a different manner, i.e. mental/service versus action.

Such terms as power, behavior, capabilities and development have been referred to throughout this chapter. These are to be understood in terms of the relationship of the planets' position to the angles. Thus planets located close to an angle represent a special development according to the nature of that planet. Consequently there is greater potential power or capability in the individual according to the nature of that planet.

Each planet relates to a particular type of development, to a particular power or ability. The Sun and Moon in Evolutionary Astrology have a different function than in Mundane Astrology, yet because they (especially the Moon) relate to the Earth plane with such importance, the discussion of planets begins with them.

The Sun and Moon are not representative so much of particular powers or abilities inherent in the incarnating soul as they are of states of awareness. To understand this concept, let's first of all consider the Sun. The Sun represents the state of *becoming*. We are all *becoming* our Sun. If the Sun symbolizes life Spirit, the God-force, or the creative force which propels this universe in which we exist, then it is a force within us which we all strive to experience to its fullest. The degree to which one experiences or understands this force determines one's capacity to achieve fulfillment. Thus the Sun furthermore symbolizes one's *path* toward fulfillment, completion, or wholeness. Each soul longs for wholeness, to no longer feel separated and apart from its experience(s). A Sun which is located near a natal angle (i.e. one who is born close to midnight, sunrise, noon, or sunset, local mean time) is likely to be more focused upon concepts like **growth**, and the **future**. There may be a strong sense of destiny with this soul, a sense that there is something special to experience in the course of this lifetime. Because the Earth is opposite this point and thus also close to a natal angle, this sense of "fulfillment" may come about more naturally when this soul understands the importance of working in harmony with natural law. Perhaps this individual experiences a sense of wholeness when close to nature (Earth).

The Moon is different. The Moon reflects, unlike the Sun which creates. The Moon represents the state of **being**. In traditional astrology the Moon is said to rule the emotions, which are **reactive** states of the mind. The reactive mind, a state in which the emotions govern, depicts an individual who is subject to repetitive patterns, particularly in intimate relationships. The Moon has a great deal to do with past relationships, and more importantly the emotional states that have been shaped from those experiences.

Yet there is a sense of comfort in these patterns. For many, the value of comfort exceeds that of growth. Familiarity, nurturing, and protection are all significant aspects of the life experience, and are characteristic of the Moon's domain. Thus those individuals with natal Moon close to an angle may exhibit a strong drive to achieve comfort, to establish roots and strong bonds with significant others in their lives. They may also be skilled at helping others to achieve these same states of comfort.

Another analogy here may be that of paternal/maternal qualities. Those with the Sun near an angle may serve as a father figure for others, constantly encouraging others to reach out, to take risks that they believe will enhance the other person's growth. Those with the Moon on an angle, on the other hand, may offer protection and nurturing to those whom they care for the most. They may instruct others on how to develop a home or center or family that will support the individual's efforts in life.

Either the Sun or Moon near the Midheaven or I. C. represents a strong state of **becoming (growth) or being (comfort)** respectively. Near the horizon (Ascendant/ Descendant axis) the same strong urges are present, but the native must be conscientious of his/her motives. For example a Sun near the Ascendant may be indicative of a strong urge to grow and undergo new experiences, but there may be underlying motives of a self-glorification purpose. Perhaps the native wishes these experiences because it will make him/her "look good" in the eyes of others. Or perhaps this soul encourages others to take risks under the pretense that it will help them grow, when actually the risks of the other person benefit the Sun/horizon individual in some personal way. Likewise the Sun near the Descendant may inspire others to grow, but they may also end up using these people for their own personal ends and needs for self-glorification (i.e. one betters their position in life through association with others).

The key to remember is that the Sun/angle person has an urge to **grow**. If on the horizon, the temptation may be for ego enhancement rather than real growth. The Moon/angle person has an urge to establish **comfort zones**, or roots. The temptation of the Moon on the horizon may be to develop unhealthy and emotional dependencies, relationships of attachment that support the native's own emotional needs more than the other person's spiritual and/or psychological needs.

Each of the other planets represents the development of specific abilities or powers. For purposes of understanding, a **power** is the result or consequence of properly applying an **ability** to one's life. Hence a **power** is representative of a higher degree of evolution than an **ability**. **Power** without a foundation in the development of **abilities** is useless in this context. **Power** in that sense might be the expression of external force or control, without conscious intent or understanding of its use. **Power** that results, or is built upon a foundation of first developing **abilities**, is apt to express itself in a far more attractive and interesting manner, one that embraces and reveres life, as opposed to one that does not.

The evolution of **abilities** to **powers** is symbolic of the evolution of a soul from knowledge to empowerment. It is also symbolic of the soul's evolution from a state of duality (or maya) to an awareness of wholeness (oneness). It is the emergence of the consciousness of conflict to that of integration. The process of this evolution is symbolized by the order of the planets in their closeness to the Sun.

As one leaves the home of creation (Sun and Moon, states of **becoming and being**) and begins the journey outward into the world of maya (physical phenomenon), there are certain principles to be learned and tools to cultivate in order to enhance (and provide for) one's very survival (or at least quality of physical existence). These principles and tools will be referred to as the **abilities** of the soul.

The first **ability** the soul develops along its journey outward is **the ability to perceive** what is necessary to enhance and provide for its survival. This ability is symbolized by **Mercury**. In traditional astrology, Mercury governs the mental realm. Mercury near any angle (the orb of influence is approximately 22-$^{1}/_{2}$° either side of angle, or one-quarter of a quadrant's distance from any given angle) suggests a soul that has a highly developed perceptual ability. This soul "senses" things before they happen, seems to "know" what is necessary in any given situation, particularly a crisis. Mercury on an angle – especially near the Ascendant – is frequently observed in people of very high intelligence. In many instances these individuals may exhibit qualities of geniusness, and a strong desire to learn, study and continuously develop the "mental" or perceptual faculties.

Perceiving what is needed to enhance survival is followed by **procuring or acquiring** the tools or means of enhancing that same survival. This ability is symbolized by **Venus**. One with Venus close to angle may have a spiritual history of developing this ability: either that soul is talented in some line of work that can be employed almost anywhere, or that soul has a knack for "knowing" people from all walks of life who can help or assist with one's survival. When obstacles arise that "block" one's efforts, this soul usually has the ability – or knows someone else who has the ability – to aid in overcoming that obstacle. Why is that soul able to do this? Because of karma. This and all abilities are the result of past efforts, and these efforts are governed by universal cyclic laws. Thus with Mercury and Venus highly developed (i.e. close to an angle), the soul has cultivated the ability to **perceive** what is necessary to enhance the quality on one's survival, as well as the ability to **acquire** the support and resources necessary to do so.

The next step is to apply and implement that knowledge and those resources in order to succeed in one's effort to enhance survival. This is the domain of **Mars**, the ability to **initiate successful effort**. Mars near an angle denotes one who has a strong drive to overcome all obstacles along the path, to conquer and triumph over all forces that inhibit or obstruct its goal. Mars indicates **action**, or the implementation of effort. However for the effort to be truly successful, one must be clear in his/her motivation, or **intention**. Mars near an angle may suggest a soul with an ability to put effort into action, but if the effort is driven by wrong motivation, the individual is simply initiating another cycle that will be governed by the cyclic law of karma. Therefore in its highest expression, Mars represents **"right action", or "right motivation"** if it is truly to be an ability in an evolutionary sense.

Thus far Mercury, Venus and Mars have been presented as the abilities to perceive what is necessary to enhance the soul's survival, the ability to procure the support for that effort, and finally the ability to initiate activity that will lead to the success of this effort. What happens after the soul succeeds in its effort to enhance its own survival in the world? The next step is to become a bridge to others in their quest to enhance survival. The soul now enters the realm of the humanitarian, or philanthropist, or even mentor. This evolutionary step is symbolized in the function of **Jupiter**. Jupiter is not really a power, but it is more than an ability because it is the first step in which the soul reaches out beyond its own personality, beyond its own immediate world. This requires another level of awareness and understanding, and to act in accordance with this principle of **giving to others** is a major step in the evolution of personal empowerment. Jupiter represents **an urge to expand one's sphere and share one's successes with others.** It is a quality of altruism that springs from a sincere desire to be charitable or generous. Jupiter near an angle is indicative of a soul who has experienced abundance and success in the history of its personalities, but who also realizes that success for oneself, by itself, is not fulfilling. There is a greater meaning to one's life that comes from sharing with others, from reaching out and providing others with the benefits of success (or understanding) that one has acquired in life.

None of these qualities, urges, or abilities represents personal empowerment yet. They are however essential in the evolution of personal power. With power one is able to facilitate change. The abilities enhance survival in the world. Powers enable one to **transcend** the world of physical phenomenon, the world of maya. They are essential to complete the "journey back to the home one never left." They illuminate the path by which one returns to its creative source, to an understanding of who one really is. Through this path, one's life changes because the soul itself evolves. Cycles are completed, patterns and scripts are terminated, and deep personal experiences of understanding unfold as the soul is released from these patterns. Those with the planets Saturn, Uranus, Neptune or Pluto near an angle may be working "their way back home" through this lifetime. They have an opportunity to express empowerment cultivated in prior lifetimes. But are they aware of this? Are they conscious of their evolution, or the process of evolution itself? If not, the consequences of using these powers without regard to intent may make the journey a very difficult one indeed. The scripts and patterns may be extremely complex and fixed, and such power may be directed in a self-destructive, rather than constructive, manner. This is to say that such a soul has lost its way for the moment (or lifetime). Such a condition can possibly be rectified, though, by the compassion and understanding of another empowered soul. And sometimes that is why the paths of two people cross. Ultimately though it is up to the one who is temporarily lost to make the choice of returning to the path that was started long ago.

What are these powers? The first is **the power of control**, symbolized by the planet **Saturn**. No empowerment comes easily or without effort. It comes first from discipline and commitment. It also requires patience and acceptance of responsibility. All of these qualities are pertinent to the principle of Saturn. The first step in acquiring power is to recognize that the world of illusion and duality is also one of conflict and inner suffering. One has to want to transcend this. This requires a

commitment, a vow. It also requires a **sacrifice**, a willingness to do without those things that distract from the goal. For some this requires a vow of poverty. At some point in the history of the soul born with Saturn on an angle, such a vow may have been taken. The well-being and salvation of the soul is of more value than that of the body (further along the same soul may realize the well-being of the body actually supports the well-being of the soul). But the commitment, the promise made to oneself (or one's higher self, or God) requires a withdrawal from the things of the world and entrance into the inner, spiritual world. Through a process of consciously denying oneself experiences of varying distractions, and embarking upon a path of rigorous self-discipline, and developing the principle of patience, one acquires **self-control**. This is the first level of empowerment in this model of Evolutionary Astrology.

One with Saturn near an angle has been working on the principle of **control**. Innately this soul understands the value of discipline and order, of structure and responsibility. This soul innately knows that in order to accomplish something of value, one must be committed and willing to work hard. This soul also understands the value of honor, of being honest in one's efforts.

What about the individual who does not seem to express these principles in this lifetime, and yet has Saturn near an angle? Control of the self, and responsibility for the self, may instead be expressed by control over others, and interference in the lives of others (i.e. taking responsibilities away from them, as in making rules that deny their freedom of choice). Such individuals may get caught up in the illusion that power is synonymous with controlling others, and the personality may regress to an "authoritarian" type. This is the danger of one born with Saturn on an angle, for it suggests very complex patterns with other people in which issues of control tend to arise. At the seat of such issues is the likelihood that this individual is expressing him/herself from a position of fear or guilt. It may take a meeting with another empowered soul to redirect this individual's attention to the source of such fears or guilt, in order to effect a "release."

In any event the process of evolution continues once the soul has developed the power of control. After rigorous discipline, sacrifice and commitment, there is finally an **awakening**. The soul finally "breaks through." This is the state of enlightenment, or revelation, and with it comes a new sense of **freedom**. Such an awakening is the domain of **Uranus**, and the result is the **power of attraction**. Once the soul "breaks through", an amazing series of events and people enter the life. There is a quickening of the evolutionary process. Time seems to speed up.

Actually time continues in the same frequency, it's just that the individual is more alert and aware of events and people than ever before. One is also more receptive to interacting with others. With the development of the power of control and attraction, one cannot fail. Failure is no longer a part of one's vocabulary, for all experiences are seen as opportunities and lessons on the path "back home."

Uranus is the first stage of enlightenment. However there is a danger with the first enlightenment. The individual may want everyone to experience what he or she has just experienced. Unfortunately such experiences cannot be easily conveyed to others. Efforts to do so may be met with rejection, or repulsion. Others may sense the individual is too zealous, or fanatical, and trying to convert them to something. The result can be disassociative; one losses closeness to those he/she knew before the enlightenment. Loneliness can then unfold. Instead of a joyous awakening, such enlightenment can turn into a terrifying experience of alienation and one without understanding. Such alienation can lead the individual into acts that disrupt the community, break the tradition, mores, or laws of the land. The breaking of such "rules" can lead to a multitude of sudden, disruptive events in the native's life, one in which nothing ever seems to proceed smoothly or in an orderly manner.

Uranus near an angle may describe both types of experiences. To the soul who is connected with its personality and possesses a deep understanding of its higher self, life seems to be a series of revelations and enlightenments. Life is an adventure, and that soul's power of attraction is truly magnetic. Others sense something unique and special about this soul who truly values its own uniqueness and individuality. This soul longs for new and unusual experiences.

On the other hand a soul with Uranus near an angle, who has somewhere along the line fallen off the path, may not hold the same degree of value toward individuality and uniqueness. Somewhere in its history such an awareness may have been terrifying, and hence difficult to accept. Instead of seeking new adventures and excitement, this soul may be caught up in a repetitive script of causing disruption and upset to those around itself. There is a need to go back and understand the principle of Saturn, of discipline and commitment. It may take a meeting with another empowered soul to illuminate this soul's path. Enlightenment without control, understanding, or responsibility can be an experience in loneliness, and instead of freedom, one may create a condition of restriction for itself.

After the soul "breaks through" and has its first enlightenment, it soon realizes that it is alone on its journey. All of one's friends and family have not and cannot yet experience the same enlightenment. It is as if the soul suddenly fell into a cave. At the end of the cave is a light which everyone can see, but only the Uranus/angle individual has ever explored. He/she liked it, but everyone else in the community or family feared it. How do you express such findings to others? How do you describe something to them that only you experienced? And what do you do when no one wants to see what you have seen, or go where you have been? It is a terrifying choice: to venture outside into a new world alone, or to return to a world that is infinitely less exciting than what you know exists elsewhere? The decision determines the quickening or the regression of that soul.

For the soul who decides to continue the journey, events and other significant people emerge rapidly. Soon the soul finds that there are others who have had a similar "break through", or enlightenment, and they too made the same choice facing the same terrifying dilemma. These souls quickly find one another because each has a powerful quality of attraction. Each has left behind something or someone that at one time was dear to them. It is possible to continue in contact with those persons, but it is no longer possible to return to the conditions defined by that prior experience—at least not without returning to karmic cycles that one has just transcended (i.e. regression). The soul now realizes that, on some level, he or she is now a minority, but he or she is not alone. The world functions by consensus and compromise, but seldom by absolute truths. This soul now seeks absolute truth, and in so doing is no longer content to accept the rules or "truths" as something imposed upon one from without. The soul can no longer endorse a reality of truths imposed upon it from the outside. It must now have a personal experience of such truths. Such a soul is now receptive to divine or universal inspiration, and must realize the distinction between enlightened and non-enlightened beings. They must and eventually do realize that their ideas are ahead of their times. Eventually their ideas will be accepted, so long as they are of truth. In the meantime, they have acquired the **power of attraction**, and others of like experience will openly receive the results of this soul's illuminations.

Uranus on an angle is very expressive and adventuresome, mentally and spiritually if not physically. Neptune on an angle represents yet another level of empowerment, yet another form of enlightenment. Whereas Uranus is very outward in its experience, or more so its expression, Neptune is more inward. The next level of evolution requires the soul to go back within. The second enlightenment is that of **compassion**. It is one of **transcendence**. Once the soul understands that it cannot convert others to its enlightening experience, it must learn to accept the uniqueness of each soul's own rhythm of self unfoldment. Until a soul is receptive and ready to understand its self, there is very little the evolving soul can do for it—other than to be patient and accepting. Any events to "force" another to grow will only be met with resistance as most force is. Uranus can be forceful, but eventually the soul learns the fruitlessness of such effort, and retreats to continue upon its own path of deeper understanding. And this brings us to Neptune.

As the soul goes back within, the heart center (Neptune) is next developed. From here the soul begins to understand the importance of compassion. Outside of the meditative state the soul becomes more accepting. As such, others are attracted to this soul, to whom they easily confide their problems. An aura of trust exudes and others do not feel threatened from these Neptune-evolved souls. Such an individual conveys tenderness, acceptance, perhaps sympathy or better yet, empathy. These are all characteristics of compassion. Others feel healed, or helped in some manner from the Neptune/angle person who is evolving. And yet there is a power that comes from this. As the individual goes deeper and deeper within the self, and is able to transcend the realm of time that governs the world of phenomena, that soul is able to **counsel, and thus heal**. That soul is able to see the higher aspect of another's being, and innately understands that each soul will, like itself, ultimately return "home." This soul therefore has evolved the **power of healing, or vision**. The ability to "see" allows this soul to help another, particularly on a one-to-one basis.

What of the individual with Neptune on an angle who is not in touch with this evolutionary power? What if such a power is not grounded in the previous development of abilities and powers? How will it be expressed, and what patterns might this individual encounter in this lifetime? An individual who retreats too deeply, or too often, and does not accept responsibilities in its current path, or does not exercise self-control and discipline, is likely to be trapped in a psychological world of paranoid delusions. If the delusions are those of grandeur, the individual may think of him/herself as some sort of savior or messiah. This individual must be careful not to get caught up in his/her ability to help and/or heal others, for taking such experiences on a level of ego enhancement may lead to the seeking of idol worshipping. To take one's talent personally instead of seeing it as the result of God's grace, or as one's spiritual and evolutionary unfoldment, can lead to very complex and difficult patterns to unravel. Neptune is inward, and to suddenly be placed (or to claim) a position of leadership over others can greatly confuse this individual. At the same time, the acceptance of such roles by this individual may lead to expressions which greatly confuse others whom the individual contacts. Where is this personality to lead others? Ultimately, when on the path, the only leadership with regard to others is back within themselves.

Each level of evolution, and hence planetary principle as one goes further and further outwards from the Sun, becomes increasingly complex when the personality and the soul are not integrated, when the personality assumes dominance over the soul's purpose for incarnating. In this case, a Neptune/angle that is more personality-oriented than soul-oriented is setting itself up for extremely complex karmic patterns. This person may avoid any kind of help from another empowered individual, for at root in this problem is a lack of trust and faith in anyone. The key principle, however, is **compassion.**

There is yet another power in the symbology of our cosmos. **Pluto** represents the power to **transform, or to change the world**. It is the enlightened being in action, in the world. This soul sees the injustices, the inequities of the system and how people relate to it. This soul has a sense of the injustice which the planet Earth itself incurs from her inhabitants. With enlightenment and power, this soul seeks to rid the planet, and the individual, and the society, of their ills. There is an awareness of those conditions which deter or destroy the natural order of evolution, collectively as well as individually.

Yet to successfully unfold such power, this soul must be grounded in all of the powers, enlightenments, and abilities just described. The power to **change or transform** will immediately be met with resistance, for individuals do not eagerly seek change or willingly accept it. That is why this soul must also have compassion, attraction, and self-control as well as patience. With all of these qualities properly integrated, a great deal can be accomplished. Without them, the individual is likely to force change and the result may be an incredibly complex karmic cycle filled with rejection and a pattern of difficult plays for power with other individuals.

As mentioned, there is a natural progression of development with the symbols of these far out planets. One needs to learn **control**, particularly of oneself, before matters of significance can be **attracted.** Once the **power of attraction** is acquired, one must learn when and how to express it correctly in order to be an inspiration, and not a distraction, to others. From this comes the **power of healing, or vision**, which comes about when one taps into that "Christ within" consciousness. With the power of vision, one then evolves to a level of seeing what is needed to heal the planet, or the community, and possibly the individual. To take the vision into the world as an enlightened man or woman in action creates the possibility of expressing the **power to change or transform the cycle**—for Earth, and/or her inhabitants.

Some of the abilities described herein will blend more naturally with certain powers than others. For instance, the **power of control (Saturn)** may be most effective when combined harmoniously with the **ability to succeed (Mars), or initiate action**. This combination is indicative of a very hard working, constructive soul, one who is willing to set forth a plan or goal and work tirelessly to attain it. Right action (Mars) integrated with responsibility and self-control as well as moral behavior will likely result in accomplishments throughout life. It is a signature of one who might be successful as an athlete, military strategist, or business executive (management).

The **power of attraction (Uranus)** may be expressed most positively if integrated well with the **ability to acquire (Venus)**. Generally speaking, this combination might be able to attain whatever it wishes (within reason) simply because both principles have such a high degree of attraction. With Venus on an angle the soul innately seems able to attract support for its projects, or else has the tools necessary to succeed. With Uranus also near an angle this soul is naturally and easily inspired, and oriented toward original pursuits. Such energy is usually very charismatic and draws other talented and original types to it. The result can indicate a most fascinating and exciting life, one filled with unusual people and circumstances (mostly positive so long as the principles are properly integrated).

The **power of vision and healing (Neptune)** flows harmoniously with the **ability to perceive what is necessary to enhance survival (Mercury)**. The combination may be remarkably gifted, either in the arts, music, writing, or intuition. The greatest form of healing is counseling, and the blending of these two planetary principles (located near an angle) indicates one who may have a natural talent in this area. Words are soft and soothing, whether spoken, written or sung. To be able to have vision (Neptune) and combine it with an understanding of what others need in order to better survive (Mercury) is a talent that suits those in the counseling or helping professions. They may be able to instill faith, in place of despair, for those who suffer greatly; they provide a sense of a world of beauty in place of hopelessness and helplessness. They may inspire others to transcend the problems of mundane existence and find stillness (Christ) within. Finally the **power to change and transform** may be most beneficial when built upon an **ability to share and expand with others (Pluto** has the power to change, **Jupiter** the ability to reach out and share charitably with others). Jupiter is the level of the **humanitarian**. It is far more constructive that one with the power to change things of the world have at center an urge to help that same world. Otherwise the combination could suggest massive destruction. The successful integration of these two planets near a natal angle suggests one who has both the desire and the power to change to community (and Earth and her inhabitants as a collective whole) for the better.

The closer a planet is to an angle the more that ability or power is likely to be developed in that soul's expression in this lifetime. It may be assumed that this soul has spent considerable effort in past lives on the principles inherent in these planets. Consequently it is that soul's karma to have such ability and power in this lifetime. This then is one of the guides by which an astrologer may ascertain the evolution of a soul. How that soul expresses these abilities and powers depends upon how well that individual integrates its personality with its soul, or how aware that individual is of its spiritual heritage as well as its spiritual destiny. It is the role of the astrologer to help put the soul in touch with this awareness, understanding, and hence facilitate that individual's empowerment.

To illustrate the principles of developed powers and abilities, let's examine the natal horoscope of a male, born January 27, 1986, 10:20 PM, latitude 42°28′ North, longitude 83°14′ West (see Figure 8). The planet closest to an angle is Neptune, just one degree from the I. C.. This is followed by Uranus, approximately 12-½° from the I. C.. There are no personal planets within one-quarter of a quadrant's area from an angle. In the model of Evolutionary Astrology there is great power here, a soul who may be well along his journey back home to wholeness. However the lack of "planets of abilities" near an angle may indicate either a lack of concern, or lack of faculty on how to enhance his very survival in the physical world. In a sense, this soul's mind may be more on matters outside of mundane focus or experience. With Neptune, his power comes from going within. This is especially so given its position on the I. C., the deepest part of the horoscope and natural day. This is further supported by the fact that his natal Sun is in the second quadrant, below the horizon and West of the meridian (yin-yin). This is a very reflective, very inward soul who has gathered great power from inward experiences.

The power of this soul is that of **healing and vision**. His power is expressed with great compassion (Neptune). His is a power that is able to uplift others by bringing forth to them a world of beauty, of inner peace and harmony. By going within himself, he is able to transcend the physical world of duality and conflict, and raise his consciousness to a level of unspeakable beauty and bliss. From this (these) experi-

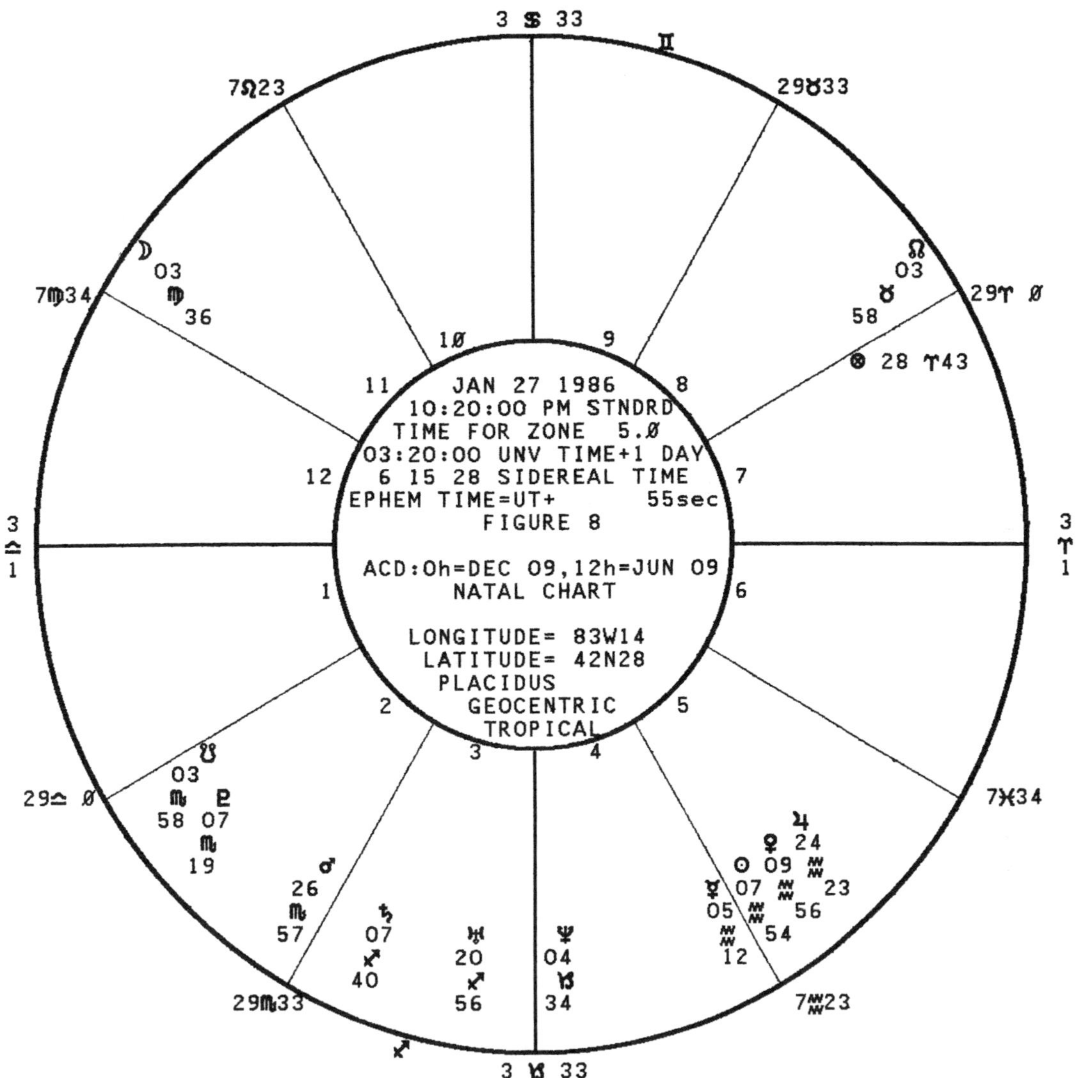

Figure 8

ences he brings forth understanding and compassion for others, particularly those who suffer in some way. His expression toward them may be soothing, sympathetic, and the result is healing to them. He may do this through music, poetry, writing, counseling, or speaking. His focus may be very spiritual, for when he enters his inner world, he taps into the heart, or Christ, spirit.

It is interesting to note that the I. C. itself is in the sign of Capricorn (Virgo decanate). Capricorn is structural. It may indicate a soul who is very aware of the need for law or guidelines, as in a government, bureaucratic or business arena. Capricorn on the I. C. may have been in positions of authority in past lives, and the challenge to integrate personal power with the needs of the collective may be present in this lifetime. Perhaps this soul was in a religious arena that had a strong influence upon the political community. Or perhaps he was formerly in the field of politics or government, but at the same time had a strong influence (positive) upon the religious community. Perhaps he brought forth the principles of spiritual law to that of the government. In any event, the principles of governing others, while at the same time counseling and/or healing others is suggested in the past, and carries over as the essence of the soul in this lifetime. Other possibilities include classical musician, poet or artist (imagination combined with structure, to yield a healing and/or transcendental effect).

Uranus is also in the orb of influence of a developed power. This indicates a soul who "broke through", experienced an enlightenment or revelation and has sought a path of truth outside of the norm. The quest for higher knowledge and understanding has (and is) a powerful magnet which now drives and empowers this soul. As such he has developed the **power of attraction**.

His ideas are unique for his past experiences are unusual and out of the ordinary. By pursuing the path of the uncommon, this soul has likely experienced fascinating lifetimes. It is likely that this lifetime will be fascinating and unusual as well, for he possesses an awareness (from past experiences) that in order to find truth and experience enlightenment (principles which he now values greatly), he must pursue a rare path where few tread. His mind will be drawn to unusual areas of study; his translations of his inner experiences (below the horizon) may be both unique and inspiring to others. He himself (with natal Sun in the fourth quadrant) is receptive to inspiration, and his inner faith in the outcome of his "risks" to pursue the extraordinary makes him unique in his community. As a result of this developed power, he attracts many interesting and unusual situations and people into his path who serve a particular purpose: to put him in touch with the value of his unique individuality, and reaffirm that the path he is upon, although lonely at times, is the one by which he returns to his spiritual home, the one that yields a sense of fullness and wholeness. For this soul to return to a life of conformity and accept truth as something imposed upon him from the outside would be difficult and spiritually regressive. Once a soul has broken through to a deeper understanding of its self, it cannot easily return to the world and accept the realm of maya, of ignorance. It must continue toward the light (enlightenment and truth) it has experienced, and in doing so, events arise quickly and in rapid fashion that support this illumination. In this lifetime, life moves quickly, and changes in circumstances are frequent (and desired). Freedom comes with movement, and this soul will not likely fall into a common routine. As a result his energy and his experiences as well as his deeper understandings of truth may enlighten the way for others whose paths he crosses.

CHAPTER EIGHT

Angular Midpoints: Crises of the Soul

"The mystery of evil is the deepest one of all. It is the mystery of the primal creative act, when God called into existence the human soul, made in His own image, and presented it with the terrifying choice: to center itself upon itself, or to center itself upon Him, without Whom it could not subsist at all. . . . Forgive us our trespasses, as we forgive those who trespass against us. And lead us not into temptation, but deliver us from evil. Amen." [7]

Evil. A word that conjures up as many negative implications and hostile reactions as any word in the English language. Some schools of thought simply refuse to recognize the existence of evil. Others, like many fundamentalist religions, use it as a basis for purporting their policies of fear and control over others. To them, it is their mission to stamp out all evil, which they interpret as anything that goes against the literal writings of their masters, such as the Old Testament of the Bible. To them evil is very real, and the cause of all suffering in the world. It is simply another word for Satan, or the Devil, the arch enemy of God and his chosen children (which is them). Evil is the enemy, that which destroys and works against all that which is good and of God. An evil person is one who intentionally violates God's word, or law.

But who is God, and what is His law? And what is one's relationship to God? The concept of God is unique to every soul, just as each soul is unique in its experience and its expression of itself. How each

[7]Morris West, *The Shoes of the Fisherman* (New York, Wm. Morrow & Co., 1963).

soul reflects its understanding of God, or Spirit, or Creative Source determines a unique quality of each individual being on this planet. No two beings are exactly alike, which is to say that no two souls are exactly alike, which is to say that the relationship, understanding, and reflection of Spirit by each soul is unique. Likewise no two horoscopes are exactly alike because the universe is in constant motion. The universe is constantly evolving and changing its structure. The relationship of the planets and all moving celestial bodies is constantly changing in its relationship to the Sun, and to one another. Hence, as Carl Jung wrote in the forward of the Wilhelm/Baynes edition of the *I-Ching*, . . . "whatever happens in a given moment possesses inevitably the quality peculiar to that moment".[8] Every incarnating soul will have a different horoscope, and therefore every incarnating soul will have a different "quality" which is peculiar to the moment of its birth.

The way in which each individual soul reflects Spirit, or its understanding of God – and hence natural law – ultimately interprets good and bad, right and wrong, evil and righteousness. According to *The American College Dictionary*, evil is: "violating or inconsistent with the moral law; harmful; injurious; that which is evil; evil quality, intention or conduct; anything causing injury or harm."[9]

In the model of Evolutionary Astrology the principle of karma is an integral cornerstone. The experiences of the incarnating soul are a result of cycles that soul has put into motion. Even the moment of one's birth, and hence one's natal horoscope, is a result of cycles that soul has initiated. Since one's birth occurs at a moment of time when all the planets and celestial bodies are in a mathematical harmony with the quality, or essence, of one's karma, that event (i.e. the birth moment) is not by happenstance. And yet the soul continues to evolve beyond the moment of birth through the experiences it encounters in a given lifetime. With each experience, which is karmic in origin, come choices: choices in actions and reactions. These choices are either consistent with patterns that created the experiences in the first place, or they are different. In the latter case, new modes of expression become active in nature – they give rise to new cycles and thus create a new karma. The dynamics behind these choices are at issue here: in the words of Morris West, the choice of the soul is either "to center itself upon itself, or to center itself upon Him, without Whom it could not subsist at all." The

[8]Wilhelm/Baynes with introduction by Carl G. Jung, *I Ching: Or Book Of Changes* (Princeton, Princeton University Press, 1950).

[9]*American College Dictionary* (New York, Random House, 1970).

former choice will ultimately initiate a cycle of distance between the soul and the personality. On some deep level the soul knows this choice is not right, that it is embarking upon a path in which it must construct very complex and elaborate defenses to protect its "error." Another entity (cycle) is being created which will separate the soul from the Spirit. This entity becomes part of the personality, the ego, and as such a "script", or "pattern" is born. As the personality grows around this script, it grows further and further apart from the soul, requires more and more energy to "keep alive". As such the consciousness begins to shift from the soul to this construct of the personality. It is, in layman's terms, a psychological defense. It is a lie, an illusion (maya), and yet the individual acts and reacts as if it is something precious and important. It will do whatever it needs to do (including violating universal law) in order to protect it, for it fears exposure (i.e. God finding Adam and Eve violating His law and thus being expelled from the Garden of Eden). In its effort to perpetrate this myth, the personality falls into a "pattern" of responses surrounding this issue. These themes repeat over and over again in the form of failed relationships, work and health problems. The individual utilizes so much energy to repress the truth, which is in violation of its own understanding of natural law, that the soul's growth becomes fixated. The pattern is crystallized, and it requires great effort to undo the pattern. However, when there is illumination and an effort to penetrate the illusion, when there is conscious effort to make choices that are "new" with regard to this pattern (and consistent with the soul's understanding of spirit), there is a tremendous release. The release is one of great compassion and love, for self as well as for others. It is a cleansing, and from it comes an outpouring of compassion.

To understand how these principles work in the model of Evolutionary Astrology, it may be helpful to again look at the four-fold construct of the angles of the horoscope (see Figure 9). The I. C. represents the point where the soul is in closest contact with Spirit, where there is a sense of oneness between the incarnating being (soul) and Creative Source (the God within). There is a sense of union here. This is the essence of the soul.

When a being expresses itself from this point of understanding, the result is the opposite point: the Midheaven. This is the potential manifestation of the highest aspect of the soul's essence in the world of form. This is a challenge for the soul to accomplish in this incarnation. The essence of the soul (I. C.) is ideally manifested in the form signified by the Midheaven. Thus the Midheaven is one's "calling in life," one's

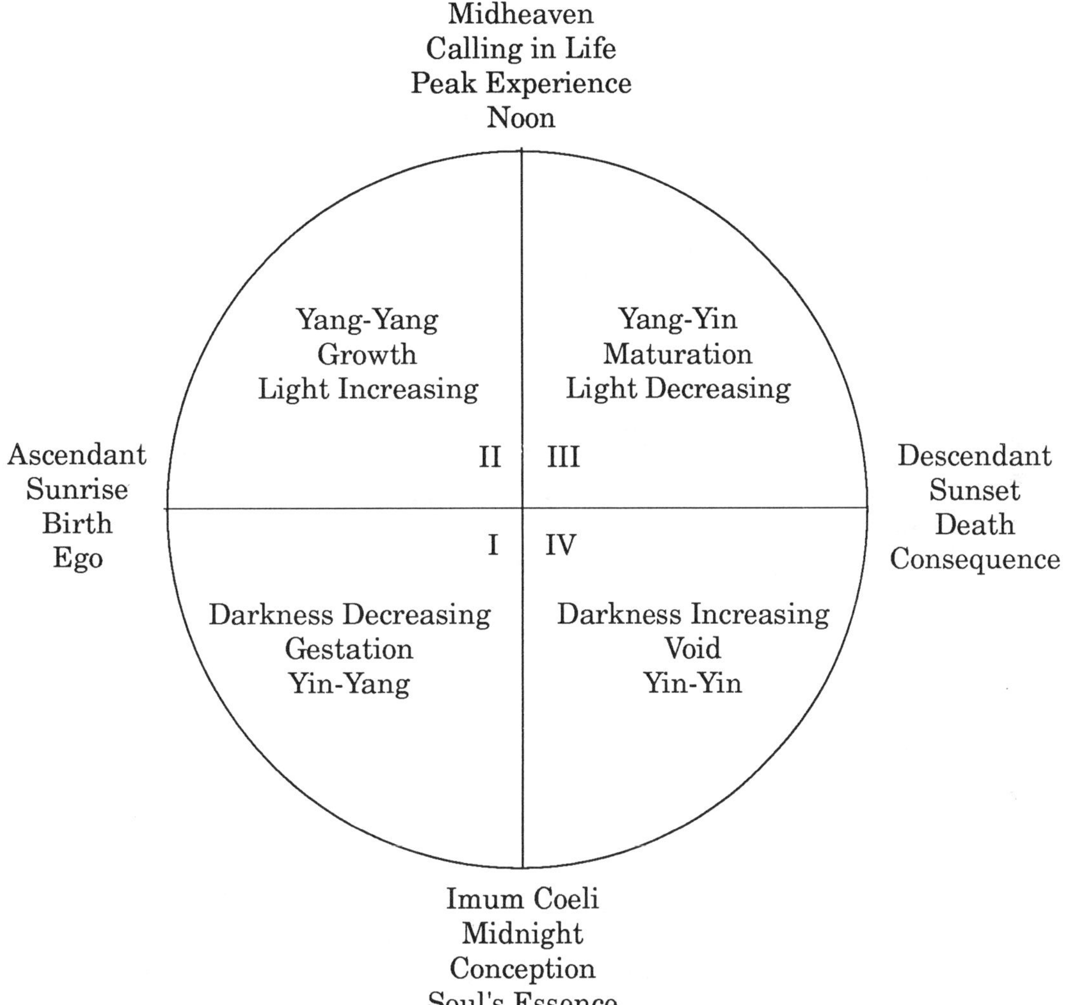

Figure 9
Daily Cycle of Sun to Earth (Rotating on its own Axis)

destiny. It is achieved by putting forth the truths reflected in the I. C., in the form indicated by the Midheaven.

The process of connecting the essence of the I. C. to the form and potential of the Midheaven is put into effect through the Ascendant. The Ascendant symbolizes the **initiation of activity**, and the consciousness of the intent behind that activity. The purpose of the activity, when the intent is pure, is to attain the form symbolized by the Midheaven. The *result* of the activity, and all the dynamics that go into initiating the activity (i.e. intentions and motivations) are symbolized by the Descendant.

The Descendant represents the consequences of one's actions initiated at the Ascendant. From one's effort and intent (conscious and unconscious) springs forth circumstances, conditions, and other people, as denoted by the Descendant. These circumstances and/or people support or reflect the **intent** symbolized by the Ascendant.

From this model it becomes apparent that the horizon, bordered by the Ascendant/Descendant axis, represents the intent of consciousness and its consequences. In the natural order of the day, the Sun rises at the Ascendant; the Earth awakens from darkness; the physical body awakens from the sleep state; the soul incarnates into the physical body; birth takes place. The soul must now make choices, between the home it came from (I. C.) and the home it will go to, or its destination (Midheaven). In the process it must protect its physical vehicle; it must struggle to survive the journey. There is a path between the I. C. and the Midheaven, between the essence of the soul and the highest potential form in which the soul comes to express itself, according to its own unique plan of destiny. Yet along the way comes challenges, obstacles and temptations that can and do distract the soul from this purpose. These arise with regard to the matter of survival, both physical and psychological.

As the soul incarnates into the physical vessel it has already contracted to undergo experiences that are reflective of its karma, or past actions that are part of a cyclic phenomenon not yet completed. From these prior experiences, and reactions to them, the soul has not only initiated various cycles, but also developed various skills referred to earlier as "developed powers and abilities." These developed powers and abilities may enhance the soul's journey. In the case of abilities they depict strengths that may enhance the struggle for survival. In the case of powers they may enhance the soul's potential to transcend the world of duality and physical phenomena and to quicken the journey back to oneness with Spirit, to experience an integration of soul to Spirit. That part of the path consists of many enlightenments.

However the incarnating soul has probably made some choices and initiated some activities which have inhibited its development. When given the choice, the individual in prior lifetimes has likely made some choices to center itself upon itself, instead of upon God; it has likely chosen at various opportunities to do that which it *knew* violated natural law, in a manner which benefited its lower self at the expense of another or others. In so doing, the individual gave rise to cycles which can be described as "patterns", or "scripts". These patterns are karmic in nature. They are reflected in relationships, work and health patterns of an inhibiting nature. They represent violations of natural law, violations of one's own understanding and reflection of its higher self. Around these cycles one has developed an ego, a personality complete with elaborate and complex psychological defenses, which the conscious mind now sees as being very real. Yet they are not.

How did the soul get to this point? What choices did it make? What choices could it have made? And finally how do these matters show up in the natal horoscope according to the principles of Evolutionary Astrology?

The midpoints of the angles represent critical points in the evolution of a soul in this incarnation. They symbolize the areas of life where one is compelled to make serious choices between what is desired for itself in a self-centered sense (and ultimately bad, or evil for itself in a spiritual sense), and good for itself in the pursuit of attaining wholeness, or oneness with its higher self. In the former case, one is creating a lie. The soul knows it, particularly if one is intuitive. On some level, it does not "feel right," and yet the individual chooses this path anyway. The result is a cycle, a pattern, in which the personality must exert great energy to defend.

These areas of choice between good and evil, right and wrong, self (ego) and higher self, is unique for each being. They may be shown within a 7-½° area surrounding the midpoint of any and all angles of the natal horoscope, according to the principles espoused here. These are the points of temptations. Any natal planet posited in this area represents critical issues to be experienced in this lifetime. They may represent patterns or scripts which the soul has created in the past, and around which the personality now struggles to defend. Transits and progressions over these points represent periods within this lifetime when the soul is confronted with significant spiritual choices, and is tempted to choose in violation of its understanding of natural or higher law. When the planets of another horoscope fall on one's natal midpoints, unique and special challenges to the integrity of the native arise. If not fully conscious of these forces, the native may be tempted to be influenced by these "others" in ways that ultimately prove distracting or harmful to its own journey toward wholeness.

Calculating the angular midpoints is not a difficult task. In a counter-clockwise fashion, simply take the sign, degree and minute of one angle from the sign, degree and minute of the previous angle, and divide by two. For example, take the distance between the I. C. and the

Ascendant and divide by 2, and add to Ascendant. Or, take the distance between the Ascendant and Midheaven, divide by 2, and add to the Midheaven (see example in this chapter). Once you find the midpoint of one angle, all angular midpoints will be the same degree and minute of the same quality. For example, if one angular midpoint is 14°30′ of fixed signs, all angular midpoints will be 14°30′ of the other fixed signs. Furthermore all angular midpoints will be located in the second, fifth, eighth and eleventh houses. Once the midpoint has been calculated, allow a 7-½° orb of influence. The closer a planet is to the actual degree of an angular midpoint, the more "fixed" that planet may be in terms of a karmic script or pattern in this lifetime.

The significance of each angular midpoint differs with each quadrant. The midpoint of the first quadrant brings into play the dynamics of the I. C. and Ascendant. The I. C. symbolizes the essence of the soul, its needs, and the point of integration between the soul and the Spirit. It is the symbolic point of "egolessness", or no ego in the sense of self relating to not-self. The Ascendant symbolizes the **intent** behind the action to be initiated. The choice is to act with an intent that is in harmony with the essence of the soul (I. C.), or in a manner that is self-centered, and perhaps in detriment to one's higher self. When a self-centered, or selfish decision is made, one is putting into motion a cycle of **deception.** One is not acting in a manner consistent with the needs or essence of the soul. There may be an attempt to represent oneself in a manner other than who one really is. Hence a script of an imposter evolves, and the temptation is to become a pretender, or a phony, to represent oneself in a false manner. The most common psychological defense here may be **denial.** The individual simply refuses to deal with attempts to look and see itself for what it is (or is not). At the root of this pattern may be a great deal of insecurity. If so this may manifest in a pattern of hoarding, or over-possessiveness of things the individual feels are needed to enhance survival (but in actuality only serve to detract from the integration of the personality with the soul, or awareness of the soul and its needs).

The midpoint of the second quadrant is located in the 11th house, halfway between the Ascendant and Midheaven. The dilemma here is between choosing to do that which is in harmony with one's calling in life, or higher purpose (Midheaven) and that which is self-centered and self-serving, even to the point of harming others in some way. When the choice is made to satisfy the egocentric self first and forfeit the choice that would support the unfoldment of the soul's purpose for incarnating, a pattern of procrastination and character weakness is likely to evolve. In a sense, this soul may be reluctant to actualize its potential.

It may create numerous obstacles to its potential success. The struggle to attain goals may be made more difficult than necessary, simply because when the time comes close to culminating the venture, the individual becomes timid and chooses a path of lesser resistance, or more satisfying short-term gratification. What stands in the way to the achievement of this soul's purpose? It may be the choice to do something extraordinary for the wrong reasons. Perhaps it wants fame, or recognition for its self, instead of seeing the value of the accomplishment for its own merits *without* its ego entering the bidding for the effort. This soul must closely examine its motives for doing things in the world, and realize the choice is between initiating the effort because the cause is right, and not because of the glory it will bring forth to the personality.

Quadrant three's midpoint lies somewhere in the eighth house, midway between the Midheaven and the Descendant. Whenever the Descendant is involved, the issue is one of **acceptance**. The Descendant represents the people and conditions the soul has drawn into its lifetime as a result of prior intent and hence actions initiated. These people and conditions serve a purpose: to facilitate the unfoldment of the soul's purpose for incarnating (Midheaven) or understanding of its higher self (I. C.). In the area of the midpoint of quadrant three, the soul may encounter a battle between attaining its contracted purpose (Midheaven) and the types of people it has drawn into its drama. Typically one tends to **blame** others for his/her failings in life. "If it wasn't for my wife, or my husband, or this condition, I could have succeeded in life." The danger is that this individual may use others as an excuse for his/her lack of commitment to do what one knows is right to do. In truth, these people or conditions may actually illuminate the soul to its higher purpose, if the individual would simply see these people and conditions in terms of **lessons** and **principles**. The major psychological defense present here is **projection**, or unwillingness to **accept** responsibility for one's own destiny. The danger is to "give up" and fall into a pattern of blame and routine as an excuse for failure. In truth there is no failure. It is simply a lapse of higher understanding, of awareness that all experiences are potential learning experiences—even the appearance of failure.

Quadrant four contains the midpoints between the Descendant and I. C. somewhere in the fifth house. The attraction of others may be in conflict with the needs of the soul. This can result in a **"groupie syndrome"**, or one who tries to better him/herself by attracting others whom one thinks are better than him/herself. In this case the individual strives to associate with situations and people who are not in harmony with the needs of the soul (I. C.). Discernment in the choice of mates and associates is critically important here. The individual must be certain that these associations facilitate unfoldment of one's true essence, and don't require him or her to be something they are not. The question to ask before engaging in intimacy may be: "Does this person inspire or enlighten me?" If one falls into this trap of **"glamour"**, great confusion can result when the individual realizes his/her needs are not being met.

Planets located in these angular midpoint areas symbolize issues of potential conflict. They are issues of conflict because of unwise choices the soul may have made, choices that may not have been in harmony with that soul's sense of truth or integrity. The choices were not consistent with the essence of the soul, or in harmony with its natural path of evolution, and the soul knew it at the time. As the choice was made, the cycle was created and the personality was likewise created, whose purpose was to defend it. The personality defends it by separating the soul from the consciousness of the ego, and building an apparent reality (script, or pattern) around this choice. An ego emerges (an aspect of the personality), and as these issues arise again and again, the individual has a choice again and again. As the choice continues to be self-centered and out of alignment with the higher aspects of the self, the personality gains greater and greater control, and the connection of consciousness to the soul diminishes. This may be reflected in the horoscope, in the position of planets near or on angular midpoints. These issues and principles are the same as described in the last section on "Developed Powers and Abilities."

To illustrate the principle of planets conjunct angular midpoints, let's look at the horoscope shown in Figure 10. This is the chart of a young lady born November 1, 1969, at 9:48 AM, at longitude 83°06′, latitude 42°20′. As of this writing in 1991, she is in law school studying to be a lawyer specializing in global natural resources. She has spent considerable time studying in France (she minored in French during her undergraduate studies), where she would one day like to live and work. On a personal level, she is friendly, ambitious, and loyal in relationships.

The midpoint of her natal angles is 4° 34′ of fixed signs. This is determined by subtracting the Midheaven from the Ascendant. This procedure may be simplified by converting signs of the zodiac to a number. For instance, Sagittarius is the ninth sign of the zodiac (the Ascendant in this example) and Virgo is the sixth (the Midheaven in this example). Also keep in mind that there are 30° to a sign, and 60′ to a degree, for conversion purposes. Thus to determine the midpoint of the Ascendant/Midheaven, one uses the following calculations:

	9S	9°	38′	(Ascendant)
+	6S	29°	31′	(Midheaven)
=	2S	10°	07′	(distance between Ascendant and Midheaven)

Divide this distance by two, and add to Midheaven, to determine midpoint of angle.

	2S 10°	07′ = 70° 07′
	70° 07′	divided by 2
=	35° 03′	

Convert this back to signs, degrees and minutes, and add to Midheaven.

	1S	5°	03′
+	6S	29°	31′
=	8S	4°	34′

This comes out to 4° Scorpio 34′ as the midpoint of the Midheaven/Ascendant, or quadrant 2. The midpoint of all other angles will be 4° 34′ of fixed signs.

Her natal Sun, Moon, Mercury and Saturn are within close proximity of these midpoints. The fact that there are as many as four planets conjunct to the angular midpoints indicates a high probability of a lifetime of major decision-making. It also indicates a great emphasis upon personal morality, very clear distinctions between right and wrong, good and evil, justice and unfairness. It is also interesting to note that at age four her parents divorced. The 4° 34′ of the angular midpoints corresponds with an important age arc – an age when an event was likely to occur that would have meaningful impact upon her life, particularly with regard to morality and/or decision-making. Another is likely to occur between ages 34–35 and 64–65 (see section on age arcs).

The closest planet to an angular midpoint is Saturn, posited at 5° 10′ of Taurus in the fifth house. This is the midpoint between the I. C. and the Descendant. The potential conflict is between the needs of her real self (soul) and the conditions as well as people who are thrust onto her path in life. The Descendant represents the results of cycles initiated prior to this lifetime. Those cycles are not yet complete. Thus conditions arise in one's life, or people enter into one's life, who repre-

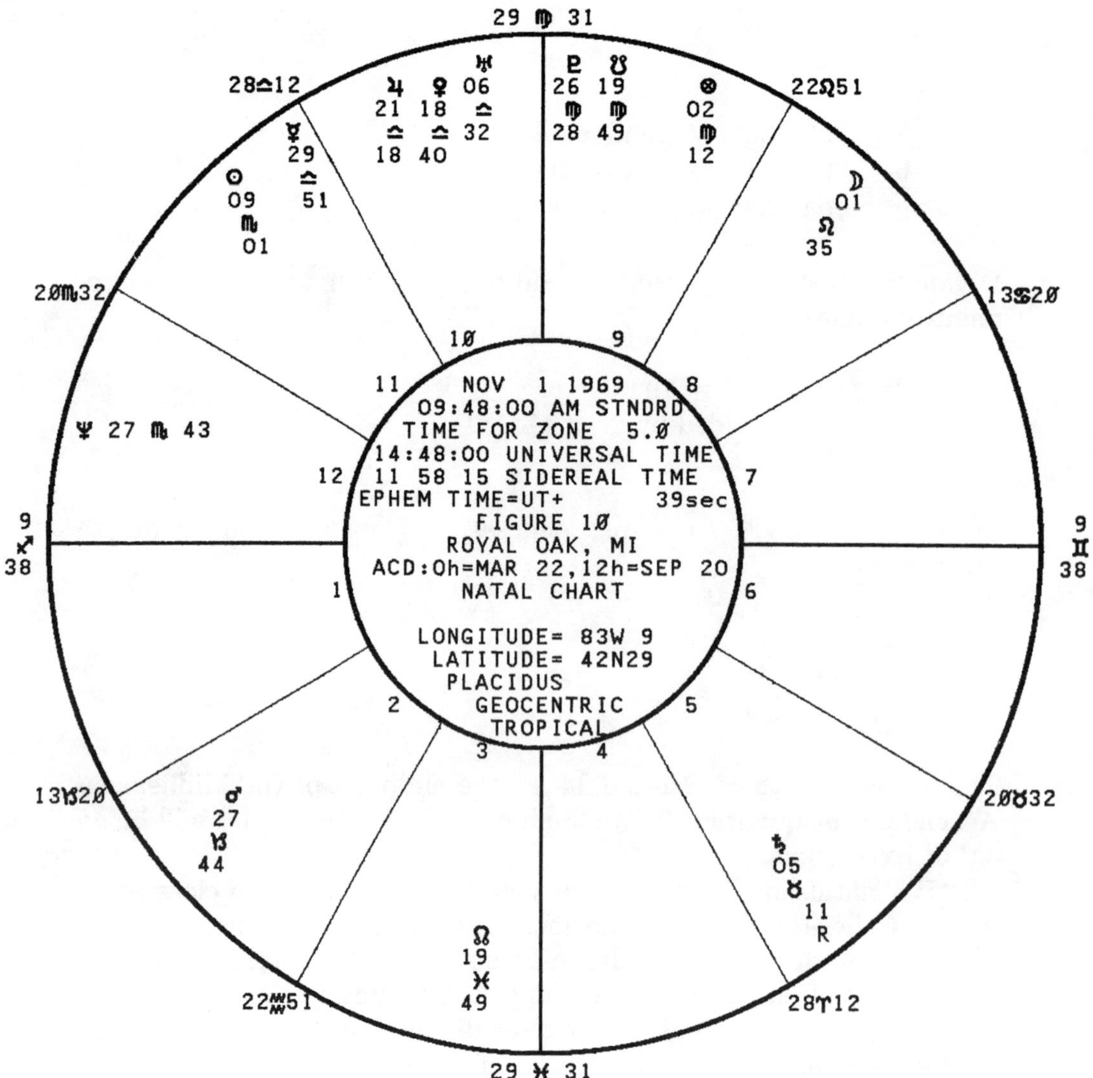

Figure 10

sent the principles inherent in the intent behind those actions initiated previously. Innately this soul understands her responsibility to these conditions and people. She also understands her responsibilities to her inner self, her inner needs. Saturn is the principle of responsibility, integrity and honesty. Conflicts arise when she must make a decision between these two responsibilities: the responsibility to her own inner needs versus her sense of responsibility to others whose needs may be in opposition to her own. It is likely that she may find herself in positions where others request her to compromise her integrity, to do something for them (out of obligation, as a favor) that is not consistent with her own set of personal principles. How she handles these situations will determine whether or not she maintains a connection with her soul, her spiritual needs. The more she compromises her integrity to please others, the stronger her ego is likely to become, thus separating her from the innermost needs of her soul. If that happens, she is likely to fall into a pattern of routine (quadrant four) in which her world becomes governed more by fear than faith. Her challenge is one of faith with Saturn situated on the midpoint of quadrant four. It is a faith that, by making those decisions consistent with her inner sense of honesty and spiritual responsibility, she will experience more reward in terms of personal fulfillment than she would by compromising her values in order to please others. This may not be easy because others may put great amounts of pressure upon her to compromise, and this pressure may translate as a sense of guilt (Saturn). Once again, in order to justify such decisions, the ego builds elaborate psychological defenses that cut off communication with one's soul.

Before making critical decisions that favor others at the potential expense of herself, this young woman would be well-advised to think the matter out clearly. In the decision-making process, she might be well-advised to ask herself one simple question: "Which decision feels right?" If she chooses this course, she may feel she is risking something the ego has determined to be of value (i.e. financial reward, acceptance, job security). From the point of view of Evolutionary Astrology, she is risking something far greater than those needs of the ego. She is risking an opportunity to evolve as a spiritual being. Within the course of this lifetime, that translates as an opportunity to experience a great psychological release as a karmic pattern is finally transcended. The result would likely be a deeper self-understanding and confidence in her ability to make decisions.

The natal Moon is located close to the midpoint of quadrant three, at 1° 35′ of Leo. This is the midpoint between the Midheaven and the Descendant. Once again the soul is confronted with dilemmas between the conditions and people it has attracted as a result of prior actions (incomplete cycles), but this time with the potential purpose for which it has reincarnated. The Midheaven represents one's calling in life, the service one may aspire to. The Moon represents unconditional love versus conditional love issues. As mentioned earlier, this individual is intensely loyal in her relationships. Yet up until this time she has had a tendency to attract mates who are not compatible with her calling in life. At some point in the relationship, it becomes apparent that she and her mate will have to part ways, either due to different choices of school, careers, or even residences. Does she choose to maintain her loyalty to these mates, or pursue the direction of her calling in life? She would be well-advised to seek out potential mates who are compatible with her calling in life, or who at least do not require her to "choose between your career or me."

The Sun and Mercury are located near the midpoint of the second quadrant. The dilemma here is between choosing that which is consistent with the unfoldment and realization of one's potential in life (Midheaven) versus doing that which satisfies a desire for immediate gratification, or the pleasure principle (Ascendant). The Sun in this position is extremely critical, for the natal Sun's location represents one's natural path toward self-unfoldment. As indicated in an earlier chapter, the area of quadrant two is where the Sun increases in light every day. It is the quadrant that suggests bringing thoughts into form, the quadrant of productivity and manifestation. In order to manifest one's ideas, it is first of all necessary to learn something, to be a specialist. In this manner a talent develops. This soul has the possibility of developing a unique talent, and through the intelligent expression of this talent, to manifest something significant in this lifetime. Both the Sun and Mercury here denote a person of high intelligence. It also denotes someone who is willing to be of service (Mercury) and has a strong sense of purpose (Sun). However issues likely arise which "tempt" her to procrastinate from the realization of these goals. The Ascendant is a point of temptation – the temptation to do that which is in conflict to one's calling in life. It is also the point from which activity is initiated that leads to karmic cycles. Therefore when this individual makes choices that provide for immediate gratification while at the same time being at the expense of one's potential purpose, she is likely to incur results that are more complex and distracting than she had thought possible. For example, perhaps she will be placed in a situation wherein she has a chance to take a trip to Europe, but at the same time she has an opportunity to start work in a field that may be helpful to her career. Which will she choose, and why? If she chooses that which provides the greatest pleasure (i.e. the trip to Europe), she might experience a whole host of results that she did not expect, results that complicate her life. In a sense, when one acts out at the Ascendant when there is a choice consistent with the I. C. or Midheaven, one incurs a karmic script.

One other issue may be important to note with the Sun on the angular midpoint of quadrant two. The native may be placed in activities whose cause is consistent with her personal recognition and glory. She must be careful not to let the praise and recognition cloud her sense of the cause behind the effort.

CHAPTER NINE

The Evolutionary Moon

> *"Without an awareness of our emotions, we cannot associate the effects of anger, sadness, grief, and joy – within ourselves or others – with their causes. We cannot distinguish between that part of us which is personality and that part of us which is soul. Without an awareness of our feelings we cannot experience compassion.*
>
> *If we are not intimate with our emotions, we cannot perceive the dynamics that lie behind emotions, the way these dynamics work, and the ends that they serve. Emotions are currents of energy that pass through us. Awareness of these currents is the first step in learning how our experiences come into being and why.*
>
> *Emotions reflect intentions. Therefore, awareness of emotions leads to awareness of intentions."* [10]

Prior to this section, Evolutionary Astrology has focused upon the relationship of the Earth to the Sun, and the cycle of the Earth rotating upon its own axis. There is another unique and special cycle pertinent to Earth, and that is the relationship of the Earth to the Moon.

As pointed out in an earlier chapter, man has created two measurements of time to which he relates: clock time and calendar time. Clock time is a function of the Earth's rotation on its own axes, while calendar time is a function of the Earth's orbit around the Sun. Yet there is another measurement of time which is not generally used by the collective, but is nonetheless consistent with various rhythms of human (and nature) activity, and this is the time measured in accordance with the

[10]Gary Zukav, *The Seat Of The Soul* (New York, Simon and Shuster Inc., 1989).

cycle of the Moon in its orbit around the Earth. The lunar cycle, as it is called, lasts approximately 29.5 days (new Moon to new Moon, or full Moon to full Moon). This cycle is divided into four sub-cycles, each lasting approximately one week each: new Moon, first quarter, full Moon, and last quarter. This lunar cycle, and its phases (sub-cycles) correlate closely to such natural activities as tidal forces and female menstrual cycles. There are several studies indicating that plants respond to changing phases of the Moon. In fact researchers are constantly coming up with new evidence that the Moon exerts an influence in a wide variety of earthly affairs.[11]

The symbolism of the Moon in its changing relationship to the Earth is another key to understanding deeper aspects of the soul. The changing phases of the Moon really are relationships not just between the Earth and Moon, but as well with the Sun. It is the interaction between all three—the movement of the Earth in its orbit around the Sun as well as the movement of the Moon in its orbit around the Earth, that creates the appearance that the Moon is constantly changing. In these relationships, what is constantly changing is the amount of light the Moon is reflecting from the Sun, based upon their respective relationships to the Earth.

The symbolism important here is the reflection of the light of the Sun. If the Sun is symbolic of one's wholeness, of the "master within", then the Moon is symbolic of one's reflection of that wholeness, or creative source. It is not the source of life itself, literally or symbolically, for the Moon actually has no light of its own. It does have an influence over the affairs of the human and nature kingdoms, for it correlates to (and perhaps even causes) fluctuations, or swings, in the status of many living organisms. As tides ebb and flow, so too do the emotional states of human beings rise and fall.

Just as the Moon reflects the light of the Sun to the Earth, so too do souls in physical vehicles reflect and respond to conditions and circumstances encountered in any given lifetime. These responses may be cyclic; they may even change in time. Yet the fact is that individual beings react and respond to one another according to their own unique level of understanding. These responses and reactions give rise to emotions, or feelings. They themselves give rise to future intentions and behaviors that follow along the lines of karma, or cyclic consequence.

As conditions arise in life, the individual responds. The result of

[11]Edward R. Dewey, *Cycles: The Mysterious Forces That Trigger Events* (New York, Hawthorne Books, 1971).

that response elicits a particular judgement in the individual's mind: perhaps it was pleasant, happy, exciting, or perhaps it was unpleasant, disturbing, upsetting. The general characteristics of the experience (the condition and the subsequent reactions) are stored in the individual's memory. When future conditions arise that are in some ways similar to the previous one just described, the individual remembers aspects of the prior experience. This in turn affects the manner in which he or she responds this time. The response and subsequent reaction is again recorded in the memory bank, and so the cycle continues. In time, general "types" of conditions elicit similar types of "reactions" which become a pattern unique to that individual. The dynamics behind these reactions are **emotions.** It is one's **emotions** that arise from certain types of circumstances that one encounters in life. It is one's **emotions** that influence the manner in which one responds to these circumstances. It is one's **emotions** that become the root of patterns or scripts that one creates in his/her life. And it is through the **emotions** that one is able to become **aware** of the various principles and lessons the soul is in need of understanding in order to integrate itself with Spirit.

There is a wide variety of emotions and feelings. Some are very energizing while others may be draining and debilitating to the individual. Gary Zukav, in his book *The Seat of the Soul*, describes it very well: **"Emotions are currents of energy with different frequencies. Emotions that we think of as negative, such as hatred, envy, disdain and fear have a lower frequency, and less energy, than emotions that we think of as positive, such as affection, joy, love and compassion. When you choose to replace a lower-frequency current of energy, such as anger, with a higher-frequency current, such as forgiveness, you raise the frequency of your Light."**[12]

In the model of Evolutionary Astrology, it is through the understanding of emotions and the subsequent scripts created around them that each individual is able to effect a release. Once the dynamics of the script are understood, the individual will be better positioned to choose different modes of expression than that dictated by the script. By becoming conscious of one's intent, by "knowing" that it is in harmony with the essence of the soul and its potential destiny, one comes closer to becoming whole. Symbolically, by understanding the reactive nature implied by the Moon, and making choices of a higher frequency, one becomes the Sun.

The lunar cycle of the Earth is only pertinent to the Earth and its

[12]Gary Zukav, *The Seat Of The Soul* (New York, Simon and Shuster Inc., 1989).

inhabitants. The Earth is a realm where souls incarnate, they become embodied. On Earth the soul has the privilege of embodiment, a privilege which all souls seek. Yet with embodiment comes the phenomenon of reaction, response in the physical, dualistic world. How the soul cares for this vehicle, both physically and mentally, is a function of its spiritual understanding. A soul exists, but the consciousness within the embodiment may not accept this. Why? Because of the elaborate defenses created to sustain choices that were made, but not in harmony with the soul's needs or understanding. From these an ego was created, and its purpose is to justify or rationalize those choices made in which the self was centered upon only itself, and not upon what it ***knew*** was right. The ego's purpose is to protect this "new self", which is not in alignment with the real self, or soul. Whenever issues or conditions arise which relate to the reason why this ego was created in the first place, lower frequency emotions are exhibited. An individual who can "feel" these emotions still has a consciousness which is connected to the soul. It has not become so crystallized and fixed that it has lost the battle with the ego. It is not yet in a state of denial, which is characterized by an unyielding pattern, script and/or routine to the life, in which the individual does not feel anything at all, does not express any emotion whatsoever. There is still consciousness that is open, and by allowing the self to feel, to become aware of its emotions, that soul can evolve. The phenomenon of evolution is evident when there is an understanding of a pattern, a release of the ego surrounding that pattern, and an outpouring of compassion where before there was self-centered protectiveness. Ultimately there is a change in choices, and hence emotions, related to the cause of that script.

For now let us look at the emotions and scripts suggested by the natal Moon. First of all, understand that the basic emotion is one of **hurt**. Behind every low frequency emotion is an experience in which the individual felt **hurt**. Close to that (and immediately following) is the emotion of **fear**. Fear also hurts, because it causes pain on some level. The individual seeks to escape pain on any level. In this context, the sign of the natal Moon may indicate where the soul is vulnerable to feeling hurt or emotional pain. Moon in **Aries**, for example, may feel hurt if it does not get its way, and may express this hurt through **anger**. Taurus may feel hurt when something it has done is not appreciated, and others want to change it. The Moon in Taurus individual may become very possessive and guarded and not let its effort be changed. Its reaction may be one of stubbornness as a means to protect itself from being hurt. What is the solution? How does one overcome these reactive states, and the patterns they coincide with? In the case of a

Taurus Moon, it may be through **appreciation** of others and what they would like. In the case of **Aries Moon**, it may be through allowing others to do things their own way rather than trying to force an issue by becoming angry (which is an effort to manipulate the external). Letting it go (i.e. the pattern, the emotion) and seeing it from the other side may be one of the ways to overcome these patterns, but it cannot take place without understanding of the pattern first. That is where astrology comes in as a useful tool for self-unfoldment.

The Moon is past experience. Where the Moon is located in the horoscope is where the soul is coming from. It describes experiences, and conditions, but more importantly, patterns of responses learned from those experiences. Even more importantly it provides the key to understanding the causes, and hence the solutions, to overcoming inhibiting patterns.

In the natal horoscope, there is the area from which the Moon came (prior to birth), and the area where the Moon is going (after birth). The area where the Moon came from will be referred to as the "Evolutionary Waning Moon." The section of the chart which the Moon will cross after birth will be referred to as the "Evolutionary Waxing Moon."

To find the "Evolutionary Waning Moon" area, begin by locating the point directly opposite the natal Moon. The area of the horoscope which proceeds from the Moon *counter-clockwise* to its opposition point is the "waxing phase of the Evolutionary Moon." The area which continues from the opposition point counter-clockwise back to the natal Moon is the "waning phase of the Evolutionary Moon" (see figure 11).

The planets in the waning segment are those which the Moon has crossed in the two weeks prior to birth (approximate). Those in the waxing segment will be crossed by the Moon in the approximately two weeks following birth. The planets in the waning segment represent the types of experiences and conditions the soul has recently undergone (prior to birth). The soul brings the tools and understanding accrued from those experiences into this lifetime. It is also possible that the soul brings various emotional patterns related to these planets into this lifetime.

The planets the Moon will cross after birth (i.e. the waxing phase of the Evolutionary Moon) represent specific types of experience, people and conditions the soul will possibly encounter in this lifetime. These experiences and people are not without purpose. To the contrary they serve a very valuable purpose. In order for the soul to evolve, it may be essential for it to undergo these types of experiences (represented by the planets). It may be necessary for the soul to encounter

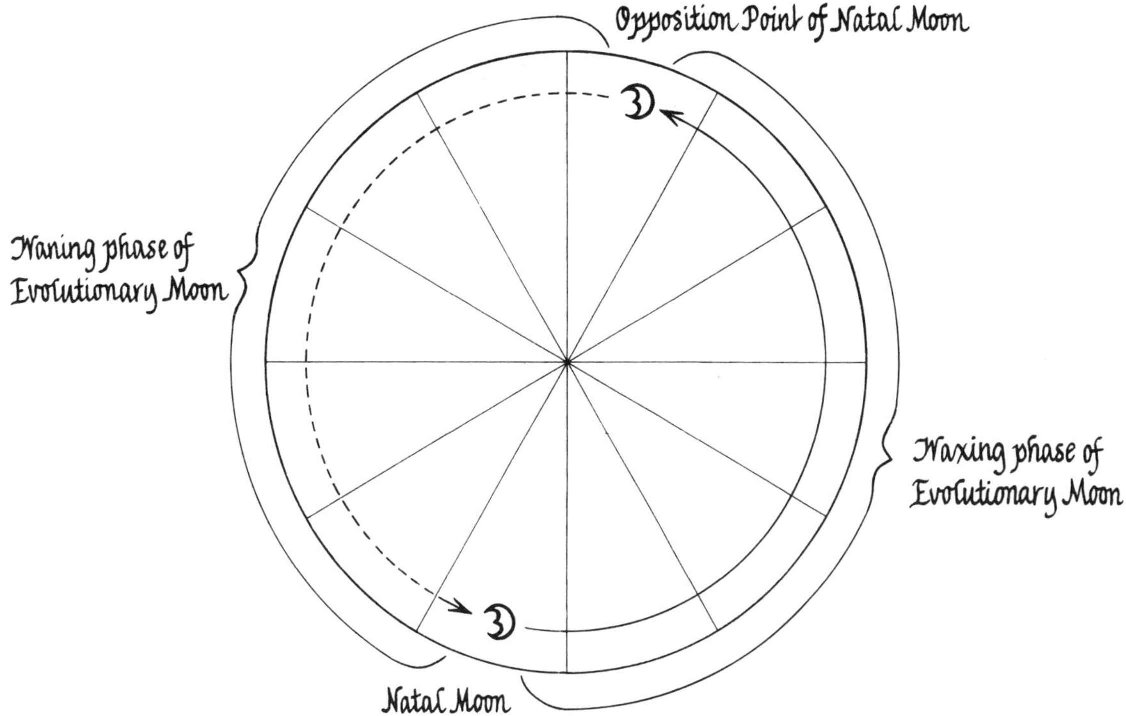

Figure 11: Example of waxing & waning phase of Evolutionary Moon.

emotions related to these planets, and meet the challenge of not succumbing to the temptation of building patterns around the lower frequency emotions related therein.

Ultimately these planets in the evolutionary waxing phase of the Moon represent new tools to be developed in this lifetime. They also represent principles which, if understood, may be applied in a manner that will facilitate the soul's release from patterns developed prior to this lifetime, patterns which the soul is in need of overcoming in order to continue its journey to wholeness.

What are the types of experiences and principles one has undergone (waning) and is to undergo (waxing), and around which various patterns may have been developed? These are signified by the planets (and to some extent the signs) that the Moon has most recently crossed (past) and will cross (this life). They are as follows:

Sun: The higher principles to learn (waxing) are unity and wholeness. When in the waning phase, the soul may have been in a position of leadership, and/or possibly one of high visibility and recognition. He/she may have had some degree of popularity amongst others. The central question is whether or not such recognition resulted in the development of an egotistical pride and arrogance, or whether the soul was able to use such recognition as a positive tool for constructive leadership in the community. On the positive side, the soul may now express confidence, vitality, and willingness to assume a leadership role for good causes. Negatively, a sense of pride and arrogance may manifest in a disdain for other people; an attitude of superiority which now results in unpopularity and being viewed by others with disdain (i.e. a fool or buffoon).

When the Sun is the first (or one of the first) planet(s) to be crossed by the Moon after birth (waxing phase), the soul may meet up with circumstances that require leadership, and may attract recognition. It is now essential for this soul to realize the purpose of assuming such positions, that it is to create a sense of unity within the group, and not an opportunity to glorify its own ego.

Mercury: The higher principles are **service and cooperation**. In the waning segment of the Evolutionary Moon, Mercury suggests a soul that was in a position of service to others, a role where planning and cooperation were essential to the success of projects. The soul may have been responsible for developing ideas that would either inspire others into action or learning. Perhaps this soul has been a writer or speaker, or possibly an organizer or planner, one who created designs or provided a service that helped others. On the negative side, the soul may have acquired knowledge or skill in order to make itself appear "superior" to others (i.e. mental arrogance, intellectualism). In this regard the soul may have been extremely critical of others, quick to find fault and blame in any effort or idea proposed by others, thereby breaking a sense of cooperation that could have unfolded. In this lifetime others may now be critical of the native, reticent to go along with his/her ideas. He/she does not seem to receive the cooperation sought from others.

When located in the waxing phase, particularly as the first planet the Moon will cross after birth, Mercury denotes the opportunity to develop the intellect or a willingness to be of service to others. Circumstances arise which require cooperation, and it is the challenge of this soul to facilitate such cooperation as a means of solving problems, either personally (i.e. family) or in the community (i.e. work place). As one becomes more and more organized, and gathers more and more information, one can be of greater service to others, and thereby enhance one's own evolution. By becoming critical of the efforts of others, one creates an uncooperative pattern in business and mental ventures.

Venus: The higher principles are **gratitude and forgiveness.** Venus also represents a strong sense of beauty and balance (harmony). In prior experiences this soul may have been an artist, or one who appreciated beauty and a balance of form. He or she may have sought to create beauty and harmony in the lives of others, offering support and encouragement whenever it was needed. It is possible that this soul had (and still has) a talent which was of benefit to others. On the positive side, the soul willingly shared this talent with others. It also understood the need for harmony in relationships of all kinds, particularly intimate ones. In this regard it developed an unconditional love for those it was related to, or involved with. It attempted to give, or be, something of value to others. It also strove to see something of worth and value in others, thereby enhancing their sense of self-esteem. On the negative side this soul may have been very possessive and not willing to share with others. This may have been most evident in relationships where one could have been extremely possessive and jealous. As such the soul may have set up patterns whereby it would be rejected, and the reaction may have been one of resentment (unforgiving). The native may also have been the one who rejected others, or entered into relationships without intent to be supportive, and now experiences the same from others in this lifetime.

As the first planet the Moon crosses after birth (waxing), Venus indicates the soul will likely enter into situations with others where success depends upon the willingness to be supportive. Harmony and balance are likely to be essential in order to facilitate one's evolution. By choosing to be jealous and/or possessive of one's mates (or things), the soul creates a pattern of unfulfilling relationships.

Earth: Directly opposite the Sun in a natal horoscope is the Earth. If Earth is the last planet crossed by the Moon prior to birth, then the soul may bring into this lifetime experiences of closeness to nature. Perhaps the soul was a gardener, farmer, botanist, or in some way connected to nature and the outdoors. Perhaps the soul was concerned with the well-being of the planet. In this setting one became close to God, and still might be in this lifetime. Perhaps through its relationship and understanding of nature the soul is able to heal others (i.e. herbs). On the negative side, this soul may have abused nature, engaged in activities that were destructive to the environment with no regard to the damage its acts would have upon the future of the land. Such violations may have set up patterns wherein the individual experiences problems with nature in this lifetime (i.e. allergies, problems with animals and/or insects).

The Moon going toward the Earth after birth signifies opportunities to work with the environment, or close to nature. By developing a love for land and ecology, the soul enhances its evolution; it may come to know itself through nature, which becomes a catalyst for spiritual experience. To be placed in such conditions and to ignore or behave in a manner that is harmful to nature and the lower kingdoms may result in personal physical problems. It may also result in patterns of hurt in personal, intimate relationships with the opposite sex. Perhaps one's parents do not get along; perhaps one experiences difficulty in marriage or family settings. If so, understanding may come from going out alone into nature and "finding God," or "finding one's self".

Mars: The higher principles are **right action and unselfish motives, combined with courage**. In prior lifetimes (waning phase) this soul may have been called upon to respond with courage and bravery, to defend principles which it strongly believed in (particularly rights of individual freedom). In this sense the soul may have assumed roles in the military, or as a strategist involved in fighting for essential human rights. It is also possible that the soul was athletic, or involved in competitive efforts. As long as these efforts were not designed to bring harm to others, this soul may have experienced the success of victory and triumph. In this lifetime there may still be the joy that comes with winning, or being best, in competitive ventures. Negatively though, such a desire to win or be first, even at the expense of others, may have created a pattern wherein others may now try to measure themselves against the native, and attempt to defeat the native's efforts in this lifetime. If the soul's activities were not undertaken with right motives, but rather with selfish or self-centered motives, then the soul likely encounters conditions wherein others are not exhibiting right motives where the native is concerned (i.e. they try to take advantage at the native's expense). It may seem like others are trying to get ahead and using the native as a scapegoat. When a soul continually wants to do things its own way, without regard to the effects this has upon others, then it sets up a pattern wherein others will resist. Such frustration of "not getting one's way" leads to **anger**, and ultimately pushes away people whom the native needed for support.

As the first planet crossed after birth (waxing phase), Mars indicates conditions may arise which require courage and right action. In order to meet these challenges, it is first of all necessary for the soul to develop a strong set of principles and beliefs which it is willing to fight for (not necessarily in a physical sense). When these principles are violated, particularly those of individual freedoms and rights, the soul has a choice of how to behave: with courage and bravery, or timidity and cowardice. The latter response will likely result in a pattern wherein the soul is "pushed around" by others. Even in the first possibility, there is a dilemma: to act with bravery and courage must not be translated to mean dominance over others, for this is not consistent with right action. The key may be to consider whether or not the activity or response is one of sensitivity or insensitivity to others. Courage with sensitivity to others leads to success and respect. Courage without sensitivity to others may lead to patterns of argumentation and dissension, wherein others are drawn into the life who "challenge" the native and his/her motives. There is no peace of mind in this case, only a life of "fighting with others."

Jupiter: The higher principles are **wisdom and charity**. If Jupiter is the last planet crossed by the Moon prior to birth, it signifies a soul which may have had the opportunity to be charitable to others, to help in their development. Perhaps the soul was a teacher, writer, or philanthropist. The charity exhibited may have been in the form of time, expertise, or financial resources, or wisdom and understanding of life. Where there was despair, this soul may have provided hope. As such this soul may have experienced the great joy of being loved by many. On the negative side, one may have been tempted to take advantage of others, receiving help and aid from others under false pretenses. The emotional pattern here is **envy**, wherein one wants more than he or she needs, even at the expense of lying to (or conning) others. A pattern may now be in place in which the soul is never content with what it has. This may manifest in physical maladies of obesity. It may furthermore manifest in relationship patterns wherein others do not take the native seriously. They give (in the native's eyes) false hope, and hence relationships never seem to turn out as positive as the native hoped (i.e. broken engagements).

When Jupiter is the first planet crossed by the Moon after birth (waxing), opportunities to develop wisdom, or to be charitable to others are presented. Perhaps the soul comes into wealth, far more than is needed, and recognizes conditions which could benefit by receipt of the native's charitable assistance. Perhaps the soul encounters conditions where wisdom or understanding are needed, where there is much despair and the community requires hope and wise counsel. Does the native help, or does the native seek to exploit the situation? By choosing to act with charity and humanity the soul creates patterns of joy and growth. By exploiting these people and conditions the soul sets up a pattern of disappointment in others.

Saturn: The higher principles are **responsibility and integrity**. As a waning planet to the Evolutionary Moon this suggests a soul that may have been placed in positions of great responsibility. Perhaps this soul was a government leader, or the head of a business, or some other group wherein it was his/her responsibility to guide and direct the affairs of others. As such, this soul was responsible for creating guidelines, rules, or laws by which the group could best attain its goals. In a very real sense, this soul now brings with it a "father figure" role in the lives of those it contacts. The key principle is the level of integrity the soul exhibited in these conditions. If integrity was high, then that soul is now trusted by others in this lifetime. In fact it may be looked up to as an authority. On the negative side, such positions may have been misused to foster one's own egocentric sense of control over others. In this role the soul may have denied others certain freedoms and privileges because it wanted to maintain tight control. The enslavement or restriction of others for one's own desire to maintain control may manifest in patterns of feeling controlled by others in this lifetime. One may feel restricted, denied, or held back in some way. At the root of these patterns may be the emotion of **guilt**, and on the surface the emotion frequently felt may be **depression**. With this may come feelings of failure and possibly inadequacy.

As the first planet crossed by the Moon after birth, Saturn brings forth conditions which require responsibility and integrity on the part of the soul. It is important how the soul chooses to handle these positions of responsibility. Does it do so with a sense of honesty and integrity, or does it wield the tight fist of control and authoritarianism? In the latter case, the individual is assuming a position of judgment over others and handing down punitive dictates. This may result in patterns wherein the native fears others, for they may challenge and overthrow the native's base of control. In the former case wherein the native handles responsibilities with honor and dignity, the eye is always kept on the goal of the group, and a respect for each member's importance is conveyed. In this manner the soul experiences a pattern of successful accomplishments in life, and is respected by his/her peers.

Uranus: The higher principles are **freedom and truth**. If Uranus is the last planet crossed by the Moon prior to birth (waning), the soul has likely developed strong values for freedom and a love for seeking truth outside of mainstream thinking. There may be a high degree of enlightenment with this soul, and if the pursuit of truth is sought there may also be a high degree of charisma that attracts others. In prior lifetimes this soul may have stood out in his or her community because of unusual interests, a highly developed mind, or talented skills. One's expression may have been highly individualistic. Negatively this soul may have been tempted to violate the rules or laws of the community just for the sake of being different. As a result, such disturbances and violations of the rights of others (and the community) may have created a pattern of ostracism in this lifetime. The soul may feel uncomfortably "strange" and alienated from his/her peers now.

As the first planet crossed after birth by the Moon, Uranus represents opportunities to choose a path of enlightenment in this lifetime. The seeking of truth and higher knowledge (knowledge not generally accepted by the masses), leads one into a direction much different than his/her background would suggest as probable. It furthermore creates a pattern of enlightening breakthroughs, which in turn leads to charisma and the attraction of unusual people (and circumstances) into one's life. If the endeavor for higher knowledge is not pure, and such knowledge is used in an arrogant manner (i.e. a need to always be right), or if one pursues a course of disrupting the lives of others under the guise it will "set them free", then the soul may create a pattern of short-term, unfulfilling relationships (i.e. separations) and experiences that are fraught with disruptions before completion, i.e. a series of shocks and unexpected surprises of a disturbing nature. The key is to seek truth without falling into the trap of trying to convert others to one's unique understanding before they are ready. To give up the seeking of truth is to give up one's freedom; to pursue it is to find one's freedom.

Neptune: The higher principles are **compassion and faith**. The lower frequency emotions associated with Neptune are grief, suffering and suspicion. Others include confusion and helplessness, and the pattern of vulnerability from incorrect choices regarding these principles is one of *victimization*. When Neptune is the last planet crossed before birth by the Moon (waning), the soul brings with it experiences of sacrifice. What did it sacrifice and why? If the sacrifices were made because of belief in a higher order (i.e. God) and adherence to the principles of this higher authority, then the soul truly learned the meaning of: "It is better to give than to receive." In giving there is great joy. In desiring to help others who are more needy and in suffering, there is the great outpouring of compassion that makes one feel close to God. In so doing the soul has created conditions in this lifetime wherein others now feel tremendous love and care for the native. There may be a saintly quality to the soul which makes others feel comfortable. There may be a warmth which brings forth the same from others now. In addition, or instead, the soul may have developed skills that enhance the imagination of others, such as acting, music or poetry. There may also be counseling skills which heal others. Negatively the soul may have been tempted to mislead others for its own selfish ends, particularly in matters of intimacy. Trust may have been created with another, and then betrayed without regard to the hurt this would cause another. Such violations of trust may have created a pattern of "betrayals" in love in this lifetime. It may also be the root for patterns of victimization wherein the native feels vulnerable around others. The result may be a pattern of withdrawal and fear of others.

As the first planet crossed after birth by the Moon (waxing), Neptune signifies opportunities to help others, to behave in creative ways that bring joy or faith to others. There are opportunities to develop the intuitive side of one's nature as a tool to helping others. But the key is **faith** in a higher order, faith that all experiences serve a purpose. In this sense there is inner harmony. Without faith, and without desire to help those who suffer, one is setting the foundation for patterns of grief and sadness, patterns of loss and disillusionment in others.

Pluto: The higher principles are **self-realization and insight**. It also represents the ability to change things for the better. As the last planet crossed before birth (waning), Pluto signifies one who may have been in situations that required transformation. This is the soul who could see what was wrong with the community (or individual, or planet) and had the courage and talent to initiate an effort to correct or improve it. This soul may have the power to rid itself and others of disease or obstacles that interfere with a natural flow of growth. Negatively the soul may have chosen to rid itself of a condition in order to enhance its own well-being, and may have done so at the expense of others. In this sense the soul may have chosen to behave in ruthless ways in order to rid anything or anyone who stood in its way. If so, a pattern of rejection, and a series of power plays with others, may be a theme in this lifetime. Otherwise a choice of using one's insight to improve or heal the community and/or individuals within the community may now result in experiences of great personal empowerment, and ease with working with authorities in order to "get things done" in the community. There may be healing or repair abilities. There may be a deep and profound understanding of human nature. Others may value the soul's insight in this lifetime.

As the first planet crossed after birth (waxing), Pluto indicates one who comes into circumstances that require transformation and improvement. There are ways to make things better, and it requires research and insight. By probing into the matter, the soul may discover what went wrong, why it went wrong, and how it can be corrected, even improved, so that the matters achieve their highest potential. Before embarking upon such a project involving others, the soul might first have to follow this course for itself. Thus there is the potential for self-realization followed by personal empowerment that may lead to healing the community, or planet. The negative side unfolds when the soul doesn't first understand the dynamics behind the situation or condition. The soul simply sees something wrong and immediately begins to force the issue. Coercion without insight leads to rejection and hostile reactions against the native. Instead of eliciting praise, the native encounters wrath and resistance, hatred and anger. One's base of power then becomes vulnerable to sabotage from others. Ruthlessness breeds ruthlessness. The key is to understand the deeper dynamics of any condition the native wishes to transform, and this process is best begun with oneself. "Who am I and why do I want to change things?" Getting to the source, or motive, one is able to understand not only the self (and empower the self), but also to understand others and thereby empower them. To do so will lead to a successful group effort. To not achieve this before undertaking the project may lead to hatred and resentment, and an abundance of power plays with others.

To demonstrate the principle of the Evolutionary Moon, let's look at the chart of a prominent astrologer and bookstore owner who was born December 30, 1947, 3:00 PM, in Phoenix, Arizona. Note that his natal Moon is located in the middle of a stellium near the I. C., with Pluto on the waning side and Saturn on the waxing. The principle of

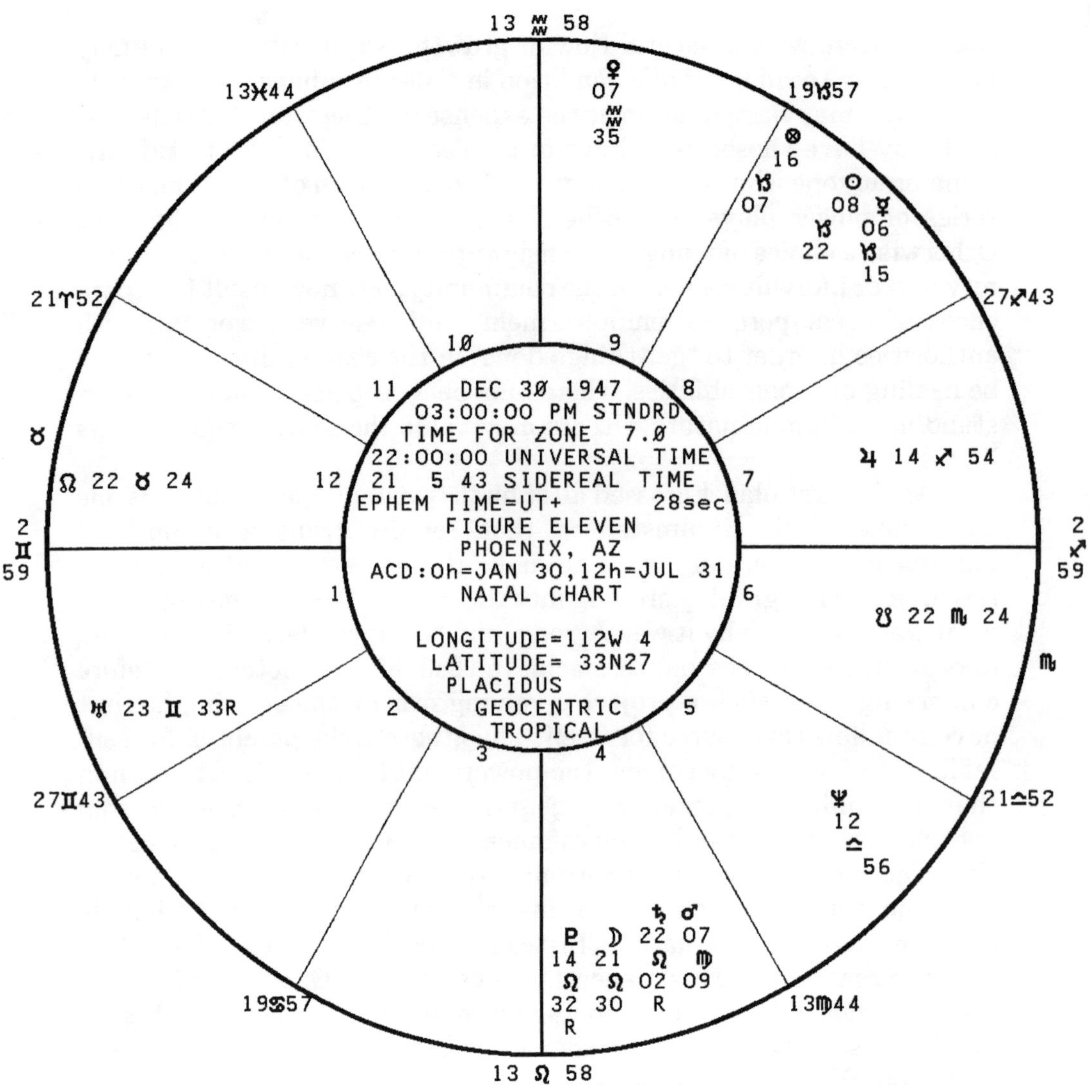

Figure 12

Pluto is doubly significant due to its conjunction to the I. C. as well as being the last planet crossed by the natal Moon before birth.

As the last planet crossed by the Moon prior to birth (as well as being close to the I. C.), Pluto represents the types of experiences and their consequent emotions as well as skills the native brings with him into this lifetime. The types of experiences suggested are those involving groups of people who possibly shared a powerful goal, or powerful experience. The principles of force and coercion may have been evident, but so too may have been the principles of reformation and healing. The symbology is that of a group whose beliefs or efforts may have been a threat to those in power, and as a result the group may have come under siege. It is possible that it may be reversed: the native may have been part of a powerful group that felt threatened by others, but rather than listening to their concerns, may have ruthlessly annihilated them. Given that Pluto is on the I. C. rather than the horizon axis, it is more likely that the former was possibly the case.

As an integral member of a group that sought to transform the community's leadership (Leo is leadership), the native innately sensed the value of secrecy. In this lifetime there is still the attraction to secret societies, to the mystery schools, and secret meetings.

In order to effect a lasting change in one's condition, Pluto requires two skills. The first is an untiring drive to get to the source of a matter, to research until the cause is determined. The second is to create something new in its place that will have value to the masses. If something is worth dying for, something new must be created that is worth living for. With these concepts in mind, then, the native brings forth into this lifetime an intense desire to understand the source. His research capacity is insatiable. The result is deep and profound insight into the existence of problems, as well as their causes. In addition he is not content merely to diagnose or appraise such imbalances. He also possesses an equally strong desire to shed light on the corrective, or healing process. There is an uneasy suspicion of leadership, particularly of the complacent kind, but as well toward that which is ruthless to others.

At its best, this placement corresponds to the native's intensity to understand life. It also corresponds to his ability to recognize wrongdoings of others who are in leadership roles, with an uncanny understanding of the motives behind these efforts. There is a power to heal, or transform, through his insight into personal conditions. At its worst, it may suggest an individual whose intensity and insightfulness can elicit a sense of intrusion into the private thoughts of others. They may feel violated on some level, as if he is entering without permission, as if he is trying to change them before they are willing to admit anything is out of balance. As a result, Pluto in this position indicates one who likely experiences a great deal of passion for life, deep and intimate relationships with others, knows that he has a transformative effect upon the lives of others, but at the same time encounters a measure of resentment from others who may feel his insights are too intrusive.

Now how can these qualities be useful with regard to the conditions one might undergo in this lifetime? First of all understand that the primary principle of Pluto is self-realization and insight. This is where the individual is coming from (waning phase of Evolutionary Moon). The first planet crossed after birth is Saturn, and this is where he is symbolically going. Saturn describes new conditions, new emotional responses, and new people he will contact in the course of this lifetime. Also inherent herein are new lessons his soul is in need of understanding. As he undergoes these Saturnian experiences, and learns these Saturnian lessons, they in turn will aid him in elevating to higher frequency emotional reactions to the Pluto principle brought over from prior experiences. What are those lower emotional responses? With Pluto it may be resentment, or an overly sensitive reaction to rejection, or fear of losing everything one has built or accumulated in life. Such fears may have been reinforced early in the life by virtue of the fact that Pluto, Moon and Saturn are all conjunct the I. C..

As the first planet crossed after birth, Saturn denotes very little that comes easy to this native in this life. Early in the life he had to fight for recognition in his own family (it was a very large family). However the key is patience, commitment and responsibility. He is a successful consultant and bookstore owner, but his reputation and success were not achieved overnight. He built his business slowly and gradually. He demonstrated great patience. He studied his craft very hard. He became very self-sufficient. All these are attributes of Saturn. As such he has become a very respected member of his community (Saturn's reward).

One of the keys for this man's success is patience. When he is patient and in control (self-control), he exhibits great wisdom. When he takes the time to appraise the situation and reflects before responding too quickly, he succeeds. Difficulties in relationships, particularly business, have come up when he fails to exercise patience. By itself, Saturn is not very conducive to partnerships, for it suggests one who may be uncomfortable relinquishing or sharing control. This issue – sharing versus control – may lead him to be critical of others when he fears his control is being thwarted. At the same time, his needs for control may make him the subject of criticism in his close, intimate relationships. The issues implied by Saturn that may need attention this lifetime are those of responsibility (Saturn) regarding the intense expression of his insight (Pluto). If he reveals (Pluto) in an impatient, critical, or controlling way, he likely experiences criticism, judgement, (Saturn) as well as resentment (Pluto). If he reveals his insight in a responsible, patient, and non-critical way, he likely experiences respect and admiration from others. In addition, when he is willing to build in a manner that is well-organized and thought-out (Saturn), he likely experiences success. When he attempts to force matters quickly and expediently, or tries to get ahead without making the proper concerted effort, he sidesteps the principles of Saturn, and likely does not experience success.

The fact that the Moon is contained by Pluto and Saturn is in itself very significant. The two planets represent power and authority. They are near the I. C., which means this is a signature of the soul. In a sense, this is a signature of a superman. There is no limit to what he might achieve in this lifetime so long as he adheres to the positive principles of Saturn. He has the drive, the passion and the intensity (Pluto) to put forth great efforts, and to see the results of those efforts manifest in this lifetime (Saturn).

CHAPTER TEN

The Karma of Identity

Sometimes things are not as they seem. Sometimes things happen wherein one cannot understand the cause. "What did I do to deserve this?" one might ask. Sometimes one seems like an innocent bystander, and yet things happen to him or her, and of no apparent cause by the individual. Why, for instance, were millions of Jews put to death during the Holocaust? What did each Jew do to deserve this fate? Why, for instance, were thousands of Iranians killed by the Allied Coalition in the Desert Storm War who had nothing to do with the war itself? Why, for instance have thousands of innocent Blacks and Whites been killed in racial riots in both the United States of America as well as South Africa?

The answer to these questions lies in the concept of the karma of identities. It would be simple if all embodied souls had no race, no religion, no national identity. However that is not the case. Every embodied soul has distinctive characteristics that separate him and her from other souls. Some of these distinctions are by choice, some are not – at least not consciously by choice within the context of this lifetime, though they are created by choices made in previous lifetimes. These distinctions that separate one from another are the basis for each soul's identity. It is these identities that become like entities themselves: they too have a karma, and anyone who partakes in that identity takes on the karma of it.

Each planet represents a type of identification, a "grouping" that each soul associates with. In association, one takes on the karma of the other. For example, all White people are not alike, yet the Caucasian race as a group identity has initiated activities with regard to other races. Because of these activities the Caucasian race has accrued karma with regard to those other races. Whether an individual has participated in those activities regarding other races is important to a degree, but even if one has not, he or she will still be a recipient of thought forms by those other races simply because of the karma of the White race.

Let's take this a little further, and relate it to astrology. Let us assume that **Pluto** represents **racial identity**. Whether one is born into the White, Black, Red, Brown or Yellow race, each has a group, or racial identity. Each group has a karma with the other. Each group has committed actions against the other, or for the other, and the cycles of those actions are not yet balanced. How do we know these cycles are not yet balanced? Because racial tensions still exist on the planet. There is still prejudice between the White, Black, Red, Brown and Yellow races. As long as there is hatred, anger, and fear associated with race, there is a script, a karmic pattern, a cycle that is still in motion and not balanced. As a result, reactions and responses are still likely to be activated when people of different races come together for anything other than a common cause. An innocent Black person may be beaten by a group of White people just for being in the wrong neighborhood at a particular moment. The opposite may also be true, and the same may be said about a Native American or an Asian. The victim may have perpetrated no offense. It is simply because he or she is White, Black, Red, Brown or Yellow and in the community of another race, and the racial karma of that community is unbalanced. The possibilities of incurring karma as a result of one's **racial identity** may be denoted by the placement of **Pluto** in the natal horoscope. For those with a difficult placement of Pluto, it may be helpful to consider your thoughts, let alone your actions, with regard to other races. Attitude is important, and if the attitude is one of prejudice, then the intent behind any actions initiated may set off the unbalanced karmic cycle between different races, and the result may be directed toward the individual.

Neptune may represent the **karma of religious identity**. Some of the souls on this planet identify themselves as Christian, some Jewish, some Muslim, some Buddhist, some atheists, etc. Throughout the ages many atrocities have been committed by one religious group against the other in the name of God, or Jesus, or Mohammed, or any other sacred diety. Today the word Jew or Muslim elicits strong reactions in the minds of many non-Jews or non-Muslims. Why? What happens when a Jew enters a room of Arabs, for which there is no common purpose for meeting? Does one not have strong feelings about the other, even though they never met as individuals before? These feelings, these attitudes, are based upon the karma that one religious group has accrued in relationship to the other. The karma of religious affiliation may be denoted by Neptune's placement in the natal chart. Once again it is important for the soul to overcome religious prejudice lest he or she becomes subject to the unbalanced karmic cycles between various religious groups. Neptune on the horizon, or an angular midpoint and afflicted, may indicate religious karma, either detesting one religion, or taking an attitude of superiority of one's own religion over others.

Uranus might symbolize **national identity**. Each soul is born a citizen of a particular country. This is his or her national identity. Yet nations, as a group identity, have behaved in specific ways toward other nations, either helping or hurting them. In this regard every nation has a group karma with every other nation. When a Russian walks into a room of Americans (or vice-versa) without a common purpose, a host of reactions from the Americans may be witnessed. They may be hostile, suspicious, or possibly threatening. The Russian, as an individual, may have committed no acts or thoughts prior to this meeting, yet because of the history (karma) between these two nations the Russian may become subjected to an attitude or worse, may even become subjected to unpleasant behavior from the group of Americans. The point is that every nation has a "national attitude" about every other nation based upon the history between those two nations. As a soul born into a nation, it takes on the karma of that nation in all of its dealings with souls of other nations. Uranus afflicted on the horizon, or an angular midpoint, might suggest one who has developed a prejudice against other nationalities, and may be sensitive in this lifetime to those of other nations who are prejudiced against his or her country.

Saturn might denote the karma of one's **vocational identity**. We are now entering the sphere of choice. Yet even the choice of one's vocation elicits certain reactions from other people. When one chooses a vocation, he or she takes on the karma which that vocation has accrued throughout the ages. Some professions may be "looked down upon" by other professions, while others may be "looked up to and admired." In a spiritual sense, all souls have the same purpose of profession: to serve one another. The idea of status of one profession over another is man-made. All service, if undertaken with proper intent, is meaningful. Prejudice based upon one's vocation is separating in nature. It gives rise to illusions and creates dualities. As a result it sets into motion cycles governed by the law of karma, and hence patterns and scripts arise in one's life with regard to his or her profession. An afflicted Saturn, possibly on the horizon or angular midpoint, may denote one who has a difficult karmic slate with regard to their profession. Perhaps this soul is not happy with his or her profession; or perhaps he or she feels very sensitive about the status of that profession. If so, that soul may be in need of exploring these feelings, and perhaps ask him or herself: "Have I been too arrogant about my worth in comparison to others regarding their career?" There may be a need to see the equal value of all service performed with right effort and motive.

Jupiter might correspond to the karma of **social identity**. Throughout a lifetime, one associates with various social groups. One develops friends, one forms cliques, or groups that he or she bonds closely to. In and of itself, there is nothing harmful about developing friendships or group associations. However when that group initiates actions toward another group or being, a cycle is started, and all those who associate with that group take on the consequences of that cycle. For example, let us assume as a teenager, one joined a clique, a group of friends who were very close. One day they decided to play a prank on another student whom they all made fun of. Let us assume this prank hurt the other student, humiliated him or her, caused the other person to break down in tears. The group perhaps took great joy in causing this emotional pain. The group, and *all* of its associates, must now bear the consequences of such action, even those souls in that group who were not even present that day. The fact is that once one has identified with a group, and that group commits a hurtful act, all members (present or not at the time of the act) must bear the reactions now directed against it from others as a result of the "group" action.

Imbalances from group associations arise when the group adopts an attitude, or initiates an activity, that is in violation of natural law. At root of all violations is generally an attitude of prejudice, a sense of: "We are better than they (or you)." Individuals of the upper financial classes of society may look down haughtily upon those less successful than they. Contrary-wise those of a lower economic class may resent those more successful than themselves. Both accrue karma of group identification. One with an afflicted Jupiter, perhaps on the horizon or an angular midpoint, may have been associated with a group (reference group or actual), and in this capacity may have developed separative attitudes about his/her group in relationship to other groups of people. Two common attitudes found here are "superiority" and "inferiority", and their consequent emotions of disdain or resentment. In an earlier chapter it was mentioned that Jupiter pertains to the humanitarian.

The solution for one with an afflicted Jupiter is to develop a humane and charitable attitude toward all groups of people, and perhaps attempt to associate with groups who have the same attitude and commitment toward good will, without the need to judge oneself or one's group as "better than" others.

Mars may pertain to the karma accrued through identification of one's **enemies**, or **opponents**. This is an interesting concept because it assumes one takes on a karma of one's adversaries, which on the surface is totally opposite to what one thinks he or she is working toward. This brings into play the law of opposites. To work **against** something is to give it life. As an example, imagine walking into a room full of people whom you like, and one person whom you do not like. Throughout the evening, whose presence are you most aware of? Your friends, or the one single enemy? You and that person have an imbalance with one another, and since the universe moves toward harmony and equilibrium, you are most aware of that one individual. An afflicted Mars, perhaps on the horizon or angular midpoint most of all, may signify one who has a tendency to put people into two camps: those who are with me, and those who are against me. The strategy seems to be one of calculating ways to bring harm and adversity to those "who are against me." These attitudes and actions further complicate a very complex script of anger and hatred. The solution is simple but hard: figure out ways to support the adversary, and avoid hostile and negative thoughts toward him or her. In addition, the individual may benefit by overcoming temptations to see people in the two camps mentioned. At its best, Mars moves forward; it doesn't waste time or energy on "making the score even."

Venus may pertain to karma accrued by **entering into partnership, particularly marriage**. When one marries, or takes on a partner (such as a business partner), one contracts to take on the karma of that other individual. In the past 2000 years or more, this has been especially true of women who married men and took on the man's name while forsaking her own. Immediately the woman elicited responses according to her husband's name and reputation. However it is also true of the man, even though he keeps his name. He too takes on the reputation of the woman. Whatever one's mate has done to others, the soul now takes on the consequences of that partner's cycles. An afflicted Venus, particularly on the horizon or angular midpoint, may indicate one who created harm or hurt to a partner previously. By not properly caring for the partner, that soul now bears the consequences of those cycles in partnerships entered into in this lifetime. Perhaps those partnerships are unsuccessful, or perhaps unfulfilling; perhaps the partner's family creates burdens to the individual in this lifetime. The key word for Venus is **forgiveness**, and that is exactly what the soul must be willing to express with regard to partnerships in this lifetime in order to transcend the pattern.

Mercury may pertain to the **karma of one's children**. Children can bring shame or praise to a family. Whether one likes it or not, the actions of his or her children reflect back upon the individual. The soul as a parent has a responsibility in the upbringing of a child. How the soul performs this responsibility (or has performed it in past lives) may determine which behaviors and attitudes the child takes on as an adult, and these reflect upon the parent. Put simply, the behaviors of each individual reflect back upon one's parents. They are either proud of what the individual has done, or ashamed. The individual's actions affect them, and possibly in the manner suggested by the placement of their natal Mercury. An afflicted natal Mercury, perhaps on the horizon or an angular midpoint, may indicate violations of responsibilities to one's children in previous lives. A pattern has been set. In this lifetime one may not have children, or may have children that do not mature in a manner that brings joy and/or pride to the individual in this lifetime. Of course the script can be broken. The key is cooperation and service to others, and in particular with regard to one's responsibilities, and even attitudes to his or her children.

The Moon pertains to the **karma of the family** one is born into. The child takes on the "sins of its parents." Almost immediately after birth the child elicits reactions from others. The reactions are almost purely based upon the reputation of the parents in the community. The first judgements of the child from others are usually based upon how those "others" felt about the parent(s). A child is judged by the career, religion, social group, race, and even nationality of the parents. It is not until later in life, when the child takes responsibility for his/her own actions, that he/she begins to become free of this parental identity. In fact it never ends totally, for whatever one's parents do the rest of the individual's life continually reflects back onto the individual's own life. An afflicted Moon, perhaps on the horizon or angular midpoint, might suggest a soul who has incurred a difficult family karma. The reputation of the parent(s), the quality of living with parents, or the stressful relationship with one or both parents may be the result of cycles initiated before this lifetime. Perhaps in a previous life one did not care for his/her parents, was not respectful or loving. Perhaps one abandoned the parents at a time of need, or in some way brought shame to the family name. In any event, the key word to overcome the script is **love; unconditional love, not a love of attachment or dependency**.

The Sun has no karmic identity. It represents the self, without any identities. The Sun is whole; the planets are parts. As parts, the planets represent separate identities, but their function is to combine harmoniously to become a whole, to become as one, to become as Spirit.

The model of Evolutionary Astrology is at its most basic simplicity in its core astrological assumption: the Sun is the master, and all souls strive toward self-mastery. In this sense, every soul is striving to become its Sun. The planets are the servants which aid the soul in its quest toward mastery, which is to return to Spirit, to selfhood, to the very creative source from whence it came.

When the soul becomes distracted by the illusion of the parts (i.e. planets), one's sense of reality becomes fragmented and separative. This is when the karma of identities becomes governed by cyclic law. Giving importance to the parts, to that which is separative, gives rise to the illusion of self-importance. At that point one is more focused upon the self than upon that which created and sustains the self. In this illusion, the soul begins to separate; that is, an ego forms, a personality develops, which distinguishes it as something separate **and with judgement** from other souls. As a reality builds upon this separative illusion, the personality defines it as "better or worse" than others it has separated itself from. Prejudices arise over these separate identities. These prejudices give rise to behaviors and intentions which are designed to enhance one's physical self at the expense or detriment of others. This is in violation of natural law, but is governed by the natural, cyclic law known as the Law of Retribution, or karma. In the model of Evolutionary Astrology, this law is measured by the heavens. It is reflected in the creation of the natal chart. "One is born at that precise moment, and exact location, when all the planets and celestial bodies are in precise mathematical harmony with the karma of that soul."

Separate the illusion from the reality, the personality from the Spirit. The purpose of identities is not to give basis for judgements of one over another. It is simply to acknowledge the difference in paths to the same end.

CHAPTER ELEVEN

Somewhere in Time

We have all lived before this time.

Spirit is a creative life force which is present in all living organisms. It is the primal creative force from which all living matter is born. Our existence is an outgrowth of Spirit, from which we came and by which we continue to subsist. Spirit is an essential part of everyone, of every living thing. In a sense we have always been, because Spirit has always been, as long as there was (is) life. On a very basic level, we are all one and the same; we are all Spirit because we all share the phenomenon of life, or Spirit.

The soul reflects Spirit, like the Moon reflects the light of the Sun. All living beings have a soul. Souls are different from one another because they reflect different levels of relationship to Spirit. Souls undergo different experiences from one another, and as individuals, make different choices from one another. As a result of these conscious choices, souls undergo different cycles of life experiences, different sets of circumstances and consequences. Because of this cyclic law, known as karma, souls have different lessons to master through different experiences from one lifetime to another.

The soul does not die once it is created. How it is created is a great mystery. It may originate with thought, particularly a desire. That desire may become a motivation, or an intention. Perhaps due to various circumstances, that desire never materialized, the intention never acted upon. Yet it was in the gestation phase, just never born. Perhaps even at this early stage a cycle may have been initiated for which a soul was created, and necessitated a physical vehicle, as well as a new consciousness, apart from the being who originated the thought but acted upon different intentions throughout its lifetime.

This is merely speculation. No one knows for certain how and why souls are created. We will allow this to be an essential assumption to the model of Evolutionary Astrology. That is, every living being has a soul, and that soul has in most cases (if not all) existed before birth, and will continue to exist (in most cases) after physical death. This is known as the principle of continuity or "soul continuity", and is the basic premise to the theory of reincarnation.

Reincarnation is the act in which a soul is reborn into a physical body. The soul "transmigrates" from one lifetime to another. It does this in order to work out the cycles it has put into motion which are, as of yet, incomplete. However not all souls earn the privilege of reincarnation into the human, earthbound, body. Embodiment is a privilege and one that is desired by most (if not all) souls. Those that are living on the planet at any given point in time have two things in common: they earned the privilege of embodiment, and they are in the midst of completing cycles governed by the law of karma. They are all in motion. They are all evolving.

In any given lifetime a soul develops a personality. More correctly, the soul develops a multitude of personality aspects. The personality does not continue from one lifetime to another, yet it shapes the essence of the soul. The personality itself is shaped by a multitude of factors: life experiences, responses to those experiences, emotions and emotional patterns developed around those experiences and responses, and most of all through interactions with significant other people. The personality may be kind or selfish, it may be loving or cold, it may be radiant or dull. It is ultimately dependent upon one's own choices in life.

Each individual chooses how to behave in any given situation in life. Each chooses how to respond to each event that arises in life. The choice of behavior or response is either in agreement or not in agreement with principles the soul has learned prior to that moment. The behavior may also be based upon one's intent to cause a certain result, which again is either in agreement or not in agreement with the soul's understanding up until that point in time. When one's intent and/or behavior is not in agreement with its understanding, then a script may be created, a pattern may be set up. In other words, at this point the law of karma commences, and an aspect of the personality is created.

The same is true when the soul responds in a manner which reflects a new and greater understanding than before. For example, if the soul finally understood it was mired in an inhibiting script as a result of a low frequency emotional response pattern, and made a conscious effort to respond with a higher frequency intent and behavior the next time (and the times after that), then a new series of consequences would begin. Likewise a new aspect to the personality would be constructed. There would occur a "release", an outpouring of a higher frequency emotion, and the soul would evolve to a new level. It would release, or shed, a layer of its "old" self.

From one lifetime to the next the soul learns of things that please and displease it. From one lifetime to the next, the personality registers experiences of pain and pleasure, of joy and grief. As the personality registers these experiences, they become imprinted on the soul. They shape, to some extent, the quality of the soul as it reincarnates from one lifetime to another. In this manner the soul gravitates toward certain likes and dislikes from one life to another. In this context it is not difficult to understand why some individuals have an extraordinary interest or ability in certain aspects of life and a total distaste for other aspects of life, with no known experience of either related to this lifetime alone. For instance, why is it that some children immediately like the taste of potatoes, and others do not? Why is it that some children learn mathematics very early in life, and others form a mental block—even in the case of two children in the same family, and each having the same teacher in school? Why do some children love animals while at the same age others are frightened? Behavioral psychologists may tell us it is due to some early generalized experience associated with pain, fear or reward. The theory of reincarnation postulates it is due to the same reason, except the experience took place in another time.

Astrology is one of the most adaptive languages known to humankind. It is a language of symbolism that can be applied to any human experience. With the symbology of its planets and constellations, astrology can address and render remarkable insight into any study or model, whether science, philosophy, religion, economics, politics, sports, etc. Every aspect of human experience which can be described, can also be put into the symbolism of astrology. The quality of kindness can be associated with Jupiter; the study of art can be ascribed to Venus; the pursuit of adventure can be related to Aries or Sagitarius; the principles of government and executive leadership can be assigned to Capricorn.

Countries and civilizations, much like individuals, are also described with certain adjectives. Countries too have certain personality attributes. For example, the Swiss may be considered very detailed and exact, while the French may be considered very romantic and passionate. Russia may be thought of as a very controlling and repressive government in the post-World War I era, while Holland very liberal. The point is that every government, every leadership, on every level, has its own unique personality. This can be interpreted in the symbolism of astrology simply by understanding the dominating features of that country or state's personality.

Let's take this one step further. As each of us studied history, there may have been certain civilizations, countries and/or time periods that were more attractive than others. There may have been others which were absolutely upsetting and repulsive. Pleasure and pain. Attraction and repulsion. What is the connection to the soul? On some level, these personalities, these times and these lands, are familiar.

The analysis of geographical and period familiarity probably best begins with an astrological assumption of the five races of humankind. Let us assume that the White, or Caucasian race is symbolized by the Sun, while the Black or Negro race corresponds to the Moon. In addition let us assume that the Red or Native American race relates to the Earth while Jupiter corresponds to the Oriental or Yellow race. If there is a separate Brown, or Latin race, it may correspond to Venus. These are only suggestions, but they are presented because in order to correlate location and period to the character of an individual soul, a foundation must be established upon which to build.

If these assumptions are accepted as a foundation, then it may be easier to understand the suggestions that follow. Each planet, and combination of planets through aspects in the natal chart, denote psychological characteristics. As races, countries, and civilizations also have personality attributes, it may be assumed that individual attributes may have been shaped greatly by the time and place of one's prior existence. If this assumption is correct, then individuals with certain types of psychological dispositions will be most attracted to those civilizations, countries, and time periods whose attributes are similar. For instance, an assertive or aggressive Mars personality may be most attracted to a time when an aggressive civilization was at its military peak. Or a gracious, charming socialite might be most attracted to a country and a time of great cultural and social value. In this case, natal Venus may be prominently placed.

Those civilizations and periods in history which are most captivating to an individual may show up by the placement of planets near the angles, or angular midpoints of the natal horoscope. They may also relate to the planets contained by the natal Moon, as well as that planet which rules either the Moon or the I. C.. Aspects to these planets may also be significant, as described below.

Sun: The Caucasian or White race. A country that was the dominant leader of its time in the world. Specifically it may relate to Great Britain, or England, which dominates the history of the White race.

In aspect to the Moon, it might pertain to a period in which Great Britain, or the White race, was involved in the colonization of African nations. In aspect to Mercury, it may denote a time when great emphasis was placed upon the literary and intellectual accomplishments of the English. In aspect to Venus, it may correspond to a time when Great Britain flourished in the arts, and social activity was held in high esteem. In aspect to Mars, it may denote a time when Great Britain was at war, particularly with the French. In aspect to Jupiter, it may show attraction to a period in which the English were colonizing Asian countries. It may also denote a period of great financial success and the center of world trade.

A prominently located Sun in aspect to Saturn may indicate a period in which Great Britain was under repressive rule, or a period of disaster and calamity. It may also indicate a period of activity with Russia. In aspect to Uranus, it may correspond to a time of revolution against the British leadership, or a time of significant political change within the British Empire. It may also denote a period of activity involving Germany, or even a time when Germany was a world power. In aspect to Neptune, one might be attracted to a period in English history when poetry and music were held in high esteem. It could also represent the English navy, or colonization of islands throughout the world. In aspect to Pluto, it may represent a period in which large numbers of people were killed, either due to plague or ruthlessness. It might also represent the Roman or Alexandrian empire, a time of great and massive world dominion.

Moon: The Black or Negro race. A country, civilization or time in which the female or mother principle was held in very high regard. Specifically it may relate to the African continent, which dominates the history of the Black race.

In aspect to the Sun, it may pertain to a period in which an African nation was involved with the British empire. It may also indicate a great African nation, one that was considered to be the leader of all African nations. In aspect to Mercury, it may represent an African nation, or period in African history, where and when great literary activity took place. In aspect to Venus, it may correspond to a period when great artistic efforts were produced. In aspect to Mars a time of war might have unfolded between one African nation and another. It may also have corresponded to a very competitive and sports-like period. In aspect to Jupiter it might correspond to a period and an African nation that was the center of world trade and commerce. It may also pertain to relations with Asian countries.

A prominently placed natal Moon in aspect to Saturn might denote an African experience of hardship. Perhaps it was during a period of famine, or even a period in which Africans were taken as slaves to other countries. One with the Moon on an angle in hard aspect to Saturn may have very strong feelings about slavery. In aspect to Uranus, it may denote a period of an African uprising or revolution, a cry for independence. Again slavery may have been an issue in the past, and still may be in the present. In aspect to Neptune it may indicate a period in which African culture, music and poetry flourished. It may also indicate an African nation that is on the coast of a great ocean. In aspect to Pluto, it might symbolize a period of a great tragedy and catastrophe, when large masses of people were put to death, possibly by cruel leaders or invaders. It might also symbolize a belief in wicca, or witchcraft.

Earth: Communities which respected and paid homage to the Earth; an agrarian community; a commune of like souls attempting to live in harmony with nature; Native Americans (Indians of both the North and South American continents). In aspect to the Moon, it may signify African nations or tribes which were very close to nature, both the animal and plant kingdoms. In aspect to Mercury it might denote intellectual communities that banded together and tried to live in harmony with nature (i.e. Brook Farm commune). In aspect to Venus, it may denote an artistic commune, or a nation which placed great value upon its art which depicted scenes of nature. In aspect to Mars, it might denote periods in which Native Americans were at war with other nations, particularly French-Indian conflicts. In aspect to Jupiter it might denote Oriental or Asian communities that lived in harmony with nature, perhaps the Buddhist monasteries. Aspects to Saturn suggest an agrarian community, a self-sufficient farm-state, and possibly an existence of slavery. In aspect to Uranus, it may denote a period in which there was a great clash between progressive reform and the sanctity of nature, a time when industrial expansion may have been at the expense of nature; it may denote a period in which White frontiersmen overtook the lands of Native Americans, as in the Westward expansion. In aspect to Neptune, it may denote a community of like-minded spiritual souls who have come together for a spiritual purpose (i.e. Essenes). In aspect to Pluto, it might suggest a secret community which worshiped animals or gods and goddesses of nature; it might also suggest a period in which nature was destroyed or abused by man.

Mercury: A small, neutral country, one that developed the intellect and placed great value on education. A country of precise, exacting people who take great pride in craftsmanship. Switzerland, Belgium, Netherlands, Austria. In aspect to the Sun, it represents a time of intellectual height. In aspect to Moon, commerce with African nations at a time of intellectual advancements, or at a time of great emphasis upon craft works, may be denoted. In aspect to Venus, it may correspond to any civilization in which both artistic and intellectual endeavors were valued, particularly of Spanish or Greek origin. In aspect to Mars, it may denote a time of intellectual expression and debate. In aspect to Jupiter, it might pertain to a period of great storytelling and folklore. In aspect to Saturn, it may pertain to a time when Russia produced literary giants, or science was held in high esteem. In aspect to Uranus, it may correspond to a time when pursuit of astrology and prognosticative studies were valued; it may also be a time of high values placed upon literary efforts in Germany or the United States. In aspect to Neptune, it suggests a time when poetry, drama, and dance were valued by the universities; it may also pertain to a small and neutral island or continent, like Australia or New Zealand. In aspect to Pluto, a time when knowledge was considered dangerous, and secret societies formed to spread knowledge underground, such as the Gnostics and other secret orders. It may also represent a period of emphasis upon the study of psychology, and the writing of horror novels.

Venus: A civilization in which art and justice flourished; the Mayan civilization. In aspect to the Sun, it may pertain to Great Britain or Spain during a time of artistic accomplishments. In aspect to Moon, it may symbolize an African nation which placed great emphasis upon art and justice. In aspect to Mars it may pertain to France during its most artistic and judicial periods, or Spain during times of war. In aspect to Jupiter it may denote a very hearty nation and jovial people; it may denote a period when Spain was the center of world trade. It may also represent a time of artistic excellence in an Asian country. In aspect to Saturn, it may correspond either to Russian artistic periods or to the Spanish people in general, as well as Mexican. In aspect to Uranus, it may denote a time in history when art led the way to a renaissance, a time when art was revolutionary and was on the cutting edge of new and bold thoughts; it may suggest a time of abstract or surrealistic art. In aspect to Neptune it may denote an island paradise wherein life was easy and relaxed; an island of great beauty and charm, a romantic setting. In aspect to Pluto, it may correspond to the region of the Mideast and a time of very elaborate and beautiful art work. It may also be a time in which art was taboo and reason for persecution, or a land in which women were punished for being unfaithful to their husbands. It may correspond to the time of the Spanish inquisition.

Mars: A nation at war; France; a nation of passionate people. In aspect to Sun, it may relate to periods when Great Britain and France were at war. In aspect to the Moon it may denote an African nation at war, particularly with France. In aspect to Mercury it may mean a small nation at war, or being invaded by a bigger nation. In aspect to Venus it may pertain to a time when France and Spain were at war. In aspect to Jupiter, a time and country in Asia at war; it may also pertain to Viet Nam. In aspect to Saturn, it may denote a very long and difficult struggle and war, a time in which the people were suppressed by the government, perhaps even punished unfairly; a time when France and Russia were at war. In aspect to Uranus, it could mean a time of revolution in which the government was overthrown, particularly in France or Baltic states. In aspect to Neptune it may denote a very hot island at a time of great tension. In aspect to Pluto, it suggests a very ruthless government which perhaps tortured its people, and perhaps used ruthless secret police forces to insure its dominance; the French guillotine.

Jupiter: A land and time of growth and expansion; a land of wisdom and religious experiences; Asia. In aspect to the Sun, it indicates an Asian country at the time of its world leadership and dominance. In aspect to the Moon, it denotes an African nation under the leadership of a wise or expansion-oriented ruler. In aspect to Mercury, it may denote a country which places great value upon literary accomplishments as well as its education and universities. In aspect to Venus, it may denote an oriental country during a time in which its art flourished. In aspect to Mars it suggests a period of war in an Asian country. In aspect to Saturn it may denote China. In aspect to Uranus it may correlate with Tibet or Nepal. In aspect to Neptune, it suggests India and the various Hindu religions. In aspect to Pluto, it may denote a time when the church or spiritual organizations punished the infidels; a time of inquisitions, such as conducted during the Middle Ages on behalf of the popes, or even the Salem witchcraft trials. Religious persecution may have been rampant, or vice-versa: the religious people may have been persecuted by the leaders who felt threatened.

Saturn: A cold country; a country whose government is very controlling; a time when law and order must be heeded or else punishment may have been forthcoming; Russia. In aspect to the Sun it may denote a period in which Russia and Great Britain attempted to form an alliance, or a time when Great Britain attempted to control its people through restrictive laws, or a time when Great Britain attempted to write new laws. In aspect to the Moon it may indicate an African nation under a strong ruler who made strong laws, perhaps the time of Moses and the Ten Commandments. In aspect to Mercury it may denote a time of scientific study, when science was king; or a time when one had to live in a monastery and study. In aspect to Mars, it may denote a time in which revolutions were squelched, or the government clashed with the military, or the military ruled the government. In aspect to Jupiter it may denote a wandering tribe with strong spiritual principles who were persecuted for their beliefs; the Jews or Israel. In aspect to Uranus, a cold country relatively new, like Canada; it may also represent a period in which new and revolutionary thoughts were punished, particularly when in conflict with religious precepts. In aspect to Neptune it might denote a cold island climate like Iceland and Scandinavia. In aspect to Pluto it may suggest the combination of power with authority and secret ritual, as in the Egyptian empire; it may also represent a time when the government imprisoned and persecuted its enemies by exile, or death penalty.

Uranus: A time of revolution or new thought; a renaissance period; a time of new discoveries and enlightenments; the United States of America; Germany; Atlantis, a land of technology. In aspect to the Sun, it may denote the period in which the United States gained its independence from England. In aspect to the Moon it may represent a time of great change in an African country, or the abolishment of slavery in the United States. In aspect to Mercury it may denote a time of enlightened new thoughts, or attraction of the society to astrology and prognosticative tools; it may also represent a time of new modes of transportation such as the automobile and airplane. In aspect to Venus, it may represent revolutionary art and new fashion. In aspect to Mars it may denote a time of great excitement and adventure to new lands, such as the discovery of America; it may also correspond to a time of overthrow of a government, as in the French revolution. In aspect to Jupiter it might indicate the period in which the West finally came into contact with the Far East, as in the days of Marco Polo, or any period in which relations between the Far East and the West took on a new understanding. It might also be the period of a "gold rush", or discovery of sudden wealth. In aspect to Saturn, it may relate to a time in which the boundaries of Russia changed, perhaps due to overthrow or expansionism; it may also be a period in which the United States ventured into the Western mountainous regions. In aspect to Neptune, it may denote a time in which one was on the cutting edge of a new religion. In aspect to Pluto, it may have been a time in which expansion to new frontiers meant displacing large segments of the existing population, such as the Native American (Indians).

Neptune: An island; a period when great emphasis was placed upon grace, culture, music, dance, poetry and spiritual thought; Greece; Lemuria. In aspect to the Sun, a period in which Greece flourished as leader of the world. In aspect to the Moon, it may signify a wet, rainy island, or coast of Africa; a time of cultural advances and dance in an African nation. In aspect to Mercury, a time when importance was given to the dramatic arts, dance, and music. It may also signify the period of the great Greek philosophers and playwrights. In aspect to Venus, a time when art flourished in Greece or an island climate. In aspect to Mars, it denotes a time of healers and counselors; also a time in which Greece was at war. In aspect to Jupiter it signifies a most religious period, a time in which religious leaders were born; special emphasis upon India; a very large island, perhaps Lemuria. In aspect to Saturn it suggests Greek law; also Scandinavia and a time of seafaring adventures (perhaps drowning). In aspect to Uranus, it signifies a time of spiritual enlightenment, the birth of Christ or similar spiritual leader; a restructuring of the church; new religious leadership. In aspect to Pluto, it denotes a time of uncovering great spiritual mysteries; an island in which magic rituals were performed; sacrifices of human or animal life for belief in gods.

Pluto: A country in transformation; a powerful leadership but perhaps one of reform or ruthlessness such as Attila the Hun; Italy; the Roman Empire; plots to overthrow; time of racial clashes. It may signify a land of volcanoes, or one in which natural calamities may have changed its structure throughout the ages. It may also represent times in which various groups of people were forced to meet in secret due to threats on their lives by the leadership. Hence there may have been associations with secret cults or groups. All nations in their history have had such groups, and have undergone such periods when the lives of many (if not most) would be in jeopardy for carrying particular beliefs. Therefore the aspects to each planet simply signified those countries and those times in which this attitude may have prevailed. For instance, in aspect to the Sun, it may have been in England. Perhaps it was the time the druids built Stonehenge, for oftentimes these periods result in great works of accomplishment accompanied by mystical ritual. With the Moon it may have been in Africa during the times of the great pyramids and tombs honoring the great pharaohs of Egypt. The same may be true with Saturn, since the pyramids were built of rock and stone (Saturn). With Venus it may have been secret societies in Spain or the Mayan Peninsula; with Mars it may have been in France; with Jupiter in the Orient; with Uranus, it may relate to Germany or the United States.

There are of course many periods in history and many countries in history which have not been covered in this short treatise. It does not mean they did not exist for any souls reincarnating at this time. The subject is simply limited due to the author's own limitations and intuitions. The purest source for these possibilities would be within the individual him/herself. Ask: "Which eras am I most attracted to? What qualities of this era am I attracted to? What are the astrological symbols that correlate to these principles?" Then read the beginning statements of each planet and see if it relates.

In trying to give meaning to these geographic and historical possibilities, it may be wise to keep a couple of points in mind. First, the planets closest to angles are probably most important. Take their aspect to other planets, but consider the planet on the angle as the key. For example if Jupiter is on an angle in aspect to Saturn, it may be more akin to China. However if Saturn is on an angle in aspect to Jupiter, it may mean one is more akin to the Jewish race. Mars on an angle in aspect to Uranus may pertain to the French revolution, but Uranus on an angle in aspect to Mars may pertain to American-Indian wars. Second, consider the last planet the Moon crossed before birth as important, and when useful associate it to the first planet it will cross after birth, much in the same manner outlined above. In other words, the Moon coming from Jupiter and going toward Saturn might be more akin to China, whereas the Moon coming from Saturn and going toward Jupiter might be more akin to Israel, or Jewish ancestry. Next one might consider planets on angular midpoints as significant, in the same way described for planets on angles. Finally consider the planets which rule both the I. C. and Moon sign.

Astrology is a symbolic language. These interpretations are based upon those symbolisms. Whether or not they are accurate in detail is unimportant. Where and when the soul lived before is not greatly important in the scheme of things. Those existences were of a personality that no longer exists. Insomuch as these previous experiences may have had a modifying effect upon the essence of the soul now incarnating, and to the extent that it is possible that current patterns may have had their origins in these previous existences, there may be value in understanding and reviewing these past lives. In this sense they are only of value if they illuminate one as to "who one is, or what one is truly here to do." One reincarnates because he or she has put into motion certain cycles which are not yet completed. The mission is to discover those cycles and learn the lessons inherent in the circumstances brought forth with those cycles. The danger of "looking back" is of course that the personality will build another false reality around the past, perhaps glamorize or dramatize it to the point of totally missing the purpose and challenge of this life. Glamour is a great temptress. It may seduce the consciousness away from the soul, and build a myth around which the personality will battle to defend. More scripts, more patterns, more complexities for the soul to unravel.

The value of this chapter is simple: it is to stimulate deeper understanding of oneself, and sometimes that is accomplished by insight into those areas and those times in which the soul may have existed. To a degree, we are all a product of the times in which we live, and our relationship to those times has great bearing on which principles we develop, and need to develop, on our journey back home.

CHAPTER TWELVE

Pre-Natal Eclipse Paths: Familiarity of Location

Determining where an individual has reincarnated on the Earth is perhaps one of the most difficult of all tasks, even in Evolutionary Astrology. The matter is complicated by several factors. First, knowledge of *civilized* humanity dates back only about 6000 years. Yet it is known that man, as a species, was on Earth much longer than that (probably much longer than most anthropologists even acknowledge). Thus it may be that astrology could be a key to the whereabouts of each individual even before 4000 BC, but since knowledge of the times before this is severely limited, it is rather impossible to correlate such times with the present chart (except in so much as one might infer the possibility of the Atlantian and Lemurian civilizations through current findings).

Another complication lies in the nature of the techniques presented here. The first, an analysis of the planets, planetary combinations and their relationship to various places on Earth, is at this time necessarily limited in scope. Not enough information is available to make this last chapter complete. The second, which involves pre-natal eclipse paths, is far *too* broad in its scope. Here is more information than can be used, and consequently the astrologer must apply his or her detective skills and intuitive faculties to limit these to a matter of relevance for the client.

There may be certain "areas" on this planet in which individuals fare extremely well or very poorly. One's reason may suggest this is coincidence. Even the astrologer may say that this is coincidence because the individual went at a time when the transits or progressions were most (un)favorable to the natal horoscope. By the very precepts of

Evolutionary Astrology, one can rule out the first possibility: it is not a coincidence. As for the second possibility, one might consider the following: assume an individual has a very favorable experience in a new setting during favorable transits. Would that individual necessarily have had the same degree of good fortune having gone somewhere else at the same time? Is *space* – locality – as important to an astrologer as *time*? If so, how can this be determined by the astrologer, particularly via Evolutionary Astrology techniques?

In response to the first question: "Would success be to the same degree in one part of the world as in another, at the same point in time?". The answer is, "No". Obviously, the scientist would agree and say this is because such differences as language, local customs, social and political mores of some places are more beneficial for certain people than for others. True, but that is not all.

The area in which one functions acquires a quality that may be described as "familiarity". The more one functions in a particular setting, the greater one's control becomes in that setting. Consequently, one's level of competency or success increases with one's familiarity of the setting. In another sense, one may say that familiarity is the equivalent of investing power, or one's energy (physical, mental, psychic, or all three) into a particular location. Whether that spot becomes one that is favorable or unfavorable to the native depends upon what kind of energy has been invested, which itself is determined by the nature of responses the native receives from others in that environment. But the fact is, familiarity with a setting produces a certain influence or power for the individual; there is a mutual, interdependent effect between man and his environment, and the effect (or invested power) continues over a period of time.

The effect that an environment might have upon an individual may continue over a period of several lifetimes. These environments – or settings – which have the greatest influence upon the individual may be referred to as "power places." They attain this influential effect as a result of the individual's investment of energy – at some point in time – in those settings. Again, referring to the example, assuming under favorable aspects an individual moves to London, England, and does extremely well, and at another time under similar aspects moves to Glasgow, Scotland, and does not do nearly so well, it may be due to the possibility that the individual in some other lifetime invested energy of a favorable nature in the area of or around London. And hence familiarity has been built.

The manner in which an astrologer may determine the points of power on Earth for an individual is by a process known as pre-natal and post-natal eclipse paths. This chapter shall deal primarily with the pre-natal eclipse path for theoretically the post-natal path has more to do with *potential* in this lifetime, and this section of the book strives for an understanding as to *how* the individual evolved up until the birth moment of this lifetime.

On the following pages are tables of solar eclipses and their paths upon the Earth[13]. A pre-natal eclipse is a solar eclipse which occurred *prior* to the individual's birth date; a post-natal is the solar eclipse which occurred *after* the birth. Listed in the tables are the latitudes and longitudes for the sunrise, noon, and sunset positions upon Earth for each solar eclipse. Taking these three points of the solar eclipse which occurred just prior to birth, and then drawing a curve to connect these three points, outlines the pre-natal eclipse path.

RULES FOR FINDING PRE-NATAL ECLIPSE PATHS

1. Find the eclipse date that immediately precedes birthdate.

2. Plot longitude and latitude coordinates of sunrise, noon and sunset points on world map.

3. Draw an arc connecting these three coordinate points. This is the path of the eclipse.

4. Draw horizontal lines through each of the three latitudes across the entire Earth.

5. Draw vertical lines through the three longitudes, from South to North poles.

6. Shade in the rectangular area that contains the most Eastern and most Western longitudes, as well as most Northern and most Southern latitudes. This rectangle should contain the eclipse path. This is known as the "rectangular grid" of the pre-natal eclipse path, and possibly describes the general area in which the soul previously moved about in a lifetime that is significant to the present lifetime.

[13]Oppolzer's *Canon of Eclipses* (New York, Dover Publications, 1962) and *The Nautical Almanac & Ephemeris*, U.S. Naval Observatory and the Royal Astronomic Observatory at Greenwich (yearly).

7. The nine points of the entire grid that intersect may also be "familiar."

8. Now find the nine "opposite points."
   A. Subtract each longitude coordinate from 180°, and change from East to West, or vice-versa.
   B. Change each latitude from North to South, or vice-versa.
   C. Now you have a set of three more longitude and latitude coordinates.

9. Repeat same steps as above with these new coordinates.

10. When you draw three more vertical and horizontal lines, you will have another "rectangular grid" that may be significant to this lifetime as a result of the soul's movement in a previous incarnation.

11. You will also now have 36 points of grid lines intersecting. Each of these points may also be "familiar" to the soul.

12. Pay most attention to those areas which compliment the planets in the natal chart in terms of "past life" possibilities. For instance, if Jupiter is on an angle, pay most attention to lands in Asia that show up on the "pre-natal eclipse" grids, and rectangular areas of same.

At this point the astrologer must begin to use his or her and the client's intuitive faculty. Obviously these twelve lines plus two rectangular grid areas are going to pass through many places upon the Earth. Not all of these will represent places of past life experiences (more so the shaded rectangular areas containing the two paths and the 36 places where the lines intersect). As the astrologer relates these locations to the client, certain places will "feel" right to both the astrologer and client. The astrologer may then further check these locations with the areas signified by the placement of the natal planets, as given in the previous chapter, and note if there are any correlations.

To illustrate this last point, assume a pre-natal eclipse path proceeds along a latitude of 20 degrees North, passing through parts of both India and Mexico. Assume furthermore that the client has strong feelings of association with both of these countries. Which should the astrologer give the greatest priority to? Assume that upon examination of the natal chart the astrologer sees that Jupiter is strongly

Table 2: Solar Eclipse Tables, used for determining Pre-Natal Eclipse Paths.

GREENWICH TIME					TOTAL or PARTIAL* ECLIPSE		
Year	Month	Day	Hour	Min.	Sunrise	Noon	Sunset
1900	May	28	14	49.9	117W 18N	45W 45N	32E 25N
	Nov	22	7	17.0	3E 6S	66E 33S	135E 18S
1901	May	18	5	38.0	40E 27S	97E 2S	157E 13S
	Nov	11	7	34.0	13E 37N	66E 12N	122E 17N
1902	Apr	8	2	05.2	*124W29 60N10	142W38 71N47	175E31 81N30
	May	7	10	34.3	*161E54 52E54	125W17 70S00	108W30 32S25
	Oct	31	20	00.3	* 19E52 58N25	100E40 70N50	106E03 33N13
1903	Mar	29	1	26.4	80E 40N	150E 65N	117W 75N
	Sep	21	4	30.4	31E 46S	101E 70S	179E 82S
1904	Mar	17	5	38.8	36E 10S	96E 6N	157E 25N
	Sep	9	20	42.7	163E 8N	133W 5S	70W 27S
1905	Mar	8	5	19.8	31E 52S	110E 43S	172E 18S
	Aug	30	13	13.4	96W 50N	22W 45N	55E 18N
1906	Feb	22	19	43.3	* 20W44 66S49	170W08 71S31	138E50 37S02

	GREENWICH TIME				TOTAL or PARTIAL* ECLIPSE		
Year	Month	Day	Hour	Min.	Sunrise	Noon	Sunset
	Jul	21	1	14.4	* 58W26 50S33	33W15 68S37	11E26 59S45
	Aug	20	13	13.4	* 48E46 71N46	66E13 70N55	113W22 46N40
1907	Jan	14	5	57.1	42E 50N	89E 39N	131E 57N
	Jul	10	15	16.7	100W 34S	50W 17S	1W 37S
1908	Jan	3	21	44.2	154E 11N	145W 12S	85W 10N
	Jun	28	16	31.9	130W 5N	67W 31N	1W 10N
	Dec	23	11	49.5	73W 23S	3E 53S	86E 32S
1909	Jun	17	23	28.8	82E 50N	173W 88N	43W 60N
	Dec	12	7	44.9	*159E06 39S01	85E49 65S03	17W28 54S53
1910	May	9	5	33.4	111E 73S		156E 46S
	Nov	1	14	8.6	*118E30 63N04	155E14 62N02	165E23 17N35
1911	Apr	28	22	25.7	148E 37S	155W 1S	90W 11N
	Oct	22	4	9.1	61E 45N	118E 11N	178E 08S
1912	Apr	17	11	39.8	61W 5N	1W 46N	89E 57N
	Oct	10	13	40.7	93W 4N	33W 35S	47E 52S

	GREENWICH TIME				TOTAL	or ECLIPSE	PARTIAL*
Year	Month	Day	Hour	Min.	Sunrise	Noon	Sunset
1913	Apr	6	5	32.9	*151W24 28N59	175E32 61N20	37E49 82N09
	Aug	31	8	52.0	* 13E16 77N36	26W36 61N36	47W05 43N45
	Sep	29	16	45.6	* 42E54 17S05	11E31 61S13	178E12 74S41
1914	Feb	25	0	1.6	30W 78S		91W 43S
	Aug	21	12	26.9	121W 71N	2E 71N	70E 24N
1915	Feb	14	4	31.4	43E 36S	118E 26S	175E 13N
	Aug	10	22	52.0	130E 23N	162W 17N	106W 22S
1916	Feb	3	16	6.2	122W 7N	62W 16N	10W 49N
	Jul	30	2	15.2	89E 28S	142E 36S	179E 63S
	Dec	24	8	46.2	* 47W40 66S32	32W10 65S43	17W43 64S02
1917	Jan	22	19	28.3	* 18E02 28N02	25E43 63N15	95E56 60N28
	Jun	19	1	16.2	*118W43 52N55	150E06 66N10	72E35 45N48
	Jul	18	14	42.5	* 93W31 53S24	101W52 69S44	129W28 68S57
	Dec	14	9	17.7	88W 59S	38E 90S	155E 56S
1918	Jun	8	22	3.2	130E 26N	152W 51N	75W 25N

	GREENWICH TIME				TOTAL	or ECLIPSE	PARTIAL*
Year	Month	Day	Hour	Min.	Sunrise	Noon	Sunset
	Jul	3	15	19.2	119W 11S	53W 36S	15W 15S
1919	May	29	13	12.3	75W 19S	18W 4N	42E 12S
	Nov	22	15	19.7	103W 31N	50W 7N	4E 19N
1920	May	17	18	14.7	* 46W28 46S11	107W32 69S05	133W03 32S07
	Nov	10	3	52.0	* 96E25 53N12	30E00 69N57	15E20 34N00
1921	Apr	8	9	5.9	43W 45N	34E 75N	152E 77N
	Oct	1	12	26.1	97W 52S	19W 84S	126E 86S
1922	Mar	28	13	3.8	76W 8S	17W 13N	47E 27N
	Sep	21	4	38.4	43E 5N	106E 12S	173E 30S
1923	Mar	17	12	51.0	76W 50S	4W 36S	57E 15S
	Sep	10	20	53.2	154E 48N	128W 38N	64W 14N
1924	Mar	5	3	43.9	*131E14 68S14	55W47 72S02	13W50 34S36
	Jul	31	7	57.9	*163E53 54S32	145E53 69S35	100E04 68S18
	Aug	29	20	22.5	* 41E35 71N49	73E05 71N32	129W23 41N05
1925	Jan	24	14	45.0	95W 48N	44W 42N	3W 61N

	GREENWICH TIME				TOTAL	or ECLIPSE	PARTIAL*
Year	Month	Day	Hour	Min.	Sunrise	Noon	Sunset
	Jul	20	21	40.3	162E 37S	148W 26S	100W 47S
1926	Jan	14	6	35.4	21E 7N	82E 10S	142E 14N
	Jul	9	23	6.3	132E 4N	165W 25N	104W 1N
1927	Jan	3	20	29.0	156E 27S	125W 52S	46W 27S
	Jun	29	6	32.0	16W 46N	84E 78N	169W 51N
	Dec	24	3	59.2	* 33W46 42S43	47E45 66S04	145E13 50S48
1928	May	19	13	14.2	11E 67S		30E 58S
	Jun	17	20	27.0	* 95W52 61N51	70W33 65N39	41W42 66N31
	Nov	12	9	47.9	* 6W04 59N54	80W59 62N40	79W09 21N25
1929	May	9	6	8.2	35E 37S	89E 1S	153E 5N
	Nov	1	12	0.6	55W 43N	1W 9N	59E 4S
1930	Apr	28	19	9.6	173W 3N	113W 45N	23W 50N
	Oct	21	21	47.2	146E 4N	155W 36S	72W 41S
1931	Apr	18	0	45.1	*100W15 26N52	58W44 61N38	80E01 76N06
	Sep	12	4	40.9	*140E27 71N18	152E39 61N24	162E29 51N10

GREENWICH TIME					TOTAL or	PARTIAL* ECLIPSE	
Year	Month	Day	Hour	Min.	Sunrise	Noon	Sunset
	Oct	11	12	35.2	* 80E24 15S40	119E37 61S22	64W30 70S46
1932	Mar	7	7	44.5	179W 75S		152E 47S
	Aug	31	19	55.3	110E 79N	109W 78N	41W 28N
1933	Feb	24	12	44.2	70W 39S	5W 24S	42E 14N
	Aug	21	5	49.1	24E 30N	94E 18N	150E 20S
1934	Feb	14	0	43.9	108E 4N	168E 19N	137W 52N
	Aug	10	8	46.2	11W 19S	43E 33S	88E 62S
1935	Jan	5	5	35.3	*106E14 65S17	110E02 64S44	113E56 64S57
	Feb	3	16	15.9	*116E05 24N48	115E19 62N33	35E53 64N37
	Jun	30	19	59.3	* 10E20 43S10	5E49 62S58	35W58 70S55
	Dec	25	17	49.6	135E 62S	93E 88S	25E 53S
1936	Jun	19	5	15.2	16E 34N	101E 56N	179E 26N
	Dec	13	23	25.6	118E 15S	173W 38S	107W 11S
1937	Jun	8	20	43.4	169E 12S	131W 10N	71W 12S
	Dec	2	23	11.5	139E 26N	169W 4N	115W 22N

	GREENWICH TIME				TOTAL	or ECLIPSE	PARTIAL*
Year	Month	Day	Hour	Min.	Sunrise	Noon	Sunset
1938	May	29	14	0.1	52W 65S	27W 52S	10E 61S
	Nov	21	23	52.0	*143W58 48N00	162E03 68N57	138E25 35N41
1939	Apr	19	16	35.2	167W 54N	79W 88N	76E 78N
	Oct	12	16	30.3	130E 60S		72E 82S
1940	Apr	7	20	18.7	174E 4S	127W 20N	60W 29N
	Oct	1	12	41.5	79W 3N	16W 19S	54E 33S
1941	Mar	27	20	14.4	178E 47S	116W 29S	57W 12S
	Sep	21	4	38.8	42E 45N	114E 30N	177E 10N
1942	Mar	16	23	36.7	* 21E51 67S51	76E43 72S16	109E07 32S19
	Aug	12	2	27.2	* 89W38 61S47	100W02 70S27	127W28 74S46
	Sep	10	15	52.6	*134E51 71N00	50W09 71N59	12W38 36N37
1943	Feb	4	23	30.6	129E 47N	176W 47N	136W 66N
	Aug	1	4	6.0	62E 42S	114E 37S	159E 58S
1944	Jan	25	15	24.6	112W 3N	49W 7S	9E 19N
	Jul	20	5	43.4	33E 3N	95E 19N	154E 7S

GREENWICH TIME					TOTAL or PARTIAL* ECLIPSE		
Year	Month	Day	Hour	Min.	Sunrise	Noon	Sunset
1945	Jan	14	5	7.0	27E 31S	108E 51S	177W 23S
	Jul	9	13	36.2	116W 44N	20W 70N	72E 41N
1946	Jan	3	12	15.7	* 91E56 46S48	177W39 67S09	86W37 47S07
	May	30	20	59.9	*165E53 52S49	101E06 64S07	85E54 27S50
	Jun	29	3	51.5	* 3E01 58N02	50E49 66N36	109E29 61N08
	Nov	23	17	36.7	*110E49 56N16	45E23 63N25	40E54 25N24
1947	May	20	13	44.1	78W 36S	25W 2S	37E 2S
	Nov	12	20	1.8	173W 41N	121W 6N	62W 1N
1948	May	9	2	30.6	77E 2N	138E 44N	136W 43N
	Nov	1	6	2.7	22E 4N	82E 37S	165W 43S
1949	Apr	28	7	48.4	* 5E20 25N15	55E56 62N04	165W55 69N40
	Oct	21	21	12.5	*154W24 15S19	107W17 61S41	55E31 66S11
1950	Mar	18	15	20.4	48E 72S		35E 50S
	Sep	12	3	29.1	67W 85N		155E 34N
1951	Mar	7	20	51.6	161E 42S	127W 21S	69W 14N

	GREENWICH TIME				TOTAL	or ECLIPSE	PARTIAL*
Year	Month	Day	Hour	Min.	Sunrise	Noon	Sunset
	Sep	1	12	50.0	81W 36N	11W 19N	46E 18S
1952	Feb	25	9	16.7	21W 1N	39E 22N	99E 54N
	Aug	20	15	21.5	112W 11S	56W 30S	4W 61S
1953	Feb	14	0	59.0	*111W00 21N55	104W57 61N59	164E08 68N27
	Jul	11	2	43.7	* 0E52 66N15	71E29 64N22	118E14 49N06
	Aug	9	15	54.5	*112E40 34S54	114E33 62S20	55E17 72S39
1954	Jan	5	2	21.8	3W 66S	31W 85S	106W 51S
	Jun	30	12	26.9	99W 42N	5W 62N	74E 26N
	Dec	25	7	34.0	5W 20S	67E 39S	131E 7S
1955	Jun	20	4	12.0	55E 4S	117E 15N	177E 12S
	Dec	14	7	8.4	19E 21N	72E 2N	124E 25N
1956	Jun	8	21	30.0	178E 55S	141W 40S	100W 55S
	Dec	2	8	00.0	* 21W29 42N54	64W32 67N52	96W45 38N09
1957	Apr	29	23	54.8	56E 66N		17E 74N
1958	Apr	19	3	24.0	66E 1N	126E 28N	164W 31N

	GREENWICH TIME				TOTAL	or ECLIPSE	PARTIAL*
Year	Month	Day	Hour	Min.	Sunrise	Noon	Sunset
	Oct	12	20	51.8	157E 1S	139W 26S	67W 34S
1959	Apr	8	3	29.7	72E 43S	133E 21S	168W 10S
	Oct	2	12	31.5	72W 42N	6W 23N	56E 7N
1960	Mar	27	07	25.1	* 14W58 65S42	151W49 72S15	129W20 30S22
	Sep	20	22	59.9	*128W45 68N56	74E09 72N11	103E49 33N06
1961	Feb	15	8	11.0	6W 46N	53E 53N	94E 72N
	Aug	11	10	35.9	39W 48S	14E 50S	51E 69S
1962	Feb	5	0	11.1	116E 1N	179E 4S	122E 23N
	Jul	31	12	24.5	67W 2N	5W 12N	51E 15S
1963	Jan	25	13	42.8	102W 35S	19W 49S	52E 20S
	Jul	20	20	42.7	143E 43N	126W 62N	44W 33N
1964	Jan	14	20	30.1	*143W39 50S59	43W03 68S14	41E09 43S43
	Jun	10	4	34.1	* 79W56 51S40	135W38 65S00	157W58 34S44
	Jul	9	11	17.9	* 99E15 56N54	173E04 67N36	118W24 54N08
	Dec	4	1	31.9	*129W19 52N27	173E04 64N18	161E35 29N35

	GREENWICH TIME				TOTAL	or ECLIPSE	PARTIAL*
Year	Month	Day	Hour	Min.	Sunrise	Noon	Sunset
1965	May	30	21	13.8	171E 36S	137W 4S	78W 10S
	Nov	23	4	10.8	65E 38N	116E 4N	175E 5N
1966	May	20	9	42.9	30W 2N	31E 41N	113E 36N
	Nov	12	14	26.5	104W 2N	43W 38S	40E 38S
1967	May	9	14	42.8	*108E12 24N05	168E30 64N37	54W34 62N52
	Nov	2	5	47.9	15W 54S		46W 69S
1968	Mar	28	23	00.5	*145W31 70S51	79E55 61S09	108E51 12S42
	Sep	22	11	9.2	108E 80N		90E 42N
1969	Mar	18	4	52.3	44E 45S	112E 19S	172W 13N
	Sep	11	19	56.1	173E 41N	117E 19N	60W 16S
1970	Mar	7	17	43.2	149W 2S	88E 25N	23W 55N
	Aug	31	22	2.6	147E 5S	157W 29S	98W 59S
1971	Feb	25	9	38.1	* 20E44 19N25	33E40 61N35	72W23 71N38
	Jul	22	9	31.9	*144E07 69N10	177W02 63N36	149W44 54N13
	Aug	20	22	39.5	*144W20 27S57	135W15 61S48	146E14 74S07

GREENWICH TIME					TOTAL or PARTIAL* ECLIPSE		
Year	Month	Day	Hour	Min.	Sunrise	Noon	Sunset
1972	Jan	16	10	53.3	143W	156W	123E
					69S	81S	49S
	Jul	10	19	39.5	144E	111W	31W
					51N	67N	28N
1973	Jan	4	15	42.9	128W	54W	8E
					25S	39S	3S
	Jun	30	11	39.1	60W	6E	65E
					5N	19N	13S
	Dec	24	15	08.1	102W	47W	3E
					16N	1N	29N
1974	Jun	20	4	55.6	59E	107E	149E
					45S	32S	53S

placed (by an angle, ruling the fourth house, or the last planet the Moon has crossed) and aspects Neptune very strongly. It is therefore more likely that the client may have had a past incarnation in India which influences conditions in this lifetime. In the same chart, the astrologer notes that Venus and Saturn (Spain or Mexico) do not strongly aspect one another, that neither planet is near an angle or ruling the I. C., and that neither is the last planet crossed by the Moon before birth. The astrologer may then conclude that the soul most likely has more familiarity with India than Mexico. Perhaps this revelation will precipitate a deeper understanding of her current psychological make-up.

To demonstrate an actual case of a pre-natal eclipse path, let's look at Figure 13. This shows the natal chart of a female born July 11, 1945, 2:15 PM, Springfield, Massachusetts. According to the solar eclipse tables, the nearest pre-natal eclipse occurred July 9, 1945, just two days before the native's own birth date.

The first step in determining the pre-natal eclipse path is to locate the longitude and latitude coordinates for the sunrise, noon, and sunset points of the July 9th, 1945 solar eclipse. This is shown in the tables to be: sunrise, 116° West and 44° North; noon, 20° West, 70° North; and sunset 72° East, 41° North. Next, draw an arc which connects these three coordinates. This, then, is the eclipse path for the July 9, 1945 solar eclipse.

The next step is to draw vertical lines across the globe through each of the three given longitudes (116° West, 20° West, and 72° East), and horizontal lines across the globe through each of the three given latitudes (44° North, 70° North, and 41° North). This then gives part of the grids across the Earth as determined by the eclipse path.

By outlining the rectangular grid which contains the eclipse path, one can see, on the globe, a potentially very crucial area for the soul of this native. This is designated by the shaded area in the map (Figure 14).

This rectangular area was determined by the extremes of the coordinates given, i.e. the Southern and Northern-most latitudes, and Eastern and Western-most longitudes.

The opposite eclipse path is then determined according to the previously given instructions. Again, vertical lines are drawn through each of the opposite longitudes (64° East, 160° East, 108° West), and horizontal lines through each of the opposite latitudes (44° South, 70° South, 41° South). Another rectangular area is shaded in to emphasize the extremes of the opposite eclipse path.

In all, there now appear two shaded rectangular areas, six vertical

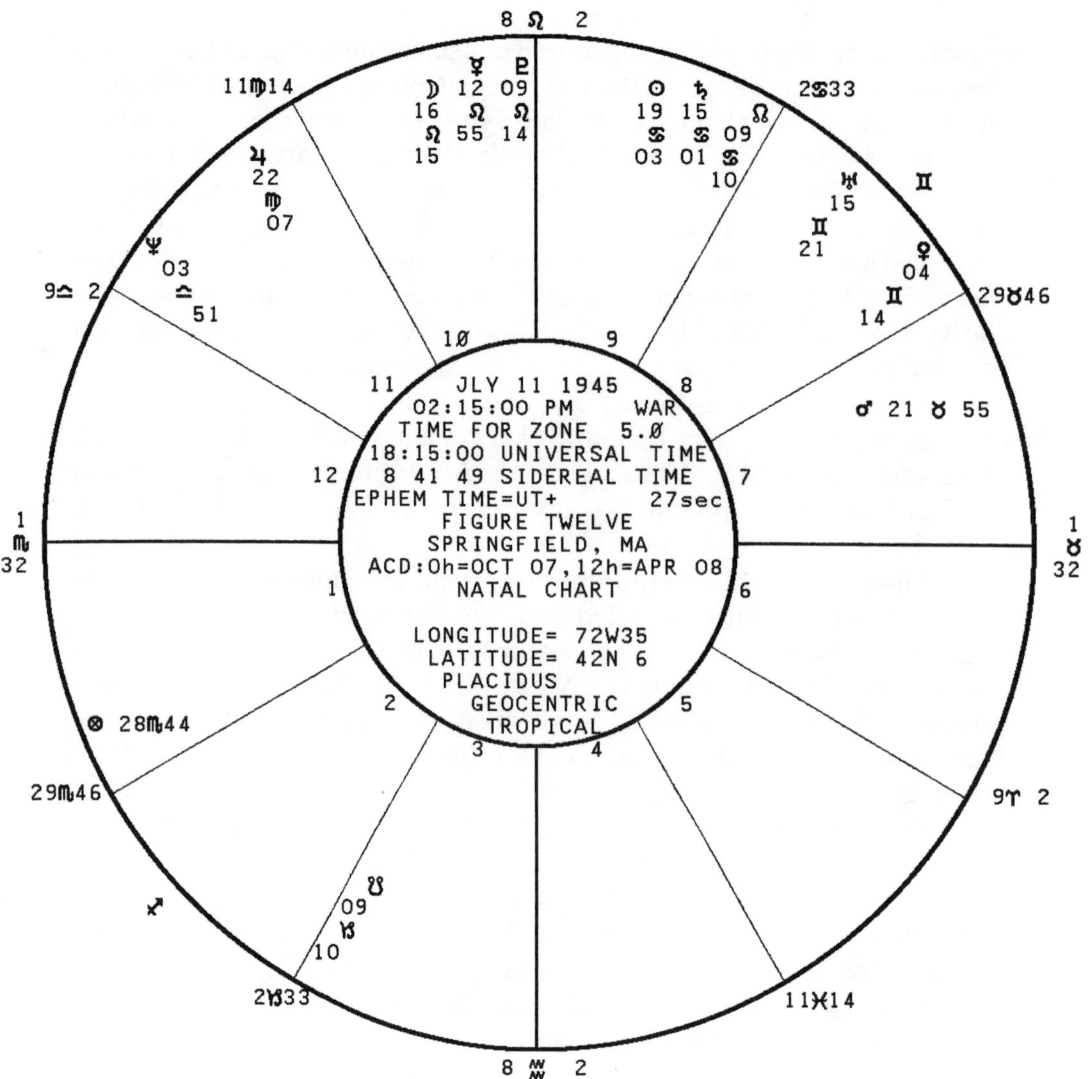

Figure 13

and six horizontal lines intersecting in 36 different places on the globe. These then outline the potential areas of familiarity to the soul.

Upon interviewing the client, it is discovered that she is an initiate of a Far Eastern Master, whose teachings are rooted in both Islam and Hinduism. In fact, one of the longitudes (72° East) passes directly through the village in which her master resides. In her natal chart,

180
75
60
45
30
15
0
15
30
45
60
180
150
120
90
60
30
0
30
60
90
120
150
180

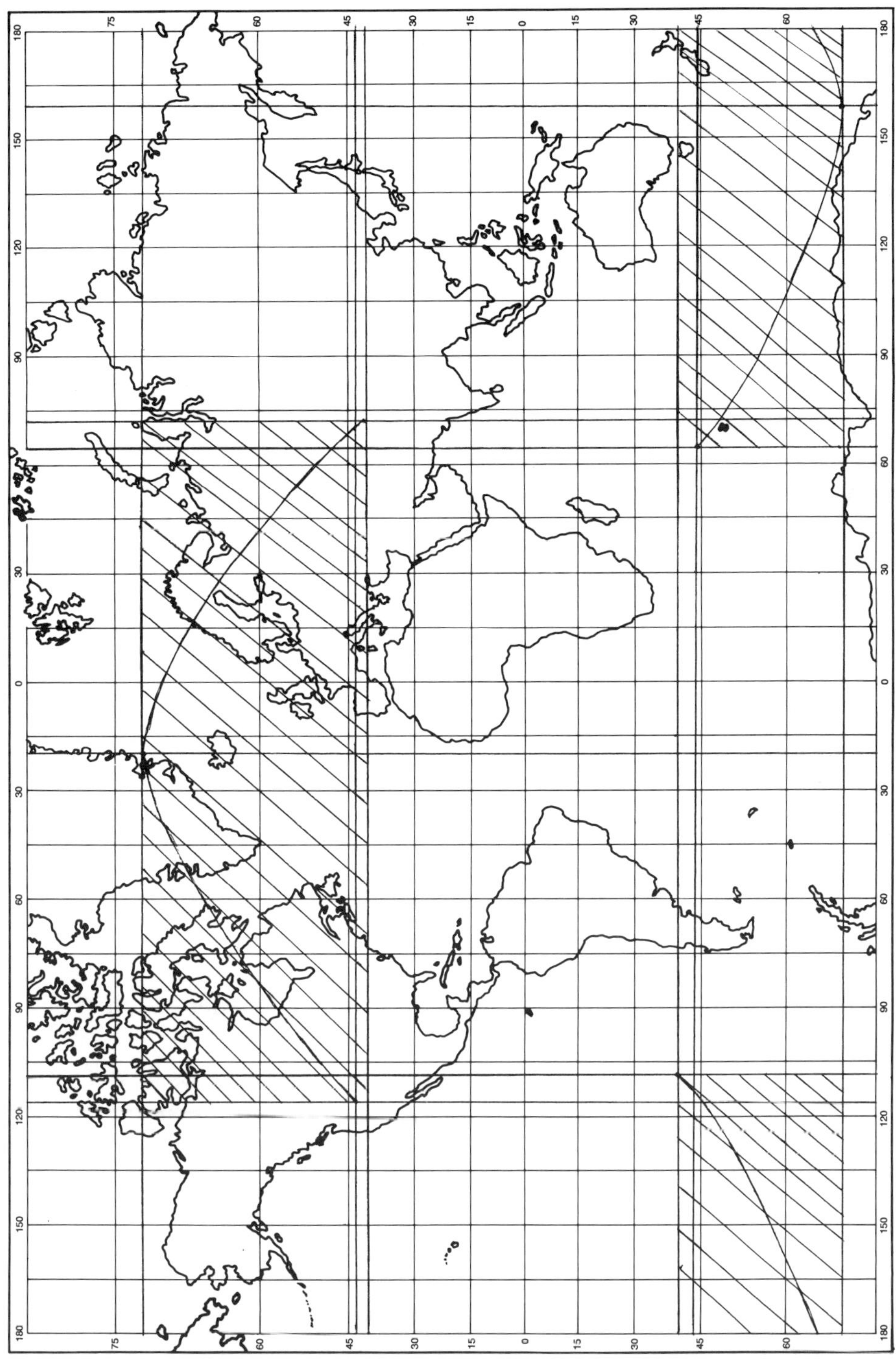

Figure 14

Jupiter is prominent because it is on the midpoint of the second quadrant.

Referring back to the natal chart, one can see that Earth (opposite the Sun), is placed in the third house near the I. C., the only planet posited below the horizon. The Earth, representing "closeness to nature", has been expressed in this lifetime in the fact that she lived for a time with a band of gypsies in the woods of Northern California, on the 41st degree latitude (also one of the pre-natal eclipse latitudes).

In the course of the interview she also related a strong desire to go to Southern France (Mars angular, and the 44th degree latitude). Her own birth place – Springfield, Massachusetts – also falls within orb of the 41 degree Northern latitude.

Considering the fact that Uranus rules the I. C., and refers to the early American Revolution as well, it is not surprising to find one of the grids passing through the New England states where she was born.

A glance at her natal horoscope shows Pluto prominent on the Midheaven, suggesting experiences in which the soul may have been part of a group whose existence may have been threatened by powerful and cruel leaders. There are many lands in the rectangular area of her grid which have a history of such regimes. The Pluto conjunct Mercury suggests a lifetime where intellectual development might have been considered a threat to the society, and study might have been forced through underground meetings. The Moon also conjuncts Pluto, so there may have been interest in pagan worship, or the study of wicca. Note that the rectangular grid and the eclipse path flows through areas of Eastern Europe, such as Romania and Bulgaria, where such experiences may have taken place.

Also note the Sun is located near the Midheaven, closely conjunct Saturn. Perhaps there was a lifetime in Great Britain during a time of close ties to Russia (the rectangular grid goes through both areas). Or it may pertain to a time the British Empire was under very strict rule, or during a time in which laws were formed.

The value of the pre-natal eclipse technique may thus be to point out those places upon Earth where the soul may have invested energy, where the soul may have a degree of familiarity due to past live experiences. By understanding the personality of those nations, and perhaps of the times one may have experienced before, one might come to a greater understanding of karmic patterns and scripts now in effect. The process of releasing these patterns and scripts might begin with identifying characteristics of their origin.

PART THREE

The Potential Blossoning of the Incarnated Soul

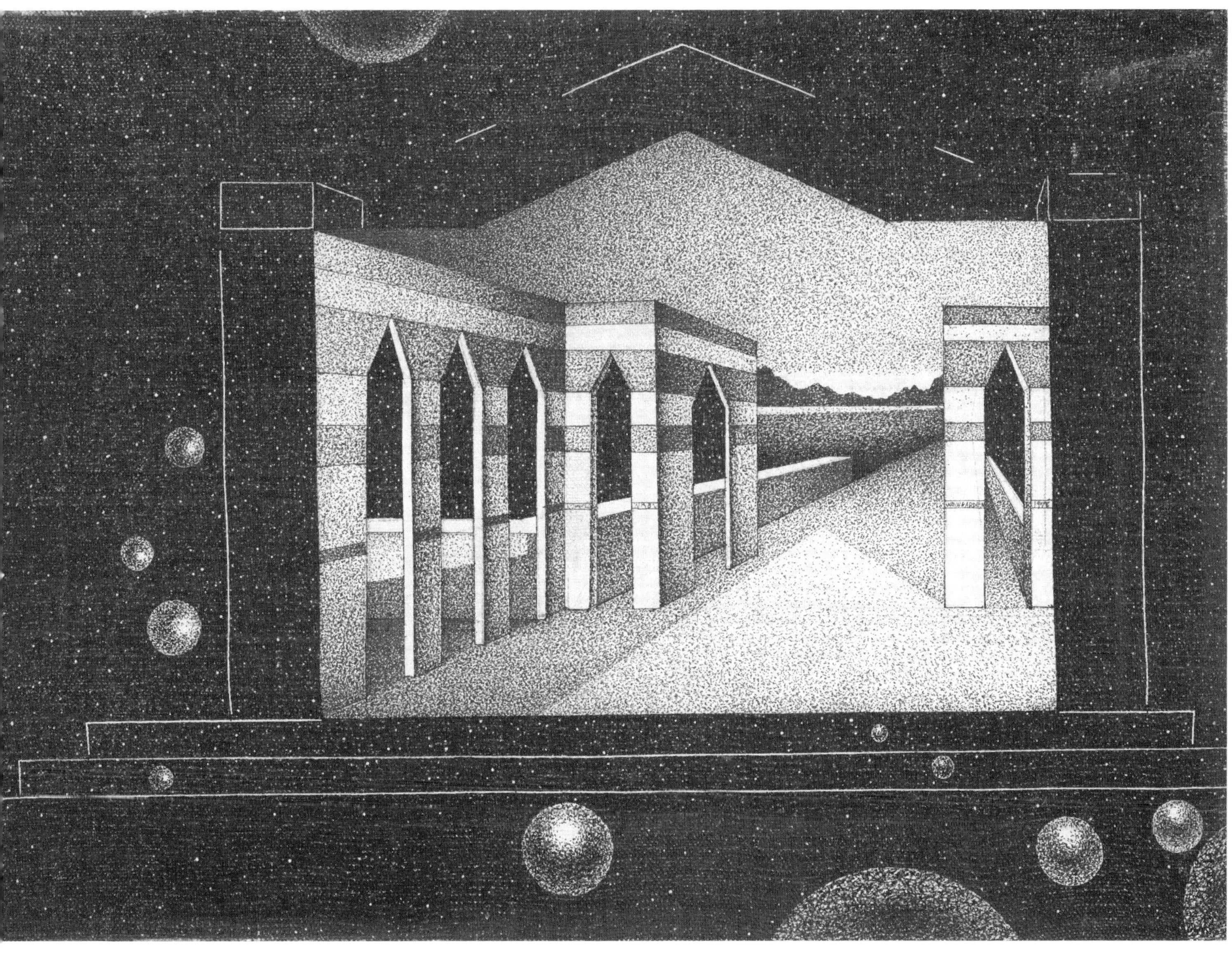

CHAPTER THIRTEEN

The Midheaven

"It is the entry into the life of non-duality where one is no longer caught by the play of opposites, where self *is not set over against* other, *nor are ideals in conflict with realities . . . As he is now one with his tasks, they are not to him mere obstacles to be disposed of so that he may begin the business of "really living." His tasks* are *his life . . . It is in the uncreative life that the doer is separated from what he does."* [14]

In attempting to show the potential path of the soul in this incarnation, one of the first points to analyze is the Midheaven. Here, according to sign and degree, the decanate and the dwadashamsa, lies the "flowering of the seed," the "blossoming of the soul's essence." With the I. C. one sees the quality, the character, of the soul as it enters this lifetime. Depending upon how the soul meets life and all its challenges, the manner in which that seed blossoms will be determined. The zenith then is *the potential peak of the soul as it manifests in this lifetime, according to character evolvement.* Furthermore, this potential is a *direct result* of past character development (of the nature of the I. C.). One does not become something that is completely contrary to one's basic foundation. Through the foundation implied by the I. C., a correct structure may be built whereby not only the native, but others whom the native comes into contact with, may benefit and grow. This *potential* structure that facilitates both the individual soul and others the soul contacts is symbolized by the Midheaven. It is one's "greatest

[14]Daistez T. Suzuki, *The Essentials of Zen Buddhism* (New York, E.P. Dutton & Co., Inc., 1962).

self," the point where the ego merges with the self's purpose, the point where one's "real self" becomes able to effectively relate in the "outer world." At this point, the soul begins to manifest its potential in this lifetime based upon a foundation developed prior to this lifetime. In so doing, the individual thereby releases a flow of energy that will generate phenomenon which may be described as "one's calling in life," if for no other reason than the soul becomes its "highest self," or its "best self possible." When one is one's "best self possible," all things are possible.

The following is an interpretation of the potential character inherent in the Midheaven signs:

Aries: The need here is to develop an honest and direct approach with others. This is potentially a pioneer, one who initiates new activities, adventurous experiences and stimulating relationships. This soul must learn to assert the self in the outer realm without becoming burdened by indecisions and uncertainties. The potential to "give life" to others is possible through new projects or even the cultivation of healing abilities. Others benefit from projects this individual begins, perhaps from the ground floor upward, because oftentimes the burden of others is carried upon this one's shoulders. The desire for truth in the most direct manner possible is strong here.

Taurus: The need here is to develop a sense of beauty and refinement, to appreciate things for what they are without trying to change them. Another need is to find the most simple way of doing things This is attained through cultivating a faith in oneself and a faith in an orderliness to the universe. Common sense and practicality are assets to this soul and those it comes into contact with. Once these qualities are developed, the individual may convey wisdom in affairs which arise and a confidence in knowing when one is right. This can be very useful in helping others realize their own inner beauty. The potential is to cultivate several talents, as it indicates a naturally resourceful person.

Gemini: The need is to develop versatility in mental pursuits and not become restricted in only one type of thinking. The potential for new and original ideas is great. The individual may be a master of many trades, having the ability to do many things at once, and all successfully. Humor is an asset which may attract many friends and lead to stimulating experiences in life. If this person can learn to relate ideas to others on their level without getting lost in philosophies and abstractions, then personal fulfillment in the world is very possible. By doing this the native brings others up to his or her own level of thinking.

Cancer: The need is to develop sensitivity to loved ones and to share loyalties and make sacrifices of oneself for the betterment of others. If positions of authority or responsibility over others is offered in this life, the native must learn to treat others with love and kindness and not with coldness. The potential is to foster and nurture growth in others and exhibit the value of loyalty, dedication and love to others without any expectations in return. Security for these persons must become a matter of healthy relationships, and not so much of material success. There is also potential to develop warmth and sincerity. There may be ability to work in a profession that benefits humanity or to serve others in some great capacity.

Leo: The need is to develop confidence among others. By asserting the personality, cultivating a knack to entertain others and learning to generously give of one's energies to others, confidence can be achieved. Once achieved, the potential to bring joy and happiness to others will manifest. There is also potential to become spontaneously creative, and hence exciting and stimulating to others. All of this comes with a positive attitude toward life, grounded in a firm and stable belief system. It may be helpful for these natives to see life as a play and themselves as actors or actresses in the play which they may also direct.

Virgo: The need is to develop discrimination in relationships as well as in one's life objectives. Rather than just jumping into situations because they look good, it is far more advisable to analyze and consider all of the consequences first. The need is also to develop common sense with critical judgement rather than chasing dreams before exploring them for what they really are. The potential for the development of exceptional reasoning powers is great, and in so doing one naturally begins to make choices that are best for all concerned. This soul may help others to examine all choices in detail, and to understand human nature more accurately. This allows them the ability to see potential in others and then bring it out.

Libra: The need is to develop a balance, or "center," in life. There is also a need to develop a sense of universal fairness and justice concerning others without a "me first" attitude. This is accomplished by the cultivation of tact, diplomacy, and grace in dealing with others, and refraining from a blunt, outspoken approach. The potential for developing an unusual and gifted approach toward seeing life in a multitude of different facets is great. Consequently many of these individuals may become great artists. They may also become excellent counselors for there is a knack of seeing the many different choices available to others. By learning to check one's own impulse to act immediately, one may learn the skill of weighing all matters first, and thus develop the need for balance in life.

Scorpio: The need is to develop the ability to bring about change rather than let matters slide into a rut. Another need is to develop a respect for the mystery of life, and a knowledge of the subtle, magical forces affecting one's life. These natives are potential seekers, healers, and magicians. There is also potential to recognize a better way of doing things and the ability to coordinate an effort involving others for the purpose of making this "better way" possible. The main thrust of such an effort must be toward change and transformation, rather than the acceptance of things as they already are. The inherent nature of practicality will likely prevent this soul from acting too rashly. As long as others are brought into the picture to share the work equally, progress will be made which will be of benefit to everyone.

Sagittarius: The need is to develop expertise in some particular area and to recognize one's ability and wisdom in that area. There is also a need to constantly expand one's horizons and philosophies. In that sense these individuals are students of life. As they cultivate an open-mindedness to all areas of thought, the potential to work effectively with others of different backgrounds and nationalities can be realized. There may be talent in bringing happiness and hope to others, to lift the spirits of those who feel hopeless or depressed. Once expertise in some area is developed, these natives may make excellent consultants, diplomats or motivators. Those who sincerely attempt to relate on the level of others, rather than trying to bring others to their levels, tend to experience great success in relationships.

Capricorn: The need is to develop order in both one's own life and the lives of others. In so doing, these individuals may become competent in getting matters successfully "off the ground." The potential is to work for the well-being of others, to develop and attain very high goals through hard work and dedication. Oftentimes these individuals seem like "parents to the world's children," for they tend to take care of others and assume responsibilities beyond their ordinary boundaries. These natives must be careful not to let feelings and emotions for loved ones, especially feelings of loneliness, get in the way. The native's road may not be easy and may not offer much assistance from others, but the rewards are great once the task is completed. Fulfillment may come by developing a task-oriented approach toward life's objectives.

Aquarius: The need is to develop a humanitarian sense of doing things for the betterment of the world and not expecting the world to do things for the native. Tremendous inspiration for great work is possible as soon as this individual overcomes any tendencies toward selfishness. There is great potential talent and unusual abilities which may bring success and fulfillment in areas where most will not even dare to tread. One with Aquarius culminating can be an example to others as to how to "make it" simply by being one's own unique self. Ingenuity and inventiveness aid in the individual's expression. Working alone on one's ideas, developing them fully without intervention from others, may produce results which will benefit others. The individual must not let pride and the desire for power (qualities possibly carried over from the last life) interfere with their unique expression in this lifetime.

Pisces: The need is to develop sensitivity and imagination in all dealings rather than attempting to control and manipulate everything under the pretense of "knowing" what is right. There is also the need for a spiritual direction or goal in order to make life more meaningful. By learning to sacrifice, to become sensitive to what others are experiencing, this native may reach his/her potential. That potential may be a very spiritual and ascetic one, and may be aided by the development of trust and acceptance of others. A naturally analytical nature will prevent foolish judgements, but a quality of faith in human nature will act as a source of inspiration in dealing with others.

In conclusion, remember that these are characteristics of a *potential nature*. They are keys to individual evolvement, to individual release. The qualities of the I. C. are already present and may be used as an aid in the expression of the Midheaven. However, too often the tendency is to rely solely upon the I. C. or Ascendant. Although the I. C. is representative of the "real self," it is not as powerful as the "real self's potential," which is the blossoming of the I. C.'s seed into the Midheaven.

CHAPTER FOURTEEN

The Moon's Nodes: A Peculiar Piece in the Puzzle of Destiny

"And she hailed him, saying:

Prophet of God, in quest of the uttermost, long have you searched the distances for your ship.

And now your ship has come, and you must needs go.

Deep is your longing for the land of your memories and the dwelling place of your great desires; and our love would not bind you nor our needs hold you." [15]

According to the American College Dictionary, destiny is "that which is to happen to a particular person or thing."[16] In this sense, destiny appears much like karma as described in this book. Both concepts refer to the idea that one will encounter certain experiences in life. Karma assumes the experiences are a result of one's prior actions, which set into motion a particular cycle whose consequences are inevitable, so long as that cycle is in effect. In this sense, the result of one's karma is destined.

A question, or perhaps a challenge, arises in the consideration of these concepts: Is it possible to alter one's destiny? Is it possible to terminate, transform or alter the character of the cycle governing one's karma? If the answer to this question is yes then it affirms the existence of free will.

The model of Evolutionary Astrology supports the concept of free will within the framework of destiny and karma. One's choices of

[15]Kahlil Gibran, *The Prophet* (New York, Alfred A. Knopf, 1923).
[16]*American College Dictionary* (New York, Random House, 1970).

behavior, and nature of intent motivating those behaviors, does set into motion cyclic laws governed by the Law of Retribution, or karma. The consequences or experiences related to these cycles are destined. In other words, one will undergo experiences in life that are a result of the actions one has initiated. However, as one undergoes these experiences, one has the free will to choose how to respond to these circumstances which are part of his or her destiny. Those responses in turn may alter, terminate, or transform the nature of that cycle. In a sense then, one has the free will to alter his or her destiny as he or she encounters experiences that are of one's destiny. The concept of destiny is fixed only insomuch as the dynamics which created the cycle remain unchanged. When one breaks through to a new level of self-understanding related to a karmic script, one may consciously choose to respond with a higher frequency emotion than the previous script called for. A different response to a cyclic dynamic will have the effect of altering the cycle. It will alter one's destiny.

All beings have inner longings. These longings are the result of very deep memories, and are the basis for creative urges. These longings and consequent creative urges are signified by the natal Sun. When one is in touch with this principle, there is a sense of freedom, vitality, radiance and wonderment. It is as if one has shed a heavy weight, and broken free of unseen constraints. The expression of the being who is in synch with the natal Sun is one of great aliveness. The energy level related to a creative expression associated with one's innermost longing is immense, and immensely transformative.

However this creative expression of one's innermost longing will ultimately conflict with the needs and perhaps love of and for others, that bind the individual. These are represented by the Moon in one's natal horoscope. Man seeks intimacy and a special bonding with others, and in the course of interacting with these intimate contacts, another dynamic is created. The challenge is to integrate the urge for intimacy and love for another with the urge to creatively express one's innermost longings.

One's innermost longings do not change. The Sun is stable, a constant source of light to any being who sets out upon the inner journey. However the journey, or the urge to seek the experience of this deep and powerful memory, loses its intensity as the being becomes attached and trapped to the circumstances of its karmic scripts. In other words, as the ego becomes stronger and stronger, the consciousness is less and less open to the counsel of the soul. Without contact or counsel from the soul, the energy of the Infinite, or Spirit, cannot be tapped. One's deep inner longings fall further and further away from consciousness, and one's creative urges retire to a state of dormancy. The memory fades and the life falls into a repetitive pattern of routine and predictability.

The longings are still there, but what changes is one's relationships. First of all there is the relationship to the soul, which is the source of that longing, for it is the soul which remembers the sweetness of the long ago experience. Second, it is the relationships of love which also change. One's needs, as well as the needs of those with whom one forms intimate bonds, either support or distract from that inner longing within each person. Just as the Sun is constant in its life giving, creative energy, so too is the Moon changing in the quality of needs encountered in intimacy. When these needs begin to bind, the path to the Sun becomes less traveled. When these needs are themselves consistent with this inner longing–when the need to experience intimacy with one's own inner creative source is powerful within each being involved in the intimate relationship–then there is the potential for a powerful release which illuminates the path of each with an incredible light.

During its orbit around the Earth, there are two times during the year when the path of the Moon will intersect with the path of the Earth around the Sun. These paths are known as ecliptics, and the new and full Moons which occur near these two times will create a phenomenon known as an **eclipse**. During a solar eclipse, the path of the Moon will intersect directly between the Earth and the Sun, blocking out the light of the Sun as seen from Earth. Imagine looking at an object some distance away. Suddenly another object, such as a bird, comes squarely between you and the object, blacking out your vision of the original object. In order to see that object again, it is either necessary for that second object to move, or for you to move around it. In any event, there is a "break" in the focus of attention, a temporary blockage.

It is the ecliptic of the Moon, known as its North or South Node, which creates this blockage of the Sun. If the Sun symbolizes one's deep, innermost longings and a source of dynamic, creative energy, and the Moon represents intimate relationships whose needs either bind or support one's inner journey, then it follows that the movement of the Moon's Nodes through the natal horoscope could indicate the time periods of destiny. Furthermore they may also time periods when one is given a choice that could alter one's destiny.

Both the natal and transiting position of the Moon's Nodes are one of the least researched area of the major astronomical cycles known to man. The cycle of the Moon's Nodes through the zodiac is about 18.54 years, which means it takes about 18 months to transit through each sign. This cycle length is greater than that of Jupiter's orbit around the Sun, but less than Saturn's. The 18.54-year cycle is one of the most dominant cycles in a wide array of human activity, according to numerous works published by the Foundation For The Study of Cycles, in Irvine, California. It is a cycle that correlates to real estate, business, the economy, marriage rates, immigration, cotton and pig prices, flood stages of the Nile River, tree rings, and stock prices, to name just a few. Is it no wonder that the same cycle would be important in the life cycle of every individual being? The answer is undoubtedly "yes", but how it relates to the individual is a matter that this work seeks to understand through principles presented herein. That is, that the principles of the Moon and the Sun come into play at the point of the Moon's Nodes. Translated in the language of Evolutionary Astrology this means the principles of one's innermost, deep longings, or one's spiritual path, come into play with the needs of others with whom one has formed an intimate bond, and these needs either facilitate one's path in a remarkable way, or they lead to complexities which bind, resulting in a fading of one's contact with the soul.

Although the Moon's Nodes are referred to as either North or South, the major emphasis of this chapter will focus upon the North Node of the Moon. Traditionally the North Node of the Moon is considered a "challenge", and the South Node of the Moon is regarded as a "path of least resistance." The latter concept may be questionable, but the idea of the North Node representing a unique challenge fits the concepts presented herein very well. That will be the direction undertaken in this section of the book.

The effect of the Moon's North Node is strongest when located in the same sign that is on the angle, and within about 22½ degrees from the angle. When posited within about 11 degrees of an angular midpoint, the individual may find the challenge an extremely testing one, as will be described shortly.

The following is a description of specific challenges for each soul based upon the placement of the Moon's North Node. Notice that the placement is not according to house position, but rather by angular relationships. These may be re-assigned to house positions if the reader so wishes, but the reason they are presented in this manner is to infer the significance of individuality, which is a matter dealing with the angles rather than house location.

The Moon's North Node located on the angular side of the I. C. (Fourth House): The specific challenge (or even duty) is to aid others in the attainment of personal enlightenment and then to act upon it. These individuals may provide the impetus as well as the security and comfort necessary to facilitate major life changes in the lives of others. They may help others to organize and establish a strong belief system for coping with life. Present here is the strong urge to share life's excitement with others, even to the point of opening their houses and allowing others to come in. These individuals are oftentimes found to be excellent hosts and hostesses, as well as creative and dynamic individuals in their own right.

The Moon's North Node located on the Cadent side of the I. C. (Third House): The specific challenge is to develop one's own personal and spiritual ideas, and then to disperse these to selected others who come into their path. Their nature is stimulating and persuasive, once their ideas are formed along these lines. As they develop these ideas, their awareness of matters around them increases greatly, and with this awareness others may benefit. Many of these individuals may be quite psychic and creative, and others may have a knack of efficient record-keeping. These are teachers, but they teach to the few (not to the masses), for their ideas are constantly expanding and thus changing. The challenge, though, is to cultivate insight and disperse these ideas to other individuals.

The Moon's North Node located on the angular side of the Midheaven: (Tenth House): This is perhaps the most potentially prominent placement of the North Node. The specific challenge is to work with others in building or organizing some great endeavor, perhaps a foundation or community. These individuals are challenged to put the ideas of others, as well as their own, into action in order to achieve some great potential. Towards this end they may find prominent individuals may be attracted to their ideals and will lend a helping hand. They tend to have tremendous determination which acts like an incentive to others. They teach the value of achievement, the joy of hard work and effort toward the accomplishment of something great. They also tend to have very high spiritual ideals and a protective nature toward others. In short, these may be the builders of a new era.

The Moon's North Node located on the Cadent side of the Midheaven (Ninth House): These may be the teachers and philosophers of a generation. The specific challenge is to first learn, then teach the highest philosophies and spiritual understandings they can comprehend. These individuals may have the ability to appeal to the higher minds of others, either through speaking or writing. It is wise for these individuals to do a great deal of travel as part of the process of learning these philosophies which they are to teach. Most of these individuals have very open minds to all areas of mental-spiritual expressions.

Those who have the Moon's North Node located near the Meridian, as described above, may indeed have very high spiritual challenges. They have earned the right to pursue these areas through their works in past lives. It is thus their destiny. In so much as they continue in these directions, their challenge will be both exciting and rewarding.

Those who have the Moon's North Node located near the horizon have the challenge of working through the will in this lifetime. Again, great things may be accomplished. But their test may lie in developing a more spiritual base to blend with a very strong will.

The Moon's North Node located on the angular side of the Ascendant (First House): The specific duty is to achieve self-understanding, facilitate the same in others, then stimulate others into action. To "know thyself", and then act upon this knowing, is appropriate to these individuals. Very strong personalities tend to have this placement. The ability to organize groups of people for some specific purpose, and usually in a pioneering type of way, may be present. These individuals may make effective leaders, but they must be careful of a tendency toward two things: 1) spiritual arrogance, wherein one believes their way is the *only* true way, and 2) manipulation of others to attain their own personal desires.

The Moon's North Node Located on the Cadent side of the Ascendant (Twelfth House): The specific challenge is to learn to treat others as equals to themself, and perhaps also to work with others who are less fortunate (handicapped or underprivileged) than themselves. Oftentimes the native's will gets in the way and a "superior attitude" is taken toward others. The result is that others may abandon, disappoint, or let the native down time and time again. By developing sympathy and compassion toward others one can overcome this affliction. There often seems to appear a karmic debt early in the life concerning one's life objectives, as early failures and disappointments may be common. This also pertains to the native's first choice of mates, where there seems to be difficulties, but of a very vague and hard-to-understand nature. It is very likely that early relationships involve karmic circumstances from the immediate past life. It also seems that before success is experienced, these natives must first "serve time" serving other people, perhaps in order to develop humility which may be lacking in the individual's makeup. These are usually secretive types with interest and potential abilities in occult and esoteric areas.

The Moon's North Node located on the Angular side of the Descendant (Seventh House): The specific challenge is to bring people together in a successful, cooperative effort. These individuals seem to have a knack for recognizing talent in others, and then helping to develop it. In fact this also seems to happen to the native – someone "discovers" them, or gives them a break in life. These individuals must be careful not to lose their personal identity in that of a great personality around them. This placement seems to be one of karmic merit, indicating one who finds many "soul mates" or kindred compatriots along life's path.

The Moon's North Node located on the Cadent side of the Descendant (Sixth House): The specific challenge is the same as the angular side – to bring people and ideas together in a cooperative effort – but the unfolding of this challenge seems a great deal more difficult than the North Node's placement in the angular side of the Descendant. There is a gift of putting ideas into the minds of others by which they may personally benefit, but the actual assistance in bringing these ideas into reality needs to be developed further. Misunderstandings in work relationships seem common here, perhaps due to a tendency of starting projects but then not finishing them. If these individuals would stick to the challenge of bringing others together to cooperate in some undertaking, and stay with it until completed, then great personal fulfillment could be attained. Another personal challenge lies in the ability to heal first themselves, then others, especially through diet and nutrition. Once accomplished, they have the gift to help others in this same area.

The Moon's North Node located near the midpoints of the angles is a most critical placement. Natural conflicts between the ego's desire and one's spiritual nature or development may exist, and the native may tend to have a life of struggle on these personal, inner planes. The individual may be put into a position of having to make several critical choices in this lifetime, choices which may relate to personal mismanagement of relationships in prior incarnations. The choices involve self-sacrifice of the ego's desires, or the realization of these self-centered desires on one hand, with a life of personal conflicts in relationships on the other hand. Not until the will, which tends to be very self-centered, is loosened up to allow a spiritual direction to take place in the life, can the native resolve the inner battle "earned" for this lifetime. Once resolved though, the native will not only experience a lasting success concerning this life's objectives, but may also find that personal relationships become an asset and not a detriment toward this end.

The Moon's North Node located near the Ascendant-I. C. Midpoint (Second House): The specific challenge is to determine one's personal values and priorities at all given points of transformation in this lifetime. The natural conflict involves one's personal ego opposing one's innate spiritual understanding. Until resolved, the native may attract partners with whom there is very little in common, who seem to confuse the native's self-concept, and who become the source of great inner turmoil. Relationships, even marriage, become filled with erratic changes and happenings until one's values are firmly established along the lines of their innate spiritual insight.

The Moon's North Node located near the I. C.-Descendant Midpoint (Fifth House): The specific challenge is for the native to determine exactly what kinds of qualities he or she would like to develop in this lifetime – goals of personal characteristics, i.e. to become kind, loving, confident, etc. Once these are determined, then the challenge is to constantly work on maintaining these without letting life's circumstances undo such development. The natural conflict is between one's spiritual understanding and the nature of relationships the native enters into with others – others who seem oftentimes to contradict the native's spiritual direction. If the native lets these relationships and romances impede the development of certain personal characteristics, then the most bizarre things may begin to happen. The native may begin acting very strangely, not knowing exactly what is wrong. A reliance on drugs, alcohol and/or sex becomes common in these addictive types. Life may become very erratic: first great success, then great loss. Even the personality may become split – a Jekyll and Hyde reaction. The key here is to either not let relationships interfere with the life process, or to choose partners who are complimentary to the native's own inner longings. Once this is done, then great success of a lasting nature is possible.

The Moon's North Node located near the Descendant-Midheaven Midpoint (Eighth House): The specific challenge is to assist others in the development of their personal values and direction in life. The natural conflict is between an understanding of one's own spiritual direction involving other people – a spiritual life objective – and the types of relationships entered into. A sense of destiny seems strong here, and if pursued in relationship to humankind, great success may be experienced. But oftentimes early experiences in relationships with others confuse this drive and results in a frustrated individual who may also act very bizarre at times. These individuals are oftentimes blessed with supranormal gifts, like healing and prophesy. But just as often they are afflicted with complex and unusual phobias, like feeling that they are possessed by some unknown, uncontrollable force. Those with this placement tend to be very intense and often experience early tragedies in life. Rejection from others may be very hard to cope with. Oftentimes there is fanaticism about matters pertaining to death (even to the point of attracting gangsters and criminals into the life). These characteristics, incidentally, are found in the Ascendant-I. C. midpoint types too, particularly concerning uncontrollable urges and feelings of possession by outside forces. When success comes close, these individuals frequently get frightened. However once the path of working in the world is accepted and pursued, and not frustrated through binds in relationships with others, then the conflict is resolved and success is possible (even probable).

The Moon's North Node Located near the Midheaven-Ascendant Midpoint (Eleventh House): The specific challenge is to define some great goal and then attain it in the outer world. The natural conflict is between attaining this objective and succumbing to one's self-centered, egotistical desires. The individual must be careful not to become too unrealistic in either their life's objectives or relationships entered into which they "think" are ideal. A crisis always seems to arise at one point in the life between a relationship and one's work. The source of this conflict is seldom ever determined (probably stems from a past life action). At this point, the native stands to lose everything by being foolish and idealistic (oftentimes in love with the "wrong kind" of person), but usually pulls out of it at the last minute (especially if there is a patient, understanding person to help). The Moon's North Node located on this midpoint does not seem quite as difficult as the others, and once the conflict is resolved, the success is just as great as in other cases.

Pre-Natal Eclipse Points and Generational Identity

The solar eclipse which precedes one's birth is known as the "prenatal eclipse point" of the natal horoscope. Great meaning has been ascribed to this point in recent astrological thought, but in truth this point is very close to one's natal North or South Node position. Since this subject matter has received little attention in the writing of astrological thought until very recently, one might consider the "pre-natal eclipse point" as significant as the natal placement of the Moon's Nodes.

One might consider the natal position of one's nodes, or pre-natal eclipse point, as relating to one's **generational identity**. It denotes how (by sign and aspect to other planets) and where (by house) one may tie into the generation into which he or she has been born. Each soul is part of a generation. Each soul has identified with various generations in past lives. What he or she contributes to that generation, or receives from that generation (both in the past and in the present) is reflected in the natal position of the North Node (and to some extent, the South Node). A Lunar North Node in the sign of Aries, for instance, relates to a lifetime of exploring and discovering new things pertinent to one's generation. It suggests an innovator, or one whose generation was innovative. One comes from a generation that was known for its introduction of "new things, new thoughts," to its society. As such, in this lifetime one gravitates to that part of its generation that is on the cutting edge of new discoveries, or explorations. In Taurus it might signify a soul who closely identified with a generation oriented toward business or economics, the accumulation of wealth, or at least the growth of resources (perhaps natural resources, as in cultivating the land). In Gemini, it might signify one who was associated with the intellectual development of a generation, and even this lifetime is attracted to the segment of one's generation that is responsible for shaping thought which others will identify as unique to that generation. The aspects formed by the Moon's Nodes to natal planets are perhaps even more important than the signs themselves. These aspecting planets describe the unique character and talent the individual may lend to the identification of one's generation. For example, a Node in aspect to Neptune will have the potential of lending a spiritual or creative interpretation to one's generation. An aspect to Uranus may denote one who adds a very ingenious and inventive quality to one's generational identity.

It may be helpful to think of the Moon's North Node as one's reference group model. Where it is posited natally describes how the soul may identify with its generation. There need not be an actual, physical "group" which one associates with, but rather a "model" one ascribes to. A North Node in Leo may mean one identifies with the leaders of his or her generation; in Sagittarius, perhaps one identifies with the novelists or philosophers of his or her generation, and in Pisces, perhaps to the poets or musicians. As such one is likely to attract others who exhibit these qualities of "reference group identification" particularly when a similar planet is involved in aspect. For example, a North Node in Gemini will identify with the intellectual parts of his or her generation even more so if the Node aspects Mercury. If it also aspects Neptune, then the quality of spiritual or creative thought may shape the direction greatly, i.e. spiritual intellectualism, or music with thought. If in aspect to Uranus, then the attraction to intellectual thought takes on a quality of the unconventional, or even the "new age." In aspect to Pluto one might be attracted toward the psychological or occult thought.

CHAPTER FIFTEEN

Age Arcs: A Time to Reap What Has Been Sown

The Law of Retribution, or karma, is cyclic in nature. Once put into motion, this law will occur again and again, at regular intervals, and in varying degrees of intensity, until the cycle is completed. Completion occurs after there is illumination, or revelation, as to the cause of the cycle. Once the cause is understood, and the dynamics behind the cause are altered (i.e. corrected so as to be in harmony with Spirit or the longing of the soul), the cycle ends. The forces (behaviors, intentions) which supported such a cyclic pattern are eliminated, and in their place are new reactions, different and more conscientious responses to the same stimuli. Hence a new script is written, and if the soul is fortunate, the new pattern will be one that is more conducive to its evolvement, and less destructive, or at least less distractive than the previous one.

The matter of timing these cyclic occurrences is a property unique to the subject of astrology. Astrology is the study of planetary cycles, and their corresponding relationship to human activity. There are many cycles in astrology, all of different lengths of time. Just as there are different lengths of time between cycles, there are also different degrees of strength in various cycles. For example, a transit to natal Venus from Uranus will take a longer time and exhibit a more pronounced effect than a transit to natal Venus from Mars.

Transits are one way in which a soul's cycles may be measured. Another is by means of progressions. A third is by age arcs. There are others, but these three means will be the subject for this discussion in the model of Evolutionary Astrology.

Each natal planet represents a unique principle, or lesson for the soul. As such, each planet also represents people and/or circumstances which symbolize the meaning of that lesson or principle. When a transiting or progressed planet aspects each planet, it "times" the cycle of that natal planet. That is, the soul will undergo a lesson, or be challenged with a principle symbolized by a natal planet whenever another planet transits or progresses in aspect to it. The natal planet is the principle or the lesson which the soul is undergoing. But the soul does not undergo this lesson all the time – the lessons come up in rhythmic cycles, depending upon which planet is in transit or progression.

That is not all. The lessons or principles signified by the natal planets are subject to different circumstances under which they are presented. The principle of forgiveness may be just as applicable in a marriage as in a friendship or business arrangement. The conditions, circumstances, or people that bring forth the challenge to learn the principle are denoted by the other planet **in transit or progressed aspect** to the natal planet. In other words, the transiting or progressed planet times, and describes, the condition or person coming into the soul's life. The natal planet being aspected describes the principle or lesson the soul is called forth to meet. How the individual responds to this challenge determines future cycles involving the same natal planet. As a corollary, the individual's responses also determine the astrological placement of that natal planet in the horoscopes of future lifetimes.

The scope of this book will not encompass the meaning of all transiting and progressed planets to all natal planets and angles. Suffice it to say that the most important ones involve transits of the power planets – Saturn, Uranus, Neptune and Pluto – to natal placements. That is because these cycles are the longest, and the corollary here is: the longer a cycle, the more powerful its effect is likely to be when it comes due.

Besides transits of power planets, there are other ways to time cycles of importance. One of these is a technique known as **age arcs**. Every planet is located in a specific degree of a particular sign of the tropical zodiac. There are 30° to each sign. In the technique of age arcs, every degree represents a corresponding year of life, and since there are 30° to a sign, this age arc repeats in 30-year sequences. To illustrate, assume a natal Venus is 18° of any sign. The technique of age arcs postulates that at age 18, 48 and 78 the individual will undergo an experience that can be described by the symbolism of Venus, i.e., marriage, love, partnership, birth of a daughter, granddaughter, etc.

Why should such events arise at these times in an individual's life? Because that is the time in which the cycle involving these planets is due, according to the rhythmic nature of the universe and the karma of that soul who initiated that cycle. Each planet's degree designates a particular year of life in which a circumstance will likely arise, according to the nature of the planet. This cycle will repeat in approximate 30-year intervals. Furthermore each period represents an opportunity to understand a universal principle inherent in that planet's symbolism.

To determine the age arcs of each planet and angle, simply take the degree of each and let them correspond to the same number of years of life. Add 30 and 60 years to each to see when they will repeat.

Let's examine the possibilities of various age arcs.

Sun: a time in which the soul may experience recognition and even fame. It is an opportunity to experience success in one's goals and to exhibit great vitality and radiance. It is a time to come into one's own, so to speak. In a woman's life, it represents a meeting with a significant man. It may represent the birth of a son, or if very young, birth of a sibling. This person, or persons, may be very significant in one's personal unfoldment. The lessons to learn are leadership and unity. The temptations to avoid are pride and a sense of superiority.

Ascendant/Descendant: a time in which the soul may change residence and/or form a partnership. It may also time a health crisis or significant change in appearance. The choices one makes now are critical. Ultimately the choice is between the self only with regard to itself, or with an understanding of its higher purpose in life. The question is: where is the attention centered? Is it upon itself, or upon some thing or some one higher than itself? The people one meets will either help the soul to understand this challenge or tempt the soul away from the correct choice. It is a time of temptation, and one needs to be clear on his or her intentions, as well as life purpose. The decisions at this time often determine the path one takes for some time to come. The effects of the decision may be noted on the physical level, i.e. good or bad health.

Midheaven/I. C.: a time when the soul has an opportunity to understand its unique calling in life; a time of personal revelation. Again the soul has a choice: to meet the challenge of its real calling in life, or pass it by. The opportunities come about through significant people who enter the life. They are, in a sense, one's teachers or guides. Through their input the individual is able to come into contact with the essence of its soul. There is an intuitive sense of the "right path" to take. The decisions made at this time also influence the crux of the individual's life for many years to come.

Moon: a time in which the soul deals with family and/or domestic issues. It may be a time of changing residence, or one's parents or children move. The period may test the bond of family love and loyalty. In a man's life it may signify the meeting or union with a significant female. If a child is born, it is likely to be a daughter. The lessons to be learned are those of unconditional love, caring and nurturing, and the importance of loyalty in forming bonds of real intimacy. The temptations to be avoided are relationships of attachment and dependency that ultimately end up as hurting either the individual, or another with whom the individual formed a bond (bind) . In this case, love could turn to hurt, which could then turn to hatred. The responsibility of cultivating a close and intimate relationship, with its consequent rewards and risks (pain), are challenges for the soul to master at this time.

Mercury: a time significant to one's mental development. During one's youth it may correspond to an event in school, such as learning a particular subject (i.e. mathematics, science, language, etc.) or performing some special creative or intellectual act (i.e. writing). Later on it might correspond to a unique work project, or new role at work, possibly even a new job. It could also coincide with the birth of a sibling, birth of a child, or ownership of a new pet. If a child is born, that child might be exceptionally intelligent (same is true with a sibling or grandchild). There is a possibility that a significant helper or assistant enters the life now. One of the key principles to be learned is that of **service**. Therefore the native meets with someone who either provides a valuable service, or finds value in the service which the native him/herself provides. It is also possible that the native develops a specialized skill or undertakes a specialized training that has a marked effect upon the life from this point onwards. If there is writing ability, a book may be completed under this cycle. The opportunity is to develop a skill, or to express some special mental aptitude. Failure to take advantage of this opportune cycle might result instead in an experience of physical discomfort, particularly to the respiratory area (failure to communicate effectively), or professional upsetment (such as one's assistant resigning or quitting). One's karma has to do with having decided to act in a cooperative manner, having given value to intellectual and mental development, and having seen the importance in constructive communication with others (as opposed to critical communication).

Venus: a time of love and compatibility. During this period one meets potential mates, usually romantic, but sometimes as in business partnerships. It is a time of marriage, or thoughts of long-lasting partnerships. It may also correspond to the birth of a daughter or granddaughter, or if very young, perhaps a sister. The principle to be learned is that of shared responsibilities, sacrifice, and forgiveness. It is also an opportunity to learn the value of harmony in order to live happily with another. Unwillingness to compromise, share, and even sacrifice for the purpose of harmony with another may result in a pattern of unfulfilled love relationships.

Mars: a time of starting new projects, undergoing accidents or injury, and possibly struggling with enemies. The people one meets who are significant to the soul's growth are highly competitive or even argumentative types. They may threaten the native. They may be or become the native's enemy or opponent. Yet they serve a purpose: to stimulate the native to develop a set of principles he or she is willing to defend (fight for). One's beliefs and morals may be critically formed now, and this may be due to a circumstance which may be supportive or antagonistic. How is one supposed to act in a situation where he or she is being attacked? The key principle is one of **right action**. One is to examine the intent behind all actions, to observe and witness the arousal of anger before undertaking action. Once action is undertaken it must not be designed to cause harm to another, or to foster one's own gain at the expense or harm of another. Having one's principles and beliefs challenged serves a purpose to create and develop strength and courage, but it is not to fall to the temptation of desiring to annihilate or destroy the person who offers the challenge. Instead one is to be grateful for the entrance of the person who issues the challenge, for without that person the soul may miss an opportunity to learn about strength and courage. Failure to learn this lesson may set into motion a Mars cycle of anger, upset, rash and impulsive reactions to others who challenge, and ultimately accidents and separations.

Mars may also be an experience of passion, particularly sexual. It may also correspond to the birth of a brother, son or grandson. Each of these people are significant in understanding the karma of one's soul. They enter the life to help the soul understand the principles inherent in the symbolism of Mars.

Jupiter: a time of growth, happiness and success. During this cycle one has the opportunity to become part of a social circle, a group. One also has an opportunity to expand his or her understanding of life, as this period may be philosophic in nature. In all activities, whether work, social, or domestic, there is the opportunity to expand. Financially one might expand greatly. It furthermore represents opportunities to travel and enhance one's education. Sometimes the two come together: one travels to learn (i.e. goes away to college out of the city of residence). The people who enter one's life now tend to be friendly, sociable, and oftentimes end up being the native's new "best friend." It may also signify an important event with a grandparent, or grandchild. A child born during this cycle will tend to be outgoing, friendly and happy in nature. The principles one is to experience now deal with charity, wisdom and generosity. As one enters a "giving" cycle, and learns the value of such, one receives from others the same. This cycle brings about joy and happiness, a sense of freedom and upliftment. Hope springs forth, and one behaves very humanely. Failure to learn this lesson may set up a script of hoarding and self-indulgence. The temptation is to exaggerate the truth, and the native may find it difficult to ever experience true friendship with others. Physically a weight problem could now develop. More importantly the native might have missed the opportunity to develop wisdom and friendship.

Saturn: a time when the soul is asked to account for things done, perhaps a time of judgement. There are a number of conditions that could arise under this cycle of accounting and responsibility: there could be a loss (financial, relationship and/or self-esteem), an apparent failure of a project, illness, difficulty with authorities or government. Positively it could represent a period of completing goals, major accomplishments, rewards for integrity and behavior with honor. The people one tends to meet during this cycle are serious and authoritative types, task masters who are demanding and perhaps even critical. Concerns for one's father or father-figures may arise (perhaps due to health or professional circumstances). A child or grandchild born during this cycle will tend to be male, and a serious, hard working soul. The principles one is learning from these events and people entering the life are honesty, integrity, discipline and responsibility. Where one has acted irresponsibly or without integrity, conditions arise for which one must now account, and it could be embarrassing. Where one has acted responsibly and with honor, there is reward and new responsibilities entrusted. One of the most important responsibilities is to one's own physical vehicle. If one has failed to care for the body properly, then the effects of stress may unfold, causing serious illness and perhaps pain. One may be forced to follow a disciplined health program in order to correct previous patterns. In the process of self-examination, one develops new rules for life conduct. Such understanding and consequent discipline allows the soul to overcome karmic scripts previously in force. Ultimately one understands that he/she is responsible for these conditions, and no one else is to blame. Failure to come to this understanding could result in more complex and difficult conditions involving future Saturn cycles.

Uranus: a time of enlightenment and breaking away from old patterns; a change of lifestyle; an awakening; a divorce or attraction to someone or something new. During this cycle one typically sees life differently. Circumstances of a most surprising and unusual nature arise. An offer for new work, sudden loss of work, new interests, or new people finding the native suddenly interesting may all transpire. One's likes and dislikes suddenly change. There may be a strong urge for freedom, a desire to leave behind a certain lifestyle and embark upon another. The power of attraction and charisma may be quite strong. There is the sense of discovery, and a desire to share this enlightenment with others. The people entering one's life may be very remarkable and unusual types, very magnetic and interesting in their thought. They may have an inspirational effect, and in some way help the individual to see life in a different manner. This may be positive or negative, depending upon the individual's understanding of natural law. The principle brought to light now is one of seeking truth through higher knowledge; an opportunity to make a spiritual breakthrough. The opportunity is to experience an enlightenment that may quicken the soul's journey back to wholeness, back to Spirit. This quickening of understanding may present problems if there are responsibilities to others involved, and particularly others who do not understand the process of change the individual is undergoing. These others may resist, putting the native in a conflict: to pursue this new enlightenment and quest for freedom against the resistance of others for whom there is a responsibility, or forfeit the opportunity and continue in one's pattern? Sometimes divorce results; sometimes families uproot and move to another community with a sense of excitement and new adventure. A degree of risk is involved, and if the native's pursuit is toward actualizing the understanding of truth, then a pattern previously shrouded in fear may be transcended. New patterns which arise depend upon the effect these decisions have upon others in the native's life. Children born during this cycle may be quite remarkable and in possession of an unusual talent. One other matter that may unfold during this period: the individual may come into contact with unusual and unconventional subjects, like astrology. These subjects could have a powerful and life-altering effect upon the individual's life pattern.

Neptune: a time of infatuation, imagination, pleasure, creative activity, deception and/or betrayal. Conditions arise that appear to be wonderful, even glamorous. However the reality may not be consistent with the appearance. This cycle may be favorable for pleasurable travel, such as a significant vacation during which one learns the value of a world of beauty, or inner peace and relaxation. It may be a time of a spiritual deepening, a religious experience, an outpouring of compassion and love for another. Significant events involving water (i.e. oceans, lakes or river) may take place. The people one meets may reflect these paradoxes: they may at first appear very trustworthy and eager to help, even sacrifice, for the native's benefit. However in time the native may learn that these people did not do what was promised. In fact they may betray and disappoint the native. The native may experience a lie, a deception, or may even be the party guilty of such an act. In any event, there may be a hurt, or disappointment, a disillusionment. During this cycle the soul is undergoing lessons in the value of trust and faith. There is also a lesson in forgiveness and compassion toward those who disappoint the native. It is important for one to act with trust and openness in dealings with others, otherwise he or she may be accused of wrongdoings, and the result could be damaging or embarrassing to one's reputation. If one is creative, it may be a time of completing an imaginative effort, like writing or producing a song, movie, or book. One may make great strides in the fields of film, photography, acting, or music. Strong feelings in love may also arise, and again the native must be aware of the reality versus the illusion of entering such relationships. Children born at this time may either be female and/or very imaginative in thought.

Pluto: a time in which the soul deals with death or the concept of termination; an experience in rejection or possibly transformation; a rebirth; a time of insight and discovery. Conditions arise which force an end to a significant matter. These may come in the form of death, or a threat to one's well being (physically or professionally). One may be exposed to deeper studies during this cycle, such as the occult, magic, psychology or some other academic pursuit dealing with the mysteries of life. Powerful people enter one's life, and these people are either supportive or rejecting of the native, depending upon the native's karma involving prior use of power. The opportunity is to see the need to make or accept a change in one's life, and in so doing, undergo a personal transformation. The process may become one of self-realization, and consequently one of empowerment. Symbolically one experiences a death in life. Some cycle has come to an end. Will the native accept this and commence a personal or spiritual rebirth? Or will the native simply move on to another situation, unchanged within him or herself? If the latter, then the pattern will arise again: there will be other power plays, other rejections, and other changes of scenes but all with the same plot and ending. The opportunity is to renew the self, to heal the soul. Any thoughts of vengeance or hateful resentment will only complicate the pattern in the future. Ultimately there must be acceptance and healing, and this comes about through deeper understanding of one's motives and patterns, and willingness to change them.

Progressions of the Sun and Angles: More Reaping

The principles inherent in age arcs are very similar to those of progressions involving the Sun and angles. Like age arcs, progressions to natal planets from the Sun and angles take place in approximately 30-year intervals from the date of the first occurrence.

The technique is simple. In the case of the progressed Sun, simply determine how many degrees forward in the zodiac the Sun must move to reach the same degree number of the planet. That will correspond to the number of years in life for the first major aspect between progressed Sun and natal planet. The same calculation may be applied to the progressed Midheaven/I. C.: simply determine how many degrees forward the natal Midheaven must move in the zodiac to reach the same degree number as a natal planet, and assume that corresponds to the age when the Midheaven/I. C. will progress to an aspect of that natal planet. For example, assume that natal Sun or Midheaven is 20° Gemini. Assume natal Venus is 4° Pisces. How many degrees forward does the 20° Gemini have to go to reach 4° of the next sign? The answer is 14°. Thus, with the rule that one degree is equal to one year of life, it may be assumed that at the approximate ages of 14, 44, and 74 the individual will undergo a Venus cycle. The nature of this cycle is similar to that described under the Venus section of age arcs. In the calculation, always remember to *add* the number of degrees to the natal Sun or natal Midheaven that it would take for each to reach the same degree of the natal planet.

There are some variations in both the interpretation and calculations between progressions and age arcs. For example, as one progresses the Midheaven/I. C. or the Sun forward through the zodiac, it will form different types of aspects to the same planet. Age arcs form no aspects whatsoever. To illustrate, use the previous example of a natal Sun or Midheaven at 20° and a natal Venus at 4° Pisces. At age

14, the Gemini will progress to 4° Cancer, which is a trine aspect to Pisces; at age 44 it will progress to 4° Leo, which is a quincunx; and at age 74 it will progress to 4° Virgo, which is an opposition. Although each age will likely coincide with a karmic cycle involving the principle of Venus, the nature of the cycle will be somewhat different because of the different aspects of each age. At age 14, the trine may be very wonderful. Perhaps it signifies one's first love experience. At age 44, the aspect is a quincunx. Perhaps an experience in love requires a more difficult adjustment, a major sacrifice, in order to experience most fully its potential reward. At age 74, the aspect is an opposition. Perhaps there is a difficult situation involving one's partner at this time. In all cases the soul is called upon to learn the lesson inherent in Venus: to share, sacrifice, and forgive, to be supportive and compatible.

The actual ages in which these progressions transpire may be less and less accurate as the years go by. The Sun does not move (progress) exactly at the rate of 1° per year, nor does the Midheaven or I. C.. In some cases they progress slightly faster, but in more cases they progress slightly slower than 1° per year. For these adjustments one requires an emphemeris. Even more accurate may be the use of a computer program which can accurately calculate a progressed Sun or angle. This is certainly true in the case of progressing the Ascendant/ Descendant axis. Their movement is very irregular, sometimes progressing as much as 2° per year, or less than 1° every two years. The average rate of progression is close to 1° per year, so even without a computer program, or emphemeris, one can still approximate those periods when the soul undergoes the consequences of karmic cycles initiated in prior lifetimes, according to the principles inherent in each planet.

Beneath these cycles the soul is challenged to understand why these circumstances, and why these people, enter into the life. In the world of maya, the outer world of illusion that "this" is reality, these circumstances and these people seem to unfold as if by coincidence. Evolutionary Astrology postulates the law of synchronisty: nothing occurs by happenstance. Everything that unfolds is part of a cyclic process, and one's responses and reactions (i.e. choices) to those events determine the quality of that script in future cyclic unfoldments. People are not just objects entering one's path. They are drawn into one's path as a result of one's actions and reactions. They are drawn into one's life because they represent or symbolize a particular principle that soul is working on. Through the people one attracts, a soul is provided an opportunity to learn something essential about its own journey. The planets are real, but more importantly they are symbols.

The people are real but more importantly they are symbols. The events are real but they are more importantly symbols. The symbols are Real because they effect the development of the Real Self. They facilitate the merger of the personality with the soul, and each degree of merging is accompanied by an experience of the soul merging with Spirit. As the symbols are understood, the boundaries separating the soul and Spirit begin to dissolve. There is an outpouring of creative force, and a new script is created, a new form is birthed. Instead of seeing and living according to the apparent differences between each living entity, this renewed soul chooses to see and live instead according to the principles and qualities which are alike with each soul. In the beginning, God made man in His image. That is to say that the Spirit of creative force is the same within each soul. Yet it is also true that man has made God in his image, but unlike God who has One image, man reflects a myriad of images which are dualistic and even separative in nature. Ultimately man, through the ego's drive toward individuality, is alienated and alone, and the freedom he/she seeks is at last only an escape from this loneliness. Ultimately such a leap in understanding requires an equal leap in faith.

CHAPTER SIXTEEN

Power Over the Angles Part One: Crisis in Consciousness

"Faith is a gift. The gift may be withdrawn, as the gifts of sight and hearing may be taken away." [17]

Every soul reaches a crossroads at various points along its journey through life. Sometimes these crossroads are precipitated by unusual and critical external events. Sometimes they are not precipitated by any specific external events, but rather the result of a long internal process that has finally made its way up into one's consciousness. Regardless of the mode by which the crossroads came into being, the soul is confronted with a choice of such great proportions that the balance of the rest of one's life is at stake. To choose one over the other, or to choose not to make a choice, determines a certain course that will mark the future character of the lifetime. From this choice, or lack of choice, there is no turning back. With this choice comes opportunity, but the opportunity is not without risk of loss. It is the value of that opportunity, as well as the value of that which may be lost, that the soul must and does measure during these periods.

The opportunity, whether understood or not at the time, is to evolve.

In the previous chapter, the subject of age arcs and progressions of the Sun and angles were discussed. For the most part these involved cycles related to the natal planets. Each planet is like a lesson. They are symbols of various experiences and people one encounters along the

[17]Morris West, *Lazarus* (New York, St. Marten's Press, 1990).

road to selfhood. These planets symbolize principles which the soul needs to master in order to transcend karmic patterns currently in effect. Each planet is a lesson, and all planets are part of a school – a school of the soul's evolution. In this sense the planets are the parts, the Sun is the whole. Furthermore the planets are the "other people" in one's life. The angles are the gateway to the soul and consciousness itself. When the Sun or angles progress to the natal planets, they refer to the people the soul encounters, and the external conditions the soul experiences. From these conditions and people the soul learns parts of the whole.

But at what times do these parts all come together and give the soul a glimpse of the greater whole? When does the soul undergo such an experience that everything seems integrated? At what point is the potential for a breakthrough in consciousness so great that the soul sees the interconnectedness of it all?

The answer to these questions may lie in the relationship of the power planets (as transits) to one's natal angles, and midpoints of those angles.

In the chapter on "The Abilities and Power of the Soul," the analogy was presented wherein the soul was on a journey. At one point in time the soul chose to separate itself from Spirit (i.e. leaving the Garden of Eden), and began a quest in which its first task was to enhance its very own survival. For this the soul required certain talents, or abilities. These were indicated by the presence of the planets Mercury, Venus, Mars and Jupiter near natal angles.

However at a certain point along this long journey, the soul realizes that no matter how well it enhances its survival, something is missing. There is a physical life, but it is not full, it is not whole. Something is empty and it cannot be measured in physical terms, or needs of the physical vehicle. There is a lack of faith, or closeness to a spiritual reality. There is a lack of meaning to the life, an absence of purpose, and in this void there is loneliness and despair.

At this point there is a crisis in consciousness. All the success in the world does not bring about inner peace, contentment, fulfillment. All the fame, recognition and material success in the world does not fill the void of emptiness, or meaninglessness to one's efforts. At this point the soul is presented an opportunity: an opportunity to come back, to return to that from which it was created. But first it must believe that such a possibility exists. There is no proof in physical sciences that such a thing exists. It requires the emergence of faith, and a belief based upon principles that cannot be measured in the physical world. Once that faith is established, personal experiences unfold (particularly of an inner nature) that cannot easily be shared with others who have not experienced something similar. There is not turning back.

But what choice is made here? Faith is not a choice, it is a gift. If not used, or if misused, it may fade away. The choice is in the form of a **commitment**, based upon an **understanding**. The commitment is to return to Spirit, to rediscover the self, to return to the home which, on some level, the soul knows it has never left. It just forgot. It just built another home in its place, but that home was built upon impermanence. At this point in time, the conscious mind may make the choice that allows the soul to return, to re-discover, that from which it came. In this sense, the choice is made to **transcend** the limitations of the outer and physical world, known as maya.

The journey back home, the journey of transcendence, requires authentic empowerment. Hence the planets of power, signified by Saturn (the power of control), Uranus (the power of attraction), Neptune (the power of vision), and Pluto (the power to transform). These planets located near an angle, and possibly an angular midpoint, may indicate a soul who has begun this journey of transcendence. It may indicate a soul who has developed a certain degree of empowerment. **Yet all souls have the opportunity in a given lifetime to be the recipient of such a choice, and to receive such an empowerment. These choices may come along during those times when the planets of power (Saturn, Uranus, Neptune and/or Pluto) transit over a natal angle, and possibly even an angular midpoint.**

Why the angles and not the natal planets? Because the planets are the "others" in one's life. They represent the karma of identities. The angles are the fastest moving points of the horoscope. Their cycle is based upon the movement of the Earth on its own axis. They are the points that relate to the individual, the self. They are the framework of one's unique interpretation of reality. Only at those points can one alter that framework of reality, or its understanding of reality. The planets may indicate the experiences, but the interpretation and importance of each experience is translated via the individual's own reference of reality, or through the structure (or glasses) of the angles. Two people may see the same piece of art work and have two totally different reactions to it. The frame of reference is the difference, not the form of the experience.

The first step toward authentic empowerment is symbolized by the planet Saturn. It represents the empowerment of control, most notably self-control. Such control comes about from rigorous discipline, and adherence to a certain code or rules one has chosen to accept for itself. At the root of control is responsibility—responsibility for one's acts and the intentions behind them. Thus when Saturn crosses an angle (or a planet), one is forced to account for what one has done. Herein lies the basis for responsibility. The temptation is to project blame onto others when there is fear of a punishment as a consequence to one's action. This is the choice: to accept responsibility for one's journey, which involves "setting the record straight regarding one's past sins", or avoiding the challenge and thereby live a life of guilt and denial. By accepting responsibility, one is making a commitment to a higher principle, and willing to accept the risk of loss (apparent loss). One commits to truth. In the words of Morris West, from his book *Lazarus*: **"He will always tell the truth, because it is his master, not himself, who must bear the consequences."**[18]

In astrology, Saturn represents the principle of authority. When an individual reaches a crossroads and decides upon a path of transcendence, he/she bows to an awareness of a higher authority. This begins the process of seeking to understand higher law, or God's law, or natural law. The first law is: "as you sow, so shall ye reap," which is another form of the Law of Retribution, or karma. Hence responsibility for one's actions is the first to be understood, and the first to be dealt with.

Saturn transiting over an angle, or an angular midpoint, presents these crises or opportunities in consciousness at regular intervals of approximately 29 years. Eight subcycles unfold within this greater cycle, or one subcycle approximately every 3.6 years. That is, approximately every 3.6 years Saturn will transit over an angle or an angular midpoint. Every 29 years it will cross the same angle or angular midpoint. With each crossing there is a crisis. With each crossing there is an opportunity. With each crossing, one's framework of reality is challenged. Yet each angle and each angular midpoint symbolizes a different aspect of authentic empowerment, a different focus upon the frame of reference of one's reality. Each crossing represents another level of responsibility and challenge to one's commitment to transcend the universal and cyclic law of karma, particularly that part which puts the soul in bondage, and separates the personality from counsel with the soul.

To more fully grasp the significance of Saturn transiting through the horoscope, it is necessary to integrate the principles outlined in the earlier chapters, specifically the relationship of the Sun and Earth as denoted by the natural order of the day. The first division studied was that which separates night from day, dark from light. In the natural order of the day, the section of the horoscope below the horizon represented night, or dark (houses 1–6). The Sun is in this section of the horoscope every day between sunset and sunrise (night time). The symbolism of the lower section of the horoscope is thus yin. It is reflective and receptive. It is one's inner world, where one interprets the meaning of his or her experiences. During the period in which Saturn transits in the lower half of one's horoscope (a period which lasts 14–15 years), the soul asks the conscious mind to study itself, to develop a set of principles by which it can best judge itself. During this period one has an opportunity to come to grips with oneself, to define and understand the needs of the soul. It is by its very nature an introspective and reflective period, when one must account to one's self for what one is.

The most critical point of all is the I. C. itself, the lowest point in the natal horoscope. In this degree and minute is symbolized the essence of the soul, the core of the being. At this point, symbolic of the conception moment and the soul's "first awareness" that it will soon reincarnate, the soul is closest to Spirit. At the point symbolic of midnight, or darkest hour, or greatest mystery, there is nothing other than self. The awareness of "other than self" has not yet commenced. In the moment of greatest darkness there is union, a sense of oneness or nothingness, at least nothing other than self. At the I. C. one is as close to Spirit, or God, or Higher Self, as one can be. Before that point, and following that point, there is a degree of light, and hence duality. But at the I. C., there is no duality, no ego, no relationship to that outside of the self.

Thus when **Saturn transits over the natal I. C.** there is apt to be a **crisis in faith**. An accounting begins of the whole life, at least the life up until that point in time. The critical issue here is: how far has the personality separated from the soul? How strong has the wall been built? How willing is the individual to tear it down in order to begin the process of re-discovering the self, of re-connecting with the needs of the soul?

In a symbolic sense, this may be the soul's "darkest hour." It is also possible that this is the soul's "greatest hour", for a choice may now be made to accept the gift of faith. The acceptance or rejection of this gift determines which path the soul takes in life: a path of transcendence or a path of increasing complexities and resultant patterns which the ego (personality) is obligated to defend. The latter choice drains more and more of the life force out of the individual as life goes on.

As in all significant Saturn transits, there are matters of responsibility and commitment which challenge the individual. The ultimate responsibility is to one's soul. What are the needs of the soul at this time? It is a time to be alone and listen to one's heart, not one's head. What feels right? When considering one's choices, it may be helpful to take inventory of how one feels given each potential choice. Which cause stress, and which produces a sense of release from tension?

The individual is now asked to make an accounting of what one has done. The choices made at this time will require another accounting. Saturn can only function at its best when dealing with the truth, and with higher law. Each soul has a code of ethics, a sense of right and wrong, which affects one's behavior. Is one acting according to these principles now? Has one been acting in accordance with these principles up until now? If not, then complications have arisen, and feelings of guilt and perhaps shame are present. The ego wants to defend these, and will flood the mind with explanations, rationalizations and justifications. The soul wants redemption, wants to confess and deal with the truth, and begin with a clean slate. However to do so is threatening to the ego. It means a loss, most certainly a loss of control. However the control it loses is only external control; the power it fears it will lose is only external power. External control and external power are part of the world of maya, or illusion, which the ego has constructed in order to justify its own existence.

The soul now has an opportunity to cultivate authentic power. The conscious mind now has an opportunity to understand deeper aspects of its being. It now has an opportunity to transform a script, and to create a new karmic script governed by the Law of Retribution. It does, however, require a leap in faith. It requires a risk of loss to things which the ego values. It requires a commitment to "clean the slate and begin anew", which itself may require a renunciation of sorts, at least a renunciation of certain behaviors and intentions behind those behaviors.

In many cases events arise which precipitate this inner crisis. It may be the loss of a parent or conflict with an authority. It may come in the form of a threat to one's work, or even a health crisis. Regardless of whether it is precipitated by an outer event, or comes about through a long internal process is unimportant (though perhaps interesting). What is important is the sense of responsibility the individual undertakes with regard to the care of its soul, and the strength of the commitment it makes to act in accordance with this set of new principles, or higher law. In a sense, it depends upon one's willingness to accept the gift of faith which is now being offered.

The level of that faith is tested again in about 3-1/2 years, or as **Saturn transits over the midpoint between the I. C. and Descendant.** Saturn is now moving "up" the chart, and the essence of the soul has recently been tested (at the I. C.). The consequences of decisions made as Saturn transited the I. C. are coming to bear fruit at the angular midpoint, located somewhere in the fifth house. Saturn is now firmly implanted in the fourth quadrant of Evolutionary Astrology's model (i.e. houses 4–6). It is still in the darkness hemisphere, but it is moving up to the sunset point, or Descendant, which begins the world of light, or form. Quadrant four is the most mysterious or mystical of all quadrants. As such the entire period in which Saturn moves from the I. C. to the Descendant is likely to be a spiritual one, a period in which the individual's level of faith is apt to be tested again and again. It is the quadrant dealing with one's greatest fears.

One of the more significant fears is likely to be confronted when Saturn transits over this angular midpoint. This midpoint brings into play the forces of the soul's needs (I. C.) and the needs of others in one's life (Descendant). How does one behave in an environment where he/she has just undergone a re-structuring of his/her own moral code of ethics, and now finds these ethics possibly in conflict with the expectations or principles of others?

One of the key lessons inherent in Saturn transits is patience. Though it is important to honor one's own code of ethics, it is also important to understand that these may not be easily accepted by others who are drawn into the native's life, particularly partners. One man's creed is not necessarily another man's law. If one is in a situation where he or she must live or work with another, then there are apt to be times when the two differ on "what's right and what's wrong", or even on who has what responsibilities. A test of control unfolds. Will the individual choose to exhibit external control, or the self control acquired from the test of faith during the period of Saturn transiting over the I. C.? The exertion of external control, wherein one impatiently tries to force another to accept his or her conditions will likely be met with coldness, even resentment. A play for control ensues with neither side moving. Ultimatums may be forthcoming: "If you don't accept my way then I am leaving," is one possible drama that results. "You'll do it may way or else," is another. Sometimes these statements are made quietly to oneself, but the consequences could be just the same. One intends to punish, or control, the other. To allow oneself to enter into such a drama can have complicated repercussions. Through thoughts, one may draw others into the life who appear to support the native's position, against the "other" person (or partner). The native may be vulnerable to seduction, or temptation. To give in to these temptations may create very complex and difficult scripts for the individual, for now there are others involved in the politics of one's integrity.

The key is patience. The individual must again exhibit the power of self-control. The difference between the individual's position and that of another is the degree of understanding. However the transit is occurring in the individual's horoscope, so it is he or she who is being challenged with these principles. By patiently and logically explaining one's position, one's understanding of truth, and openly listening to the other's position, a level of mutual responsibility may be achieved. It may not take place overnight. It may take time for each to understand – and accept – the other. By patiently applying these principles, both parties may be able to understand patterns involving "control" that have plagued the lives of both. In this understanding both parties may begin to empower themselves, and as a result the relationship itself becomes more empowered. Both individuals may experience a spiritual release, and neither party violates principles it holds sacred. Furthermore neither party acts in a separative manner which incurs greater karmic complexities. The Saturn transit is thus a karmic experience, but an opportunity of self-unfoldment as well, as are all Saturn transits over angles and angular midpoints.

As **Saturn transits over the Descendant**, the soul is squarely in the middle of the Western Hemisphere, or at a point of dealing with results of past actions involving significant others in one's life. The Descendant is the natural part of the day where the Sun is located at sunset. Light gives way to dark. In this case, the transit is coming out of the dark part of the chart into the world of form and duality. The Descendant furthermore represents the people and conditions drawn into one's life as a result of actions initiated prior to this lifetime. This is the point which most symbolically describes the results, or consequences of past life behaviors whose cycles are still in motion, not yet complete. It is thus one of the most significant periods in an individual's lifetime, at least from a soul point of view.

Put simply, Saturn transiting the Descendant represents the consequences of commitments made and responsibilities assumed with regard to others. Did the soul make a promise, or take a vow, or make an agreement with another? Did the soul fulfill its responsibilities with regard to these commitments, vows or promises? If so, the consequences are likely to represent some sort of mutual attainment or achievement, a perfection of a union or partnership. If not, the individual must now account and be judged accordingly. The ego will seek to defend itself, for there is again risk of loss. The soul wishes to tell the truth and clean the slate.

The opportunity is to understand how one is responsible for the evolvement of others as well as oneself. When one enters into a union or partnership, one takes on the karma of it. As such one has a responsibility to not only enlighten oneself as to one's own karmic scripts, but as well to help enlighten the other to the same. Again this is not accomplished by the exhibition of external control or acting as an authority. That may simply aggravate the script. It is not accomplished by abandonment and withdrawal, although separation is sometimes the agreed upon end result. It is accomplished through patience and tolerance, of mutually defining shared goals and responsibilities. It is then necessary to commit to these responsibilities, and accept the consequences which come from them. Failure to do so could result in loss. The loss may take the form of self-esteem, respect, or even the relationship itself. In many instances the partnership dies, figuratively or literally. If literally, then that event stimulates the soul's focus upon these issues. He or she does a thorough accounting of how the relationship was handled, how one behaved during its existence, and then pronounces judgement upon oneself. Whether the relationship figuratively or literally died, the individual is then likely to go through a period of loneliness, perhaps even grief. Again the soul is at a crossroads: "Do I focus my attention upon my self, or upon the Creator?" A focus upon one's purpose for living, or calling in life, might evolve out of this crisis in consciousness. So too may a commitment to honor one's agreements more completely in the future, particularly with regard to partnerships. Of course the ego may win this battle as well, in which case the soul is cut off from any further contact with the conscious mind, as the individual begins a moral sentence of coping with the results of guilt and denial.

From here Saturn begins a 5–9 year sojourn through the third quadrant (houses 7–9). It is also above the horizon for the next 14–15 years. As such Saturn is entering the "light" part of the chart, that reality which is expressive and interactive. This is the realm of the soul's dealings with the outer, physical world. It is yang. Here the soul must learn the rules and laws of man, both in a legal sense as well as a figurative sense. There are rules of interaction with others which govern social behavior. One's skill in interacting with the world is cultivated as Saturn transits above the horizon.

Quadrant three is specifically a maturation period. The individual is now likely to undergo a series of crises in the outer world. The purpose of these crises is to gain experience, and from these experiences to gain understanding and wisdom. Ultimately the result is to transform the personality. In the scope of Evolutionary Astrology, it is hoped that the transformation will be one in which the personality forms a union with the soul, one in which the light of the soul is accepted by the personality.

This quadrant is furthermore symbolic of one's role as student-teacher, or master-apprentice. Typically during this 5–9 year period the soul comes into contact with its teachers, or if a teacher itself, then its students and apprentices. There are rules by which the outer world functions, and the individual is in need of learning and even mastering those rules if he/she is to attain the purpose for which the soul has reincarnated. It is not possible to succeed in one's calling in life if one does not learn the ways of the people he or she must interact with. Those who can help the individual now appear in the life. Symbolically they are to facilitate the unfoldment of one's calling or purpose in life, as signified by the Midheaven. Because the transit at this time is Saturn, these people, or the situations in which they arise, are Saturnian in nature. That is, they are older and more experienced. If younger, then the native is to play out a fatherly role to them. Others may also play the role of authority figures who force the native to account. Consider this as a period of training. Literally one may be in school or college, trying to learn a skill or master a study that is to be a part of one's potential destiny.

The first crisis point for transiting **Saturn** above the horizon is during its **transit over the midpoint between the Descendant and the Midheaven**. This brings into play the commitment to a purpose versus the commitment of agreement with others. Typically one is striving to attain a goal. At the same time one has entered into a contract or a responsibility to another, and the two may be incompatible. There are perceived obstacles to the attainment of one's purpose or goal, and they may involved obligations or responsibilities to others. Sometimes the demands of others are perceived as obstacles to unfolding one's higher purpose. Does the native shirk his/her responsibilities and commitment to others in order to attain his/her goal? Or does one give up the goal in order to fulfill his/her commitment to others? An example would be the career woman who marries and becomes pregnant. Does she give up her career to mother the child? Or does she continue the career and make other arrangements for the daily mothering requirements of the child? Another example may be a man who receives a promotion that requires moving to another location, but his wife refuses to move. Does he sacrifice his career advancement for the sake of his marriage, or the other way around?

At this time the soul is challenged to define the real purpose in life, to outline what is possible, and to determine if such potentials have a realistic chance of attainment given the relationships one has entered, or wishes to enter. Secondly the individual needs to determine how to integrate these goals with responsibilities undertaken with regard to others. Usually these are very difficult dilemmas for the individual. Oftentimes there are serious financial concerns to take into account. This period can make or break a union. It can also make or break a dream. As a result, a personal transformation usually transpires. It would be helpful if the individual would seek the counsel of someone wise.

The opportunity at this period is to meet a teacher, a wise counsel who may guide the individual through these turbulent waters. The opportunity is to learn how to accomplish one's goals in life without causing pain or harm to another, or even to oneself. Once again the value of self-control is evident, as loss may be brought on by exhibiting only external power and control over others. The commitment must be to the goal, to the purpose for one's embodiment. But one needs to be clear on what that purpose is. Furthermore, in the pursuit of this purpose, one must be careful not to bring pain to others, but rather patiently give them (and oneself) time to adjust to this purpose. If someone forces the native to choose between him/her and someone or something else which the individual values and knows to be of truth, then the individual cannot choose that person which asked him/her to choose. To do so would only create a pattern based upon resentment and frustration. Ultimately the relationship would die anyway. Its illness, or bind, began at that moment. In order to grow, there must be understanding followed by acceptance of the potential or the inevitable. Without this the opportunity for real transformation succumbs to a debilitating karmic script, and all of one's intimate relationships may be seen as unsupportive to the native's goals. A pattern of blame and projection sets in where the native refuses to accept responsibility for his/her own shortcomings and unfulfillment in life.

Passing this crisis point puts the soul on path to a major accomplishment in life. This is signified by the **transit of Saturn over the Midheaven**. The apprenticeship is now complete. The training or education is now over. It is time to embark upon one's calling in life. The Midheaven represents a peak experience, and Saturn's influence is to define a goal whose attainment will facilitate that peak experience.

This period is approximately 14–15 years from the time that Saturn transited the I. C., the "dark point" of the soul, the period in which one's faith was tested. The foundation laid at that time may bear fruit now. If one made a vow, or made a commitment to conduct oneself in accordance with his/her highest understanding of truth, and in accordance with the needs of the soul, then this period will likely bring forth great success. If one has not acted in accordance with its understanding of natural law, did not take a leap in faith, then the fruit that is harvested may be very meagre. Instead of fulfillment with one's accomplishments in the outer world, one may instead feel unfulfilled, frustrated. One's work may not be rewarding, and one may wish to be free of his or her work responsibilities. Since thought is the harbinger of experience, the wish may manifest. There may be a loss in one's career. There may be a loss in the form of an authority figure, or with regard to one's status in the community. Instead of a graduation (from training into career) it may coincide with a period of frustration and despair, a lack of contentment regarding one's responsibilities.

The reasons are again karmic, as are all periods outlined by the position of one's natal angles. How has one handled the concept of his or her life purpose? Did one choose to work in a calling consistent with the soul's needs and purpose? At root lies the question: "Did the soul live up to the contract made prior to embodiment (reincarnation)?" Embodiment is a privilege, and to assume a body means the soul has agreed to undergo certain experiences of a purposeful nature. The purpose is to facilitate completion of karmic cycles. Did deep understanding result? If the answer is "yes", there is a fulfilling type of experience encountered as Saturn transits the Midheaven. If the answer is "no", then there is an unfulfilling and frustrating condition encountered.

Even if the answer is "no", this period still presents an opportunity. Saturn's nature is to define. The function of the Midheaven is to call into question one's purpose. Sometimes one comes to a point of understanding through an experience of frustration or despair. By acknowledging that one does not feel fulfilled by his/her work, one may be propelled to embark upon a course that will be compatible to one's purpose. Sometimes a loss of work will set off a series of decisions, choices and events that lead one to illumination. From this point onwards, Saturn enters the Eastern Hemisphere, the sector of creativity and responsibility for oneself. It is a very productive 14–15 year period, and one in which the soul has the choice to make something significant happen with his or her life. Instead of being on the receiving and effectual end of circumstances as in the past 14–15 years, the soul now has the opportunity to re-shape old patterns and create new ones simply by initiating new activity.

The second quadrant (houses 10–12 in Evolutionary Astrology) is potentially the most productive of all periods. During the 5–9 years that Saturn transits through this sector the soul has the opportunity to express its talent, to manifest its potential for which it was called into being. Projects are likely undertaken. The responsibility for the completion of these projects is solely the native's own. Does he/she meet the challenge to complete these efforts? Does he or she accept the challenge to greatness and accomplishment, and the results that come from such accomplishments? Or does the individual let the challenge pass by, preferring instead to seek a path of less challenge, less resistance? Does the native choose a course that provides more immediate and temporary gratification, preferring to indulge itself for selfish reasons, or does it take on a sense of responsibility and higher purpose to its work? The answers to these questions determine the nature of the experiences one undergoes during this period.

Once again a commitment is required. This time the commitment is with regard to one's calling in life. **There may be a vision of what one can accomplish, of what one's purpose might be, as Saturn transits over the Midheaven.** A commitment is made, or the challenge is passed by. Either way **the vision of potential is tested again as Saturn transits over the midpoint of the Midheaven/Ascendant quadrant** (somewhere in the eleventh house). The crisis comes in the form of a test to one's sense of purpose and potential. It comes in the form of involvement with a project that has a dual-edged sword. On the one hand the project may be consistent with the principles one espouses as representative of his or her truth. It is a project one believes in. Yet to be involved in the project may mean either interacting with others with whom there is a play for control or power, and/or may mean personal recognition bestowed upon the native for his or her efforts. In the latter case the individual must be careful not to confuse the purpose (higher purpose) of the project with the ego's need for recognition. This is the point of recognition-hunger, and to do something for the glory it will bring on a personal level may interfere with the proper unfoldment of the project. Furthermore it may bring forth power plays between the individual and others who perceive this need for recognition hunger, or may in fact represent someone else who has these same needs whom the individual draws into battle.

At the heart of the matter is the purpose, the successful completion of the project. If the individual is falling prey to the attractions of the ego, then the soul might be grateful if its being is confronted by others. It presents an opportunity to examine oneself and one's motives, to make certain that one is acting in accordance with an understanding of these higher principles. Although one may be looked upon as an authority in the matter, one must also not forget that there is yet a higher authority to whom he or she has made a vow, made a commitment. To understand this principle at this time may clear the way for a greater test which comes about as **Saturn transits over the Ascendant**.

If all has gone well up until this point, the soul is about to complete a cycle and begin yet another. The individual typically seeks a greater challenge as **Saturn crosses over the Ascendant**, and begins another 14–15 year cycle in which it will be below the horizon.

This may be a dangerous period. The individual is now entering the realm of darkness again, leaving the outer world of man's law and embarking upon an inner journey for which it might be unprepared. The rules are not the same. The results are not so easily controlled. The magic is gone.

The danger is that the individual may take on more than can be handled easily. The transit of the 10th–12th houses may have fostered a "superman" complex, and it could have been highly productive. A creative sense is still extremely strong, for the Ascendant is perhaps the point most symbolic of greatest creativity. Here one is the initiator of activity. One is aware that he or she is the cause behind what happens. As Saturn enters the first quadrant, the individual is apt to want greater results or rewards for his or her efforts. He or she is also apt to want to do fewer activities with other people. As Saturn falls below the horizon, there begins a period of withdrawal and introspection, one of greater self-sufficiency and less dependence upon others. One may try to do too much, take on too many responsibilities, and thus bring strain to the body or mind.

Ideally this is a preparation period. In quadrant one it is in the gestation phase. Contemplation and rest are required; otherwise there is fatigue and exhaustion. The challenge of this period is to come to grips with one's own sense of self-mastery, and as a result one will find that rules which worked before are no longer valid. One must discover new rules and new laws. This precipitates a spiritual crisis. The question is: "Who do I rely upon? Myself or God?" Coming out of the quadrant of manifestation and productivity, one may have been blinded into believing that he or she alone was responsible for all those accomplishments. Faith in a higher order or authority may have been "given up." The personality may have developed quite a wall between the ego and the soul. One may have bought into the illusion that he or she was (is) godlike. If so, this period of Saturn transiting over the Ascendant may provide a grim reminder of one's humanness. It may bring about an experience of humility. As one wants to become more and more self-sufficient, one may experience loss of significant others in his or her life. One may come also to grips with the mortality of the physical vehicle.

Saturn on the Ascendant is an opportunity to begin an inward quest, a quest that may bring the individual back into contact with its soul. All the rules and laws by which one has lived in the past 14–15 years are now tested. It is as if they must be experienced in order to become real. One is keenly aware of when he or she is veering "off the path" now. There is an intuitive sense developing, if only the native would listen. As Saturn descends below the horizon, there is a temptation to develop an overly material side to the nature. A conflict between the material and the spiritual unfolds as **Saturn crosses the midpoint of the Ascendant/I. C. angle**.

The challenge is to define what is really of value. Is it money and material possessions and things of the world? Or is it spiritual qualities like compassion, love, forgiveness? The ego wants the things (Ascendant); the soul (I. C.) wants illumination and understanding. The individual is presented with a choice between doing that which enhances its own survival, or that which facilitates its transcendence above worldly concerns. There is risk of loss on the material plane. There is risk of compromise on the spiritual plane – a compromise of truth, which is no truth at all.

It is important for one to keep in mind his or her responsibility to the soul, and the soul's contract upon re-entering the Earth plane as an embodied being. Attachment to things of the world is an attachment to an impermanence, an illusion. This does not mean that one should not work and earn an income and assume responsibilities for children and spouse as well as one's own physical self. Those responsibilities are part of the contract. One is to be thankful for the opportunity to fulfill these responsibilities as they enhance one's spiritual journey. They are part of the agreement to complete those cycles one has set into motion, which until completed, stand in the way of union with Spirit, of realization of self.

But one must not lose sight of the commitment. Again one must now account for these dilemmas. Since Saturn is below the horizon, the accounting is to one's self. If one has become materialistic to the point that it is inhibiting inner fulfillment, then one has an opportunity to refocus his/her efforts as well as motives. To do so brings one to the I. C. with a clear conscience. To not do so brings one to **a crisis in faith as Saturn transits the I. C.**, and the whole foundation must be rebuilt, for the life will be seen as empty and void of meaning or purpose. The soul calls forth for an accounting. **Moreso the soul calls forth for redemption.**

Much importance has been given to the transit of Saturn as a key to timing the cycles of unfoldment. That is because the path to self-unfoldment begins with a commitment, a promise, or a vow. Once the word is spoken, the contract is made, and the soul becomes responsible. In the course of a lifetime, these agreements are tested, the vows are challenged. The temptation to fall is great, yet the rewards of honoring one's commitments are also great in ways that cannot be described, only experienced. These begin with the experiences of Uranus, Neptune and Pluto. The rewards of these are simply limited in nature without the completion and understanding afforded by the cycles of Saturn. Saturn gives the opportunity to open the doors. It prepares one to cope with the experiences that lie beyond those doors. It is the doors that separate the personality from the soul, and hence the soul from the Spirit. The reality on one side of the doors is totally different than the reality beyond these doors.

Beyond these doors is another consciousness. The events may appear to be the same, but the interpreter of those events sees more than the appearance. The interpreter sees the relationship, the cause and the purpose. As such there is more reverence and appreciation. The journey is both more simple and more exhilarating.

CHAPTER SEVENTEEN

Power Over the Angles Part Two: Breaking Through

In the physical solar system, Saturn is the furthest-out planet the eye can see without the aid of a telescope. It represents the limits of the physical, five-sensory, world. To get beyond the world of the five-sensory reality one must undergo a transformative enlightenment. One must "break through" the illusion of the five-sense world as being the only reality.

There is no personal empowerment in the belief of the outer, physical world as being the only world of reality. There is external power wherein one can force others to his or her will, but the exercise of such external power simply falls into the law of karma: it initiates and sustains an inhibiting pattern or script to one's life. It does not "free the soul"; to the contrary, it keeps the soul in bondage to the pattern, to the cycle. The individual suffers in relationships of all kind: marriage, love, children, work, etc.

The awareness of the suffering, the emptiness created by living and re-living these scripts, is most acute when Saturn transits over the natal angles or their midpoints. These represent opportunities in faith. It is apparent, at these times, that efforts of external control simply do not work. They do not provide fulfillment; they do not provide a sense of meaning and purpose to one's life. To the contrary one may now recognize that one's life is not fulfilled, is not meaningful, and in this awareness there may be despair and frustration. Something is missing. Something is lacking and the individual longs for an opportunity to redeem him/herself. The opportunity arises, but it requires the emergence of faith and the necessity of a commitment, two things that may threaten the ego.

The battle that ensues is one between the ego, or personality, and the soul. The soul does not actually battle the personality, it is the other way around. The soul will continue, it will survive, but the ego also knows its existence is only temporary, and fears it's death. As mentioned in the previous chapter, the individual encounters opportunities to evolve on a regular cyclic basis: eight times every 28–30 years, or an average about every 3.6 years, when Saturn crosses one of the points related to the angles. Yet in many, if not most, cases the personality refuses to surrender external control to the opportunity, or gift of faith when it is offered. **Until it accepts the vital principle of faith, makes and carries through with a meaningful commitment, there is no "real" change of script. There is no "real" breakthrough in consciousness.**

However when there is a voluntary act of faith, and a commitment of responsibility, breakthroughs will follow. These breakthroughs are most likely to unfold during the transits of Uranus, Neptune and Pluto over the natal angles, their midpoints, and to some extent even over the planets which rule the angles, particularly the Midheaven and I. C..

In a given lifetime it is possible that none of these planets will cross all of one's natal angles. The cycle of Uranus is 84 years, while that of Neptune is 164 and Pluto 248 years. Some individuals may live to experience Uranus crossing each angle, but it is doubtful that many will live to see Neptune or Pluto crossing more than two or three angles in a lifetime. These periods are extremely significant in the evolution of a soul, for they portend the times in which the personality may truly "break through", when there is truly a crisis in consciousness, which is in effect an opportunity for real transformation. In a sense, the personality may integrate with the soul, and the soul may thus have an experience or glimpse of oneness with Spirit. If one has prepared properly under the Saturn transits, that is if one has accepted the gift of faith, then the crossings of Uranus, Neptune or Pluto may precipitate incredible experiences in consciousness, and their consequent results in outer experiences of a remarkable nature. If one has not made or honored the personal commitments required under Saturn transits, then the experiences encountered at the time of these more major transits may be equally remarkable, but the reactions of the native may be like those of one who is totally unprepared to meet a remarkable force – they could be shocking to the personality.

As presented in the chapter on "Developed Abilities and Powers of the Soul", Uranus pertained to the first enlightenment, the first breakthrough in consciousness. It symbolized a point in consciousness when the soul became aware of a reality beyond the five-sense physical world.

Truths were discovered that did not fit with the definition of reality one was taught. This new knowledge, or higher truth, arises when **Uranus transits any angle or ruler of any angle, especially the ruler of the I. C. or Midheaven It may also arise when Uranus transits over an angular midpoint.**

What happens when one is introduced to a "different" and "new" reality? What happens when one sees or feels things differently than before? What happens when one's awareness of things is suddenly changed? If the soul is prepared and receptive, and this might be best measured by determining the reactions to the last period in which Saturn transited over an angle or angular midpoint, then there is a heightened sense of energy. The feeling is one of excitement. It is as if an electrical current has been turned on within the soul, and it is eager to venture into new risks, new settings. Suddenly life is an adventure waiting to be experienced. The soul is ready to test its new understandings in the world. As such there may be a change of residence, jobs, even relationships. One wishes to explore this new sense of freedom, to approach new people, new work, new areas.

How does this new awareness come about? It may be through the introduction of some new thought. It may have come through reading a book, taking some class, meeting some fascinating person. It happens at a time when the soul is "ripe" for the introduction to this new thought, perhaps because one has fulfilled the responsibilities of its Saturn commitments made previously. A cycle may have been properly completed, a script finally transcended, and now it is time for the next level of evolution. The soul is prepared for a breakthrough, and the appropriate circumstances, conditions, and people are drawn into the life to offer such a possibility. The soul is introduced to the thought, given the keys, and willingly opens the door. The new world is bright, certainly in comparison to the old. The whole frequency of the soul's energy is changed. There is a quickening. New people, new situations are quickly and suddenly attracted. The whole pace of one's life quickens.

As mentioned, this enlightenment can happen anytime Uranus transits over a natal angle, ruler of an angle, or even an angular midpoint. However the experience is not always positive and exciting. For the personality who is not prepared, these sudden new thoughts and the sudden emergence of new people and new circumstances can be terrifying. Perhaps in this case the soul is still attached to the illusion of external control. Perhaps there is no acceptance of faith offered under the Saturn transits. Perhaps one did not make a commitment, or failed to live up to the responsibilities of a commitment that was made.

A rigorous refusal to let go of the script and transcend the karmic patterns of suffering when it was offered may now have the consequence of a more powerful and disruptive force in the native's life. Circumstances arise in which the native is forced to accept change. Those things he or she was attached to may now be separated. The individual may experience divorce, loss of job, loss of significant relationships, even a change in residence not desired. A multitude of sudden events arise in the life which disturb the native's desire for control, or so-called stability. In these cases it would possibly behoove the individual to study subjects that represent another way of viewing the universe, perhaps the study of philosophy, psychology, religion, even astrology. It may be helpful to consult with someone who can assist the native in understanding what is going on, perhaps even assist the native in seeing the value and excitement of the growth potential now offered.

Uranus crossing these angular points is indeed a crisis in consciousness, but the crisis may be one of welcomed excitement for the personality open to the needs of its soul.

Neptune transiting over an angle, ruler of an angle (especially I. C. or Midheaven), or angular midpoint represents the second level of enlightenment. Like Uranus, the experiences of a Neptune transit depend greatly upon what transpired during the previous Saturn/angle transit. If the gift of faith was accepted, and the commitments made were honored, then the Neptune transit is likely to be an experience of great compassion. Neptune represents the possibility of inner peace, a great inner calm. It is, potentially, a heart experience. During this period one may have vivid and prophetic dreams, a heightened sense of intuition, a burst of creative and imaginative energy. One might feel like writing poetry or music. One's mind may be very romantic, and speech may be very eloquent. There is a grace to one's actions, a tenderness and healing effect of one's expression. Others feel calm in the native's presence, and there is a pure joy in helping others. It is a most unselfish period, one filled with faith and closeness to "Spirit."

Conditions are apt to arise wherein things just seem to "fall into one's lap." Relationships are entered into of a very special quality, perhaps the feeling of a soul-mate. Creative efforts come easily, whether through music, writing, or some other form of art. Others wish to "give to the native", for they have faith in him or her. If one has faith and is worthy of trust, then the experiences with others are very special and rewarding.

If one does not have faith and/or has not been trustworthy, then the experiences encountered at this time are likely to be of an entirely different nature. Instead of faith, one may be plagued with fears of suspicion and betrayal. Dreams may still be prophetic, but instead of pleasant, they may be disturbing. In fact sleep may be a problem: too much or too little. One's reputation may be questioned, for this can correlate with a scandalous or even libelous period. One's intents may be entirely misperceived by others, and one may be the subject of accusations and slanders, not to mention betrayals and deceptions. One must ask and understand "why" he or she is subject to these circumstances. Has one been deceptive or unfaithful? Has one slandered or libeled others? Has one's intent been dishonorable and harmful to others? Has one refused to help when asked by those in need? Has one been perpetrating some falsehood?

Instead of experiencing something blissful, it is possible for one to experience great confusion. One might feel as if he or she is "losing my mind." There seems to be little control over one's life. All of one's control is dissipated and like a flood, circumstances wash away everything the native has built. Literally there may even be problems with water, i.e. plumbing, roofing, boating or swimming.

Still there is an opportunity. In the midst of chaos there is a person or a condition that can instill the value of faith. One may have to ask in order to receive. Furthermore one might be best advised to make a conscious effort to reach out and help others in need, instead of focusing all of one's conscious energy on one's own plight. Self-pity may be an initial reaction, but it tends not to rectify the suffering. In fact it only exaggerates it, for instead of creating a "safe space" for others to enter into one's sphere, it creates a sense of drowning, thereby "pushing away" others who might be helpful. By reaching out and offering to help another, one is sacrificing, and this is a key to mastering the challenges presented by Neptune. There is now the opportunity to develop a special healing gift, a gift which is imparted through consoling or counseling others. But one must make the effort to use this gift, otherwise it will not bring forth inner peace.

At its best, Neptune transits coincide with religious or spiritual experiences. As the personality surrenders all the defenses the ego has built, there is an experience of merging with the Christos, one in which the soul experiences a oneness with Spirit. There is a cleansing. There is an illumination of faith, a vision of one's higher Self. In this experience, one is at peace, one finally comes to an understanding that all is in divine order. There is no struggle, just inner joy. And the experience radiates out to others, who are in turn "moved" by contact with this illuminated and gentle soul. There is an outpouring of compassion that cleanses the native and heals others.

Pluto in transit over natal angles, their rulers, or angular midpoints offers yet another profound enlightenment. This third level is a deep understanding of what it will take to remove obstacles to wholeness and well-being, both on an individual level as well as a community (or even planetary) level. When Pluto transits these critical points, one goes deep within in an effort to understand the source, the cause. The process is insightful, and the result is one of exposure. What is exposed cannot be ignored; it must be dealt with. Failure to do so means death on some level. Willingness to do so requires power, and to succeed in eliminating or transforming that which comes to light means healing and rebirth. Pluto as a transit over these sensitive points empowers one with healing ability, providing that soul has prepared properly under the previous Saturn transit over an angle or angular midpoint.

Pluto transiting over these sensitive angular relationships brings forth profound and deep understandings. It is a period of discovery, and with discovery comes self-realization. The effect is personal empowerment. There is knowledge where before there was none. Furthermore there is an opportunity to exercise this knowledge, this power, in a manner that corrects or benefits the situation(s) now brought forth into the native's life. Will the individual meet the challenge to "repair" or heal the situation(s)? If so, one may experience a personal rebirth, a personal resurrection, a personal healing. In other words, one might have a spiritual experience, a closeness with Spirit, an experience of channelling inspirational ideas.

For one who is unprepared for the Plutonian experience, these periods might be terribly disturbing. One's ego may feel a threat to its very survival. There may be an encounter with death, and one fears his/her own demise. Perhaps there is a serious illness, one that is life-threatening. Perhaps there is an encounter that threatens the very fiber of the physical life itself. One may be in a situation(s) of feeling "forced" to do something against his/her will (i.e. being drafted, being rejected in a marriage or job). A symbol for Pluto is metamorphis, and as such a metamorphis is required of the personality at this time.

The concept of renewal is also an opportunity. One now has the chance to terminate unhealthy and debilitating cycles, particularly in relationships to others. To not do so is self-defeating, or self-destructive. It is not so essential that the relationship be terminated, but rather that the cycle which this relationship has symbolized be terminated. To continue in a situation that has already served its purpose prevents healing, inhibits renewal and rebirth. To understand the purpose of this situation and these people can bring forth a sense of thankfulness, even gratitude, instead of the debilitating karma brought on by the response of revenge and hatred. In most cases there is a sense of an enemy present at this time, one who seems bent on destroying or bringing harm to the native. The lower frequency emotion is one of vengeance and hatred. The higher emotional response is gratitude, for only through these enemies can one see the need to terminate the pattern, the fruitlessness of trying to exhibit external control in a setting where one is not given the power to act as such. Yet one can empower the self by accepting the gift of faith again, by taking the risk of entering into a new set of circumstances with a new awareness and commitment to ethical and responsible behavior. If there is an opportunity to heal and correct the situation, one should do so. If not, then one still has the benefit of deeper self-understanding, and one can then correct him or herself with regard to issues of power with others. This itself is empowering, for self-realization coincides with renewal of Spirit within the self.

Under a Pluto transit, one is wise to explore the depths of one's thoughts. Ultimately it is a period of self-discovery and authentic empowerment. It is also the potential termination of a karmic cycle and death of an aspect of the personality. One is reborn. The slate is cleansed.

CHAPTER EIGHTEEN

Transits of the Moon's North Node: The Thread of Destiny

Every play has a setting, characters, and a plot. As the play unfolds, the characters are identified with distinctive personality features which tie into the plot. These characters generally display certain principles which either support or disrupt the life flow of the story's main character or central theme. At various stages in the play, events involving the characters lead to a crisis point, sometimes called a climax. How the main and supporting characters deal with these climaxes determines the ending of the play.

Life is like a play. In fact, plays and stories are imitations of life. Each individual is located in a setting which influences his or her position at the moment. Within this setting various other individuals enter into the life, individuals who either support or distract one's efforts. At various points in life, the individual reaches a moment when everything seems to climax. There is a crisis which requires a decision, a response, and the consequence of this decision will determine the ending to that part of the native's personal drama.

Let us return to the assumption that the Sun represents the natural path of one's evolvement. It also represents a deep longing within each soul, a longing for union with Spirit remembered from long ago. When one is in touch with this longing, and is creatively expressing him or herself from this point of awareness, there is great vitality. There is a sense of freedom and great energy.

However one is not always in touch with this creative urge. Just as the Moon constantly changes in its reflection of the light of the Sun, so too does the consciousness change the focus of its attention, sometimes upon the spiritual (Sun), sometimes upon needs of others (planets) with whom one has developed a degree of intimacy (Moon).

When the Nodes of the Moon intersect the Sun, as in eclipses, there is symbolically an interruption of one's focus, or attention. As the North (and South) Node of the Moon transits through one's natal horoscope, it may identify times when the individual faces a crisis, a climax in the life. There is an interruption of the flow, and in this interruption someone or something may enter the play. The native has a decision to make. The results of that decision potentially alter one's destiny, or the ending to a story.

First of all consider that the Moon relates to significant relationships in the life cycle. These are relationships with whom one potentially forms a strong bond. These relationships are destined to arise, but how one responds to the conditions brought forth as a result of these relationships is purely a matter of free will. Yet their results can change the script, transform the destiny.

The transiting North Node of the Moon is like the theme in the play, the thread that ties it all together and allows the parts of the play to appear "connected." As important as the transits of the "power planets" were to the natal angles, so too is the transit of the Moon's North Node over these same points. Unlike the transits of the power planets, the Moon's North Node traverses in clockwise fashion through the horoscope, just as the Sun does in its symbolism of the natural day.

The Nodal cycle begins when the North Node transits over one's **natal I. C.**. In some cases it may seem as if the life starts when it transits over the **natal Midheaven**. From this point, a plot begins to unfold that describes a story of one's life. With each angular point in the horoscope touched, the drama reaches a major climax – at least so long as one's inner longing (the Sun) is not totally dormant. At this point, it would be helpful to chronologically list the dates in which the Moon's North Node transits over every angle and angular midpoint on the natal horoscope, starting with the I. C. or Midheaven (which occurred first in life?). For purposes of this book, the interpretations will begin with the I. C.. In all cases, allow a time span of six months.

Transit of North Node over I. C.: a period when the pathway to the soul opens up. One has the opportunity to receive a special spiritual experience, a glimpse of one's true spiritual self. It is a period when one may come into contact with a special calling in life. It may be a period of channeling, when one's intuitive qualities are especially heightened. Individuals and circumstances come forth into the native's life which are part of the individual's spiritual purpose. In a sense, the individuals may be viewed as soul mates, though not necessarily from a romantic point of view. They are simply there to foster the individual's spiritual unfoldment. This may coincide with a period of changing residence or careers, or both.

Transit of North Node over midpoint of I. C./Ascendant: A time when the individual is confronted with a choice between the spiritual and the mundane or material. The needs of the soul may be in conflict with the desires of the ego. Individuals again enter the life who are symbolic of this conflict, as well as representative of the opportunity to resolve it. One relationship may come to an end as another begins. This is a special crossroads, and the choice made will have a major influence on the future course the native's life will take.

Transit of North Node over Ascendant: An opportunity to develop a skill or a means to accomplish one's calling in life. This is a period of potentially great creativity, a period in which one might feel an urge to commence something new. Perhaps one starts a family, buys a home, changes residence, and/or begins a new direction in career. Once more significant souls and/or conditions enter into the native's life that represent temptations of the ego, or means to fulfill one's calling. These people may be helpful or distractions on one's path. Even as distractions, they serve a purpose.

Transit of North Node over Midpoint of Ascendant/Midheaven: A period when one is faced with a choice between his or her purpose in life (spiritual) and desires of the ego. This is the point of recognition-hunger of the ego, but it is also a crossroads one must come to in order to ascertain whether or not he or she is truly ready to meet the challenge for which the soul was embodied. Typically there is a power play entered into with another over the native's intentions or abilities. Individuals enter the life who symbolize these challenges, and others enter into the life who may help the native focus on the higher plan.

Transit of North Node over the Midheaven: A time in which the native lets go of the past and begins a new future. The purpose (or *a* purpose) is made known to the soul. It is a time to begin one's calling in life, or one of the callings in life. There is a purpose made known, or at the least there is an awareness that the current direction has come to an end, and a new one is to commence. This may coincide with a new career, a new direction in one's career, a major accomplishment in life, and/or a change in residence. Again individuals enter the life who are important in the soul's unfoldment. These are karmic relationships, and their purpose is to help the native understand his or her purpose in life. This period may represent the fruits or rewards for decisions made and efforts cultivated over the past 9-1/2 years, or from the time the North Node transited over the I. C.. The key is to understand that this is a period when one's purpose in life may change, or take a significant turn.

Transit of North Node over the midpoint of Midheaven/Descendant: This period symbolizes a conflict between one's purpose in life and the nature or responsibilities of one's relationships. Relationships entered into may be at odds with one's sense of purpose. It is also possible that relationships arise with others who confront or challenge one's commitment to that calling or purpose in life. In this case there may again be a power play. Oftentimes conflicts or struggles arise over finances. As with the opposite quadrant midpoint, this one too presents a choice between material and spiritual desires. An individual comes into the life who can help the soul through this choice.

Transit of North Node over Descendant: This is the most karmic point in the horoscope, the point of consequences to one's prior actions in previous lifetimes whose cycles are not yet complete. One's karma unveils in the form of relationships and circumstances, particularly circumstances of karmic relationships. One must now make a choice with regard to these relationships: to stay with them or break away. There is likely a relationship that wants to be developed, and perhaps another that needs to end (the Descendant is the point of death, or sunset in the natural day when light goes into darkness). Ultimately one has a responsibility to complete the karmic cycle with another. To do so keeps him or her on the path toward self-unfoldment. To avoid this responsibility, or ignore the opportunity, may mean complications of this script later on in life. There is a special person now present, one with whom there has been a shared experience in a past life of a very special quality. There may also be those with whom one has shared a past life experience which was not beneficial to either party, and the cycle was left incomplete and unfulfilled. It is the duty of the soul to identify both, and furthermore to respond to both in a manner that is consistent with its higher understanding as well as higher purpose. To respond with selfishness or purely self-interests would likely result in great inner and outer struggle with the next transit. Once again, a significant soul enters the drama of one's life.

Transit of North Node over midpoint of Descendant/I. C.: This is a period in which one might experience a conflict between the needs of others in one's life and one's understanding of the longing of the soul. Power plays may abound again. It may be necessary to release a relationship which has become detrimental both to the native and the other person. The native him/herself may be the subject of such a dismissal from another person. There may be contact with someone who simply does not like the individual, perhaps at work or in love. This relationship serves a purpose: it forces the individual into self-examination, to see what and who is really there. The choice is how to respond according to one's deeper understanding of the soul's needs. Ultimately the pursuit of truth will win out. The people in one's life either represent a challenge to this truth, or support the native in his or her belief of this truth. Again there is an individual in one's life who helps one make the correct choices. If the soul is receptive, a process begins which leads into the transit of the node over the I. C., a time of spiritual awakening when the whole cycle begins over again.

As mentioned earlier in this chapter, these periods require a six-month time window. During that period there will be one or two solar eclipses that will transpire near these natal angular points. Perhaps it is the eclipse more than the nodal transit which stimulates these events and opportunities, for the symbolism of a solar eclipse is quite unique in astrology. It is the point that the Moon enters into the plane of the Sun and Earth, thereby blocking out the Sun. This symbolism cannot be ignored. The Sun, one's sense of wholeness and one's path to mastery, is "eclipsed." There is a new potential path toward wholeness that is revealed. One's karmic scripts may be transcended as a path is embarked upon that is consistent with one's inner longing. It may also be that the old path is just renewed. After a period of darkness in which one took life for granted, the light may have been suddenly taken away. Just as suddenly it comes on again, and this time the soul is grateful and awakened.

PART FOUR

Evolutionary Phases of the Collective

CHAPTER NINETEEN

Seasonal Ingresses: Shifts in Collective Consciousness

Throughout this book on *Evolutionary Astrology*, the relationship between consciousness – or one's reality – and the angles of the natal horoscope has been postulated. How one "sees" life, and how one "experiences" life, seems dependent upon the relationship of the natal angles and their midpoints to the planets (and Moon) of our solar system. Shifts, or breakthroughs, of this reality, and consequently the patterns of experience known as karma, seemed to be timed by the slower moving transits over these critical angles and their midpoints. Such opportunities come up every so often in one's lifetime, and if one is receptive to the counsel of the soul, a new cycle may be initiated and an old cycle completed. Learning takes place. Evolution is resumed.

Shifts in consciousness, and breakthroughs in patterns, also occur on a collective level. This happens primarily in two ways: either leaders of large groups of people (i.e. rulers), or large numbers of a specific group (i.e. the population of a land) experience a sudden shift in consciousness. The timing of such periods is in many ways similar to that which occurs on an individual level, as described in the last section. Let's review some of those ideas.

In one of the earlier chapters the concept of time was discussed at great length. The movement of the Earth rotating on its own axis (approximately one revolution per day) is the basis of "clock" time. Individuals organize their daily lives around this framework of time. From the moment one awakes (usually soon after dawn) until the time one retires for sleep and rest (shortly after sunset as a rule), one's daily activities are generally governed by the relationship of the Sun to the angles of the Earth.

Group activities, on the other hand, are based on yet another concept of time. This involves the relationship the annular orbit of the Earth around the Sun. This is the basis for "calendar" time, and is the foundation upon which seasons of the year unfold. During the Winter season, growth in nature usually slows. Planting generally commences in the Spring as the days become longer than the nights. During the Summer the plants are usually in full bloom, while shortly after the Autumnal Equinox the grain is harvested.

Just as the four points of the day (i.e. midnight, dawn, noon, and sunset) coincided with the four angles of the natal horoscope, so too do the four seasons of the year correlate to the four most important ingresses of the zodiac. Just as the four angles of the horoscope represent the foundation for individual consciousness, so too do the four seasonal ingresses, known as the solstice and equinox, correspond to the consciousness of the collective. Just as the midpoints of the natal angles correspond to individual moral issues, so too do the midpoints between the solstice and equinox correspond to collective moral issues. Thus there exists an analogy between the angles of the natal horoscope, and the beginning of seasons in the tropical zodiac year (See Figure 15).

In the individual's horoscope it was seen that the I. C. corresponded to the principle of midnight in the order of the natural day. This is the beginning point of the soul's journey through this lifetime, and is symbolic of the conception moment. At this point in time the soul becomes aware that it will soon incarnate into a physical vehicle. This I. C. is also symbolic of the needs of the soul. Consciousness from this point represents the wise counsel of the soul, a counsel which is based upon the soul's understanding of what the individual needs to learn in life in order to evolve. In a sense conscious awareness, from the perspective of the I. C., allows one to complete and transcend karmic scripts in effect prior to and during this lifetime. Through the wise counsel of the soul one makes choices that are centered not just upon one's own self interests, but as well the interests of all those identities that he or she is associated with.

In the annular orbit of the Earth around the Sun this same point corresponds to the Winter Solstice, or 0° Capricorn. Just as the I. C. represents the darkest part of the day as the Earth rotates on its axis, so too does the Winter Solstice correspond to the darkest day of the year in the Northern Hemisphere upon Earth, where the vast majority of land and people exists. Thus 0° Capricorn has a potential impact upon the collective similar to that of the I. C. upon the individual. As major planets cross into 0° Capricorn, the "essence of the collective

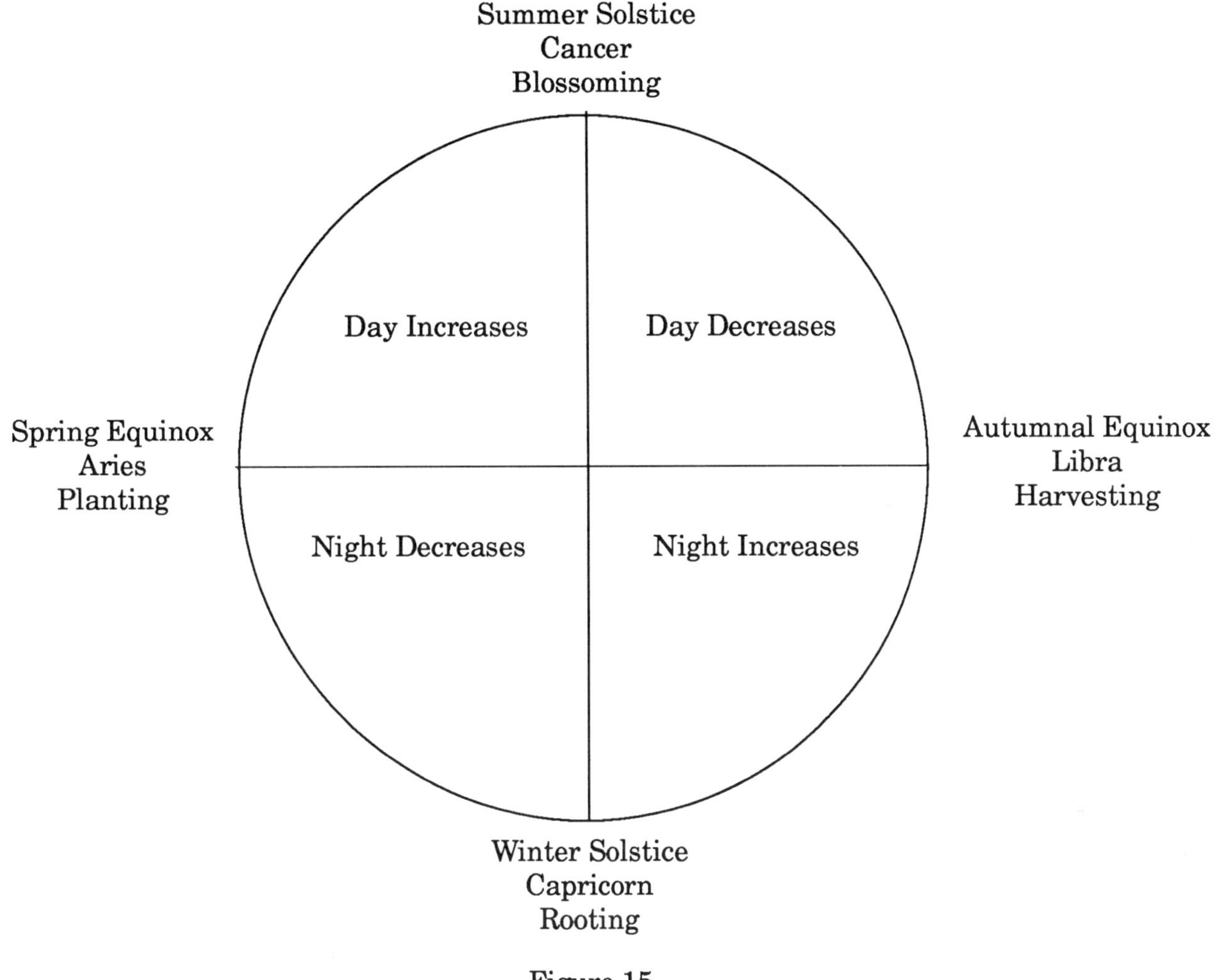

Figure 15
Seasonal cycle of Earth to Sun
(Annual orbit of Earth around the Sun)

soul" is touched. A conception takes place that potentially influences the whole of humanity. For the next several years this idea, or conception, will enter the gestation or preparation phase, until the same planet enters into 0° Aries.

From midnight until dawn the Sun (actually the Earth by its own rotation) appears to move "up" the horoscope, from the I. C. (4th house cusp) to the Ascendant (1st house cusp). This section of the sky is known as quadrant one in Evolutionary Astrology, and corresponds to the part of the day where darkness is decreasing. Symbolically this represents the period in which the soul's body, having been conceived at the I. C., is being prepared for existence upon the physical plane. The being is in a state of development, or preparation, known as the gestation phase. How this phase is handled determines whether or not that which is being conceived ever comes into form.

The same process takes place on the collective level. At 0° Capricorn, an idea that may potentially affect humanity is conceived, according to the nature of the planet entering this degree. Of most importance are Saturn, Uranus, Neptune, and Pluto (the North Node of the Moon is also important, but its natural motion is retrograde through the zodiac).

As one of these planets crosses into Capricorn, the point representative of the darkest day of the solar year, the soul of the collective is crying out to be heard. Humanity has gone as far as it can from its roots, and it longs to return to "basic fundamentals", or principles. The collective life has become, as a rule, extremely complex, and now longs for a return to simplicity. This oftentimes corresponds with a very nostalgic period, one in which times of the past are fondly remembered and rekindled. At the same time, however, something is being conceived that potentially impacts humanity in a dramatic way. The period of time that planet moves from 0° Capricorn to 0° Aries (or in the case of the Moon's Nodes, to move from 0° Capricorn to 0° Libra) may be referred to as the gestation or preparation phase for this new idea which may possibly impact humanity. How that idea is now handled will determine whether or not it is ever really born, whether or not it will ever achieve the potential for which it was destined (i.e. at the point of the Midheaven, or 0° Cancer).

Just as an individual experiences a moral crisis as planets cross the midpoint of the I. C./Ascendant, so too does humanity experience a crisis when these major planets cross the midpoint of the solstice/equinox. The first crisis is when the planet crosses 15° Aquarius, the midpoint of the Winter Solstice (0° Capricorn) and Spring Equinox (0° Aries). At this point the leaders of the land, or the majority of the people, have a major choice to make: to continue with the idea conceived at 0° Capricorn, or to return to the complexities and habitual patterns that were so dominant before that time. In other words, the "new idea" may abort here and the old order may be restored. The longing of the collective soul (0° Capricorn) may be dismissed by the ego of the leadership, or the fear of the majority. An opportunity for collective evolvement may be assured or renounced, at this critical point.

As this book is being written, humanity is entering into such a critical period known as the Capricorn Climax (see Chapter 21). In the late 1980's, Saturn, Uranus and Neptune all crossed into 0° Capricorn, and the same is true of the Moon's North Node in 1992. During this period an entire part of the world order, known as Communism, was transformed. However this movement toward individual freedom and rights is not without problems. It will be interesting to note the reactions that may be forthcoming as Saturn, Uranus, and Neptune transit 15° Aquarius, as well as when the Moon's North Node transits 15° Scorpio.

Even more exciting may be the period during which these planets reach 0° Aries, or 0°Libra in the case of the Moon's North Node. This is the degree of the Vernal Equinox, and is similar in nature to that of the Ascendant in one's natal horoscope. In the natural order of the day, the Sun rises at the Ascendant. Darkness gives way to light, and that which was conceived at the I. C. takes on a physical form. This is the birth moment, and that which is initiated here takes on an entirely new momentum.

That which is born and takes shapes now has a new primary purpose: survival, and better yet, the enhancement of its own survival. There is now a form to the idea, but it is far from perfected. In the natural order of the day, the period of time from dawn to noon is when light is increasing. At first the form is not clear (12th house). There is much hope and "dreaming" of its potential. There is much idealism. Eventually the form takes a more permanent shape, and as it does it becomes more and more applicable to the human condition. It becomes more and more useful, and with it, more and more things (or progress) are accomplished. This is truly a potential "boom" period for humanity, assuming the idea conceived at 0° Capricorn made it to the birthing stage.

As major planets move from 0° Aries to the Summer Solstice degree of 0° Cancer, there is a midway point, a crisis point. This occurs at 15° Taurus. It is midway between birth and perfection, between initiation of the project versus fulfillment of its potential. At 15° Taurus, there is likely some kind of power play over the control of the matter which was born at 0° Aries. It is now a given that this matter can be useful, potentially very beneficial. A purpose is known by all, or at least the leaders of the land(s). A conflict is now likely to arise as to how it should be used. One group wants credit and perhaps glory for it, while another wants only the purpose for which it was designed to be utilized. A fight for control or power over this concept or matter likely ensues. It may be helpful for humanity to remember the context in which this matter was originally conceived, and the purpose for which it was designed. Just as individual souls have a "calling in life", so too does each group of souls. The souls who are presently embodied upon Earth have a collective purpose, a collective calling. Decisions made at this time will either be in agreement with this group "calling", or else the will of a few may supersede. The result may be either a new era of repressive leadership and misuse of this matter's purpose, or else it will represent a period in which, after some battle and conflict, this matter will be directed and used for the purpose it was originally conceived. In the latter case, a period of great progress (evolvement) unfolds.

At the Summer Solstice degree (0° Cancer), the purpose of the matter or idea conceived at 0° Capricorn may be actualized. Its purpose, like that of individuals, is ultimately to be of service and benefit to humanity. This is the brightest time of the year in the path of the Earth around the Sun. From this point onwards, light begins to decrease, and the idea or matter enters a period of maturity or a period in which its usefulness to humanity is completely integrated. It has now become a part of life. It also now enters a long period in which "consequences" related to its creation and development will now be experienced. Just as the period of noon until midnight represents the latter half of the day when light decreases, so too does the period from Summer to Winter (in the Northern Hemisphere) represents that part of the year when the days become shorter and nights longer. It is the harvesting period, when the fruits of one's creative efforts initiated earlier determine whether or not it was a "good year." If one prepared and planted properly, then the harvesting season is usually one of abundance, and the rewards for such an effort generally carry one through the season of darkness (winter). If one did not prepare and behave in accordance with natural law during the Spring and Summer seasons, then the harvest will be meager, and suffering will be the result as Winter approaches.

As the major planets move from 0° Cancer to 0° Capricorn, humanity (the collective) is undergoing a period of collective karma. The first phase of this is between 0° Cancer to 0° Libra (0° Aries in the case of the Moon's North Node). This is a learning as well as a teaching phase. Typically humanity is entering a philosophical or even spiritual period. There are efforts to expand the use of the original matter or idea that has now been perfected and adopted in the everyday lives of many people. At a certain point in time, as planets cross 15° Leo, another crisis for humanity may arise with regard to the application or direction of the original matter or idea. It may be that some leaders misinterpret the original meaning, or misuse the rightful application of the matter. Others may be fearful of the motivation of those in control of the matter. The dilemma is between what the rightful purpose of the matter is, versus the direction those in control are now steering the matter. This represents a period of conflict between the leadership and the purpose, and frequently signals a time of change in the leadership.

As planets leave the Summer Solstice section of the heavens and approach the Autumnal Equinox area (0° Libra, or in the case of the Moon's North Node, 0° Aries), the idea or matter has likely been adopted as an integral part of society or the system. The collective has pretty much assimilated the matter into its everyday routine. An order has been established around this concept, and it affects the lives of all involved. It is soon taken for granted.

Perhaps the most interesting phase of the cycle commences as the outer planets cross into 0° Libra, and enter into the Autumnal section of their journey (i.e. from 0° Libra through 0° Capricorn). During the annual course of the Earth around the Sun, this season corresponds to Fall, or that part of the year in which darkness increases in the Northern Hemisphere. In the natural order of the day, this corresponds to the time between sunset and midnight, or quadrant four (houses 4–6) in Evolutionary Astrology. As one goes from light into darkness, there is typically a period of fear. It is a fear of the unknown, and when such a fear is present, the mood of the collective (or at least the leadership) tends toward caution or conservatism. In order to strengthen one's control of the matter, alliances may be formed with others, or agreements may be made to protect one's position. The fear of the unknown can be equated to a fear of losing control. The cycle is now old, and those who have been with the cycle since the beginning may also be aging. There may be a wind of change in the air, though it certainly is not clearly defined yet.

The key for successfully navigating through these times is open communication between the leaders and the populace. In the midst of the larger group are a number of new and perhaps revolutionary ideas that are being bandied about. There is likely to be evident new and growing social, political, and economic problems that concern the masses. These problems may be a direct result of the direction the idea or matter has taken over the past few years. In a sense this is still a period of karma, or consequence, to the activity undertaken with regard to this idea or matter that started when the planet(s) entered 0° Capricorn. These new problems will require new ideas, and these new ideas may be threatening to those who are presently in control. It is a time that not only requires communication between apparently diverse groups, but as well a time requiring a great deal of faith and willingness to take risks. Willingness to do so sets into motion a period of original ideas being exchanged, a time of great inspiration. There may be strong concern for the well being of the planet, or the collective. It may be a very humanitarian period. Failure to communicate honestly and openly, and failure to take risks at this time may lead to serious conflicts and tensions between groups. The result in this case may be wars and change of leadership.

The 0° Libra point represents a time period that is extremely critical. Relationships, alliances, and agreements or understandings between groups of people may be imitated. This sets the stage for a new order that may be forthcoming. If the relationships are based upon principles consistent with natural law (i.e. for the betterment of the whole as opposed to that which benefits only a few at the expense of the greater), then this period may usher in an exciting era of new thought and exploration. If the alliances are formed under deceptive or selfish motives, then the relationship will likely come under review during the time in which the planet(s) cross into the middle of the next fixed sign (i.e. 15° Scorpio, or in the case of the Moon's North Node, 15° Aquarius).

When the furthest-out planets reach the midpoint between the Autumnal Equinox and Winter Solstice, humanity is presented with yet another opportunity to shift its collective consciousness. The crisis is between the real needs of the group soul (i.e. 0° Capricorn) and the alliances and agreements made previously (0° Libra). Are these relationships and these agreements in the best interest of the people as a whole? The populace themselves may be asking the same questions of their leaders: "Are our leaders truly representing our collective needs?" If not, changes are likely to take place, and along the lines that will reflect the needs of the greater number of people. This is a very inspirational period, and leaders who are both intelligent and inspiring stand the best chance of playing a longer-lasting role in the drama of humanity.

The decisions made at this time are either consistent or incongruous with the needs of the group. If the decisions are repressive to the cry of the group, then the seeds of rebellion will be firmly planted. The overthrow of the "old guard", the "outdated system," will gather momentum as planets move closer to 0° Capricorn. Conflicts between the needs of the populace (collective soul) and the direction of the leadership of the land grows at an increasing rate as the new cycle prepares for its advent. Both fear and stress are at a high pitch if there is great division between the leadership and those who wish to be properly represented.

On the other hand, this may be a profoundly spiritual period. A great number of individuals tend to simultaneously undergo a spiritual awakening. When an old order comes to an end and a new one is about to commence, there is a very intense and special feeling in the air. It is an electric time. The potential for new and deeply insightful ideas is powerful. Radical approaches may be suggested in many areas of life, from education, to government, to economics, philosophy and religion. If the leadership is receptive to these new insights, then tremendous progress may commence. It is potentially a period of evolution for all of humanity, and decisions may now set the foundation for a long-term and new world order.

It is significant to note that the 0° Capricorn point is very close to the Galactic Center (27° Sagittarius) and the Solar Apex (2° Capricorn). These two points in the universe symbolize the "universal mind" and the "potential direction (destiny) of humanity" respectively. Individuals with planets near 27° Sagittarius have a natural empathy for the human condition, a natural understanding of the vast array of human experiences. In short, there is a "deep understanding" of human nature implied by this degree. Those with planets near 2° Capricorn have an innate sense of the future, particularly as it relates to groups of people, or humankind. There is a sense of the direction in which the country or the world is headed. As planets cross these two degrees, plus the Winter Solstice degree of 0° Capricorn, humanity is given a rare opportunity of profound understanding, as well as a rare opportunity to act upon this understanding in a manner that potentially has a powerful effect upon the next several generations. It is a time of conception, and in that moment lies a magnificent potential for humanity, if properly nurtured and cared for. It is a time when group consciousness may come into touch with its collective "inner longing." It is a time when a great number of individuals experience an intense and powerful revelation, a revelation that may lead to a "breakthrough" not only in the patterns of their own individual karma, but also in the patterns of others with whom one associates.

If the minds of the leaders are open, then the quality of the moment is transformative, and the needs of the collective soul are heard. The counsel is wise, and that which is initiated in response to this counsel has powerful and positive possibilities for humankind.

At each step along the planets' journey through the zodiac from 0° Capricorn all the way back to 0° Capricorn, there are many crossroads in which the idea can be aborted or affirmed. There is perhaps no single cycle in the history of humanity where a brilliant example can be cited, for history is filled with examples of "missed opportunities." Unfortunately historians also may not clearly depict the nature of choices presented to leaders throughout the ages, but rather contain their writings to only end results. Mankind can never know fully what would have happened if another (or other) decisions had been made. There is very little mention in history of decisions by world leaders made on the basis of understanding natural law.

Nevertheless, one can go back in time and review what is written about history as the various outer planets traversed through the zodiac. From these events, perhaps one can imagine the possibilities present at the time. As an example, let us look at the planet Uranus. In the early 1900's it moved into the sign of Capricorn. It did so at the time of the Wright brothers invention of the airplane. This closely followed the invention of the automobile, and while at the time it was unknown, the whole fiber of world society was about to embark upon a new order. This was the beginning of the end of an agriculturally dominated world economy. It was also the beginning of a more efficient and closer communicating world.

The transition from the agrarian community to the manufacturing community was fully birthed as Uranus entered 0° Aries in the late 1920's. It was an incredibly creative period (remember, the Ascendant, or 0° Aries, signifies the most creative part of the horoscope in Evolutionary Astrology). This was the time of the "Roaring Twenties," when Hollywood introduced the talkies, Lindbergh successfully flew over the Atlantic (perhaps the "real" birth of aviation), and the world economy collapsed in the greatest depression ever to hit humankind. Were the world's government and banking leaders taking into account the needs of the collective soul, or were they primarily operating from a point of "self interest?" The Ascendant, or 0° Aries is perhaps the point of greatest temptation to act in a self-centered manner without regard to the consequences of one's actions upon others. It is a time of great pleasure, as indeed most of the 1920's appears to have been. But the consequences of such self-centered decisions resulted in great suffering over the next two decades.

Uranus then crossed into 0° Cancer (equivalent to the Midheaven in an individual's chart) in the late 1940's. This is the result of the seeds planted in the first decade of the century. The automobile and airplane were fully incorporated into the lifestyle of the world's population. Jet planes were invented, Isreal was born, and Blacks broke through a racial barrier in professional sports. Society began the process of integration, the seeds of which may have been planted long, long ago.

Manufacturing became very big business, especially with regard to the automotive and airplane industries. The nation's, if not the world's economy became greatly dependent upon the inventions that took place in the early 1900's. These ideas now became very integral parts of mankind's life as Uranus reached its seasonal "zenith point" at 0° Cancer.

The most turbulent decade of the twentieth century was perhaps the 1960's, and in particular the late 1960's when Uranus crossed into the Autumnal Equinox segment of the zodiac. Once again humankind was presented an opportunity to shift its collective consciousness. However, in order to do so, it was first of all forced to confront the consequences of prior actions. These consequences came about in the form of the Viet Nam war, the assassinations of Martin Luther King and Robert Kennedy, the Russian invasion of Prague, and the landing of the first man on the Moon (perhaphs this was karmic merit related to the "original idea" of the airplane back in the early 1900's). In retrospect, historians have labeled the 1960's as "The Decade of Dissent," as both civil rights and anti-war movements were spawned across the globe. Agreements were very difficult to come by, yet powerful relationships and alliances were formed in all walks of human experience.

In 1988, both Uranus and Saturn (as well as Mars) entered 0° Capricorn within a 10-day period, thus initiating the "Capricorn Climax" (see Chapter 21). Within months the collapse of Communism had commenced. An old order had come to an end, a new world order was conceived. For the first time in the history of humankind, nearly all of the world's countries banded together in an "Allied Coalition" whose primary purpose was to deter naked aggression and war from one country (Iraq) onto another (Kuwait). As the 1980's came to an end and the 1990's began, as Uranus and Saturn and the North Node of the Moon all crossed the Winter Solstice, Galactic Center and Solar Apex within a short time span, an air of enlightenment engulfed the world. The needs of the collective soul were being heard and a new world order perhaps entered the conception phase, much like in the early 1900's when Uranus last entered into Capricorn.

As an old cycle comes to an end, a cycle which outwardly began with the Wright brothers invention of the airplane, a new cycle begins as rocket ships fly to the outer limits of the solar system, sending back photographs of distant celestial bodies that reveal workings of a universe that will require an entirely new set of models for explaining creation itself.

Like the last Uranus revolution, this one too will undergo severe tests. The first will likely come about as Uranus transits 15° Aquarius

(1999–2000). How humanity and the leaders of the world cope with this and future tests will likely determine the types of experiences the collective will undergo when Uranus crosses its zenith and Descendant (2032–2033, and 2051–2053 respectively). One of the most creative periods in this evolution will likely come about as Uranus enters 0° Aries (2010–2012).

Bear in mind that each of these periods brings forth a fertile era for enlightened thought. The needs of the soul are clear to those who would but listen. These are not only periods of crisis, but they are also opportunities for both individual and collective evolution, a time in which repetitive and debilitating karmic patterns may be transcended.

CHAPTER TWENTY

Planetary Pair Cycles: Breaking Through the Collective Pattern

"Liberation of creativeness should be the principle of reform." [19]

The concept of seasonal ingresses pertains to a relationship between a planet and a sector of the heavens. By itself this is a somewhat static concept. That is, a planet/sign relationship correlates to an "idea", or a shift in consciousness. Insomuch as changes in behavior or patterns must begin with such a shift in consciousness, these periods are extremely important. However, the dynamics of change also involve the activation, or manifestation, of these ideas. Such physical changes, or events that oftentimes seem to "force" such changes in human activity, are more the domain of interaction between two planets, rather than simply planet-to-sign changes.

In astrology, the interaction between two (or more) planets is most notable at an aspect. An aspect between two planets is a specific spatial relationship existing at various points along the orbit of each planet around the Sun. For example, when two planets "come together" (as seen from Earth), they are said to be in *conjunction* aspect. The longitudinal distance between the two appears to be 0° in a 360° orbit, or circle. When one planet is rising and another is setting, as seen from Earth, they are said to be in *opposition* aspect. They are 180° apart.

[19]Bertrand Russell, *The Autobiography of Bertrand Russell* (Boston, Little, Brown & Co., 1951).

When one is culminating and the other is either rising or setting, the two planets are in a *square* aspect to one another, or 90° apart.

These three aspects – the conjunction, opposition, and square – are considered the most powerful of all aspects between any two planets. In addition, these aspects correlate to the four-fold model of Evolutionary Astrology presented throughout this book. For instance, the conjunction is akin to the I. C. (the beginning point), while the opposition may be likened to the Midheaven. There are two square aspects which planets may form to one another in their circular orbit around the Sun: one is 90° from the conjunction while the other is 270°. The first correlates to the principles of the Ascendant, while the second to the Descendant, as presented earlier.

In between each of these aspects are the 45°, 135°, 225° and 315° aspects, known as *semi-square* and *sesquiquadrate* aspects. They correspond to the principles of angular midpoints presented in previous chapters.

The study of planetary pair cycles begins with a conjunction of any two planets. Put simply, when any two planets form a conjunction, the principles involved in those two planets begin a new cycle that will continue in effect until the next conjunction unfolds. During this planetary pair cycle, events or activities will likely take place when the two planets involved in the planetary pair cycle make their consecutive 45° relationships to one another.

The most familiar of the planetary pair cycles is the lunation cycle. The new Moon, or conjunction between the Sun and Moon, is a 29-day planetary pair cycle. Once a month the Sun and the Moon come together, forming a new Moon. Traditionally the period of time between the new Moon and first quarter (90° square aspect) is considered an excellent time to initiate activities. The fulfillment or completion of the activity is considered most propitious if realized by the full Moon (180°, or opposition aspect). From the full Moon back to the next new Moon is a period of realizing the rewards or results of the initiated activity. Along the way there are two critical periods that potentially alter the course of the idea: the first and last quarter Moon (90° and 270° aspect). Conflicts also arise with the 45°, 135°, and 315° aspects. These periods challenge the moral issues involved in the implementation of the idea conceived at the conjunction.

This same process flows with any planetary pair cycle. During the conjunction phase, a new idea is conceived according to the principles of the two planets involved. Since the principles are planetary-based (as opposed to sign-based), there is likely to be a major event that precipitates the birth of this new idea or order. Even the event is within the

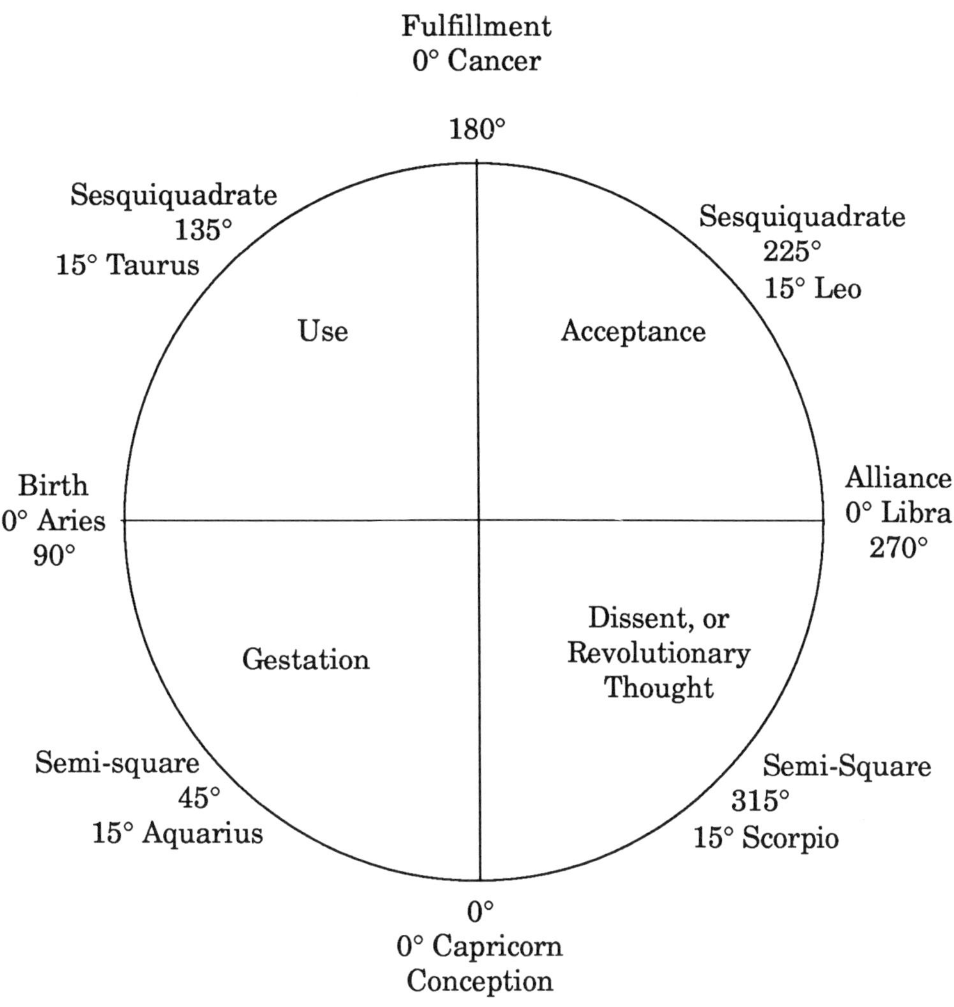

Figure 16
Cycle of collective evolution and/or change in societal structure, via Planetary Pair Cycles and/or ingresses of major transits.

language of astrology. For example, if the idea relates to aviation, it is probably a planetary pair cycle involving Uranus, the planet which correlates to aviation. If the concept relates to music or poetry, then Neptune is likely involved in the planetary pair cycle.

During the first 45° aspect between these two planets, moral issues arise with regard to the concept originated when the two planets were in conjunction. At the first 90° square between the two planets, some form is birthed which relates to the conjunction point. At the 135° aspect, a power play may unfold with regard to the matter that has now taken shape. At the 180° opposition aspect, the form may reach a pinnacle in its usefullness, or its destiny. It may finally achieve acceptance by the collective group. When the two planets reach the distance of 225° apart, another powerful conflict may arise over the application of the matter, or the people who control the application of it. At the 270° square aspect, the consequences or karma of the matter are brought to full light. If the activities related to this matter have been in violation of natural law, then major problems erupt for the leaders as a period of dissent begins. If the criticisms are not heeded properly, then the period of disintegration proceeds in earnest around the time of the 315° semi-square aspect. Finally a new idea or order is conceived as the two planets return to conjunction again (360°, or 0°).

Not all planetary cycles are equal in their potential impact. Some are potentially more powerful than others. This leads to a basic assumption regarding planetary pair cycles: **The longer the periodicity of a planetary pair cycle, the more profound and long-lasting its potential impact is likely to be upon the affairs of humankind.** There are also two corolaries to this assumption:

1. The point of conjunction between the two planets involved in a planetary pair cycle becomes a "charged" point in the zodiac. That degree of the conjunction takes on a synthesis of the two planetary principles involved, and will remain in effect until the next cycle of the two planets commences. At this time the degree of the new conjunction becomes the "charged" point of the zodiac for that planetary pair cycle.

2. Every time a major planet transits in aspect to this "charged" point, it potentially coincides with an event related to the nature of the planetary pair cycle.

An example of these principles is perhaps most recognizable with a solar eclipse. A solar eclipse is a new Moon that conjuncts or opposes the Moon's North Node. The degree of the solar eclipse becomes a "charged" point of the zodiac. Whenever major planets transit in aspect to the degree of the solar eclipse, a major event may arise that relates to the situations present at the time of the solar eclipse itself.

Given this assumption, the most significant planetary pair cycles will be those involving the farthest-out planets. Those involving Saturn, particularly with Jupiter, are extremely critical for humankind. They involve crises in faith for the collective. They present opportunities for humankind to take a more spiritual or moral approach to problems affecting large numbers of people, to correct inequities in the present collective behavior. This is oftentimes implemented in the form of new laws or policies.

However the most significant breakthroughs, or changes, for humankind are those that relate to the planetary pair cycles of Uranus, Neptune and Pluto. In earlier chapters, these planets were shown to correlate to opportunities for profound changes in one's karmic patterns. When these planets form a conjunction to one another, there is an opportunity for profound changes in the karma of the collective pattern. In addition, every time a major planet transits in a major aspect to the conjunction point of this planetary pair cycle, it is as if the conjunction itself is being set off.

To illustrate this point, let us consider the longest (and hence the most potentially profound) planetary pair cycle known: Neptune and Pluto. These two furthest-out planets of the solar system come together every 492 years. The current cycle began in 1892-1893 as Neptune and Pluto conjoined in 6-8° Gemini. During the last decade of the 19th century and first few years of the twentieth century, a profound change did occur which effected the entire planet. A communications (Gemini) revolution commenced as both the automobile and airplane were conceived. It was a period which saw the African continent conquered by several European countries and the rise of the "White Man's burden" ideologies. It was the beginning, and hence the foundation, of the modern interdependent world economy. In the United States, a panic ensued in 1893 that led to a four-year depression. In literature, naturalist writers pushed realism to extremes by writing about formerly taboo subjects such as sex, crime and poverty. This was the time of Sigmund Freud's revolutionary ideas pertaining to the repressed psychological mind which revolutionized that study. All in all, the Neptune/Pluto conjunction began a cycle that was one of the most profound in the history of civilization.

The first 45° aspect between these two planets unfolded from 1929–1933. From the point of view of Evolutionary Astrology, this would represent the first major crisis of the concepts originated during the conjunction phase. There would be a number of moral issues that might threaten the "birthing" of those matters conceived at the conjunction. During this period the so-called modern interdependent world economy almost collapsed as the world entered the worst depression in modern day history. This is also the period in which Adolph Hitler came to power (i.e. form of a "White Man's burden"), and physics became the dominant study of the sciences, both challenging the concepts originated in the 1890's. Intellectually, morally, politically, and economically, the world was faced with major conflicts. The choices were clearly becoming organized in terms of "good versus bad", "right versus wrong", and even "Black versus White." Symbolically, the needs of the soul were coming into conflict with the desires of the collective ego, the latter being represented in the form of self-centered and power-driven leaders of government and economics, not to mention science and literature. The conflicts present during that period were some of the most intense witnessed in the twenteith century.

The 90° square aspect between these two planets will not unfold until the last half of the 21st century. Until that time, the Neptune/ Pluto cycle continues in the gestation phase. A birthing process related to the ideas of the last decade of the 19th century will take almost 200 years to manifest. When these two planets do eventually enter into their first square aspect, perhaps a true global economy will take form. Perhaps the ideas of transportation conceived back in the 1890's ultimately leads to space expeditions to the Moon or other planets. Perhaps by the time of the opposition, these celestial bodies may be colonized. At this point in time, these ideas are mere speculation. However, if the principles of Evolutionary Astrology are valid, then it may be ascertained that something will take a form, something will be birthed in the latter half of the 21st century. That which will be birthed will be seen to have its roots as far back as the late 1890's.

In the meantime, 6-8° Gemini is now a "charged" point in the zodiac with a quality that synthesizes the principles of Neptune and Pluto. Every time a major aspect between a significant planetary transit or combination occurs to this degree, something related to the principles of these two planets potentially unfolds. To show how this concept works, let us consider just one aspect of the 1892–93 conjunction – the revolution of transportation, and most notably, the airplane. First of all, consider the fact that many of the early pioneers in aviation were born during the 1890's: Amelia Earhart, Eddie Rickenbacker, James Doolittle, Roy de L. Monro, Wiley Post, to name a few. The following is a list of some of the most significant dates in aviation history, and the corresponding transits to 6–8° Gemini:

1. The Wright brothers first flight, December 17, 1903. Mars and Saturn both in trine aspect to 6–8° Gemini.

2. The Wright brothers first officially recorded flight, September 9, 1905. Jupiter stationary 6° 30' Gemini.

3. The first international air flight, August 22, 1909. Mars stationary in exact sextile to the Gemini point.

4. In 1919, three major aviation events occurred: Walter Hinton completed the first transatlantic flight; the first air mail service commenced; and the first passenger service by air transport was initiated. Neptune sextiled the Gemini point.

5. The first major aircraft explosion, June 5, 1921. Uranus squared the Gemini point.

6. Charles Lindbergh flies solo over the Atlantic, May 21, 1927. The new Moon a couple of days later was 6° Gemini, as was transiting Mercury.

7. The most productive year for the construction of single engine Lockheeds was in 1929. Uranus sextile the Gemini point.

8. In the early 1930's, as Neptune squared the Gemini point, and the first semi-square unfolded, missiles and rockets were created.

9. Sputnik and Explorer satellites were launched, October 4, 1957 and February 1, 1958, thus beginning the space race. Uranus sextile the Gemini point.

10. The Soviet Union put the first man into space, followed by the United States, on April 12 and May 25, 1961 respectively. Pluto square to Gemini point. During the same aspect, U. N. General Secretary Dag Hammarskjold died in a plane crash.

11. Man lands on the Moon, July 20, 1969. Jupiter and Uranus trine to Gemini point.

12. U. S. astronauts take mankind's first ride on the Moon, July 31, 1971. Saturn conjunct Gemini point.

13. U. S. A.'s Apollo Moon program comes to an end with last visit, December 19, 1972. Neptune opposes Gemini point.

14. Soviets shoot down Korean Airlines flight 007 and 269 people die, September 15, 1983. Uranus oppose Gemini point.

15. Space shuttle Challenger explodes 74 seconds after liftoff in the worst accident in the history of the U. S. space program, witnessed by millions of viewers on television, January 28, 1986. Saturn oppose Gemini point.

The aviation and subsequently the space programs were not the only areas of human activity affected by the Neptune/Pluto planetary pair cycle. As Pluto pertains to power over the masses, and Neptune corresponds to either religion or delusions, it is not suprising to find many spiritual leaders and ideas born of this period, as well as many delusionary claims to great world power.

Some of the power struggles in politics affected by this cycle include the following blunders:

1. In 1893, as Uranus formed a quincunx to the Gemini point, the United States intervened in the Hawaiian Revolution, and assumed control over the islands.

2. In 1900, two very important wars were staged in the human drama, as Uranus opposed the Gemini point: The Spanish-American War and the Boxer Rebellion in China.

3. The outbreak of World War I in 1914 had a strange twist: in one sense it was a breakthrough for the aircraft industry (Uranus trined the Gemini degrees), and yet there were many underhanded and deceptive activities (Neptune semi-square).

4. On May 29, 1938 a total solar eclipse occurred right on the Gemini point. During the forthcoming year, Adolph Hitler proclaimed his right to rule the World with his " Master Race". During the same year, Jupiter squared the Gemini point, corresponding to great exaggeration. Incidentally, the Nazi triumvirate of Goebbels, Goring and Hitler were all born during the period of the Neptune-Pluto conjunction.

5. As the heaviest fighting during World War II took place in 1942–43, Saturn and Uranus both formed conjunctions to the early Gemini degrees.

6. In the early 1950's, the drama continued as the Korean conflict broke out, and France made her initial entrance into Viet Nam. During this period Neptune formed a sesquiquadrate and Uranus a semi-square to the Gemini point.

7. When the Commander-in-Chief of the United States ordered an attack on the Gulf of Tonkin, and hence unofficially declared War on Viet Nam in 1964, Uranus squared the Gemini point, while transiting Mercury was retrograde and also squaring the Gemini degrees.

8. In 1973–74, as Neptune opposed the early Gemini point, one of the greatest scandals ever to afflict the United States broke out with the advent of the Watergate tragedy. The very day that Richard Nixon resigned, August 9, 1974, transiting Mars squared the Gemini point from early Virgo.

There were also many gains brought forth from this same cycle, as these two powers suggest great breakthroughs on mental and spiritual planes as well. Astrology was reborn thanks to the efforts of many astrologers who were born in the early 1890's, i.e. Dane Rudhyar, Vivian Robson, Marc Edmund Jones, Ernest Grant, Cyril Fagan, Charles Carter, just to name a few. In fact in 1942, when Pluto and Neptune were both favorably aspecting the Gemini degrees by sextile and trine respectively, the United States commissioned an astrologer (Sidney Omarr) to advise them as to what information Adolph Hitler may have been receiving from his astrologer. In 1969 when Uranus trined the Gemini point, astrology became more than just an interest to many – it became a serious study once again.

In the spiritual-religious realm itself, at least three great mentors appeared upon the Earth plane under the Neptune-Pluto conjunction: Meher Baba, Jeddu Krishnamurti, and Paramahansa Yogananda. Perhaps more than any others (with perhaps the exception of Vivekananda's address to the World Council of Religion in the early 1890's), these three have brought the "East to meet the West". Much of the Western interest in the Far Eastern lines of thought can be traced to the efforts of these three. In 1920, as Neptune exactly sextiled the Gemini point, Yogananda introduced Kriya Yoga in the United States.

As one can see, the great planetary pair cycle of Neptune and Pluto has already had incredible influence upon the affairs of humanity. As transits continue to aspect 6-8 degrees of Gemini, one can watch as the drama continues to unfold as part of the scheme of the collective destiny.

Neptune and Pluto are but one of the three planetary cycles formed by the farthest-out planets of the solar system. The other two are Uranus and Pluto, which started in 1965–1966 at 15–17° Virgo, and Uranus to Neptune, which will commence a new cycle in 1992–1993 between 18–20° Capricorn. Like Neptune and Pluto, these two planetary pair cycles also represent potentially profound breakthroughs for humanity.

The late 1960's brought forth critically significant changes in a wide array of human activity, as Uranus and Pluto began their new cycle. It was the time of the Viet Nam war and the consequent anti-war demonstrations throughout the world. It led to the demise of many leaderships. It also correlated to a revolutionary change in music with the formation of such groups as the Beatles and Rolling Stones. The so-called "New Age" was birthed at this time, as a whole new generation incorporated a value system that was in complete opposition to earlier generations. This led to numerous racial, social, and political conflicts, particularly in the United States.

These two planets met their first 45° test in 1986–1987. This was a particularly dangerous and revolutionary period for humanity. Ferdinand Marcos was overthrown in the Philippines; Jean-Claude Duvalier was ousted from dictatorship in Haiti; Americans bombed Colonel Muammar Khadafy's quarters in Lybia; a major nuclear disaster occurred at the Chernobyl plant in the Soviet Union; Oliver North implicated his bosses in the secret Iran arms sales; and the world stock markets suffered their worst one-week crash in history. All of this was part of the birthing process as these two planets moved through the midpoint of their gestation phase. The birthing itself will take place in 2012–2015. Perhaps the ideas and ideals that were conceived in the late 1960's will finally manifest during this period. In the meantime, events related to these ideas of the late 1960's will tend to arise whenever major planets transit in aspect to 15-17° Virgo. As an example, consider the period in which Saturn transited 15-17° Gemini (square) and 15-17° Virgo (conjunct). The first occurred in late 1972-early 1973 as then President Richard Nixon became involved in the infamous Watergate scandal that led to the first resignation ever of a U. S. president. The second occurred in late 1979–early 1980 (along with a stationary Mars at 15° Virgo) as U. S. citizens were held hostage by Iranians, and eventually led to the defeat of U. S. President Jimmy Carter. It was also the time in which Russia invaded Afghanistan. In 1987 Saturn squared the Uranus/Pluto 15-17° Virgo point from Sagittarius. This was during the same time that Uranus and Pluto formed their first 45° aspect, as described in the previous page.

The final major planetary pair cycle commences in 1992–1993 as Uranus and Neptune form a conjunction in 18-20° Capricorn. This will end the previous cycle which unfolded in 1821 as these same two major planets conjoined at 1-3° Capricorn. That period brought forth a major shift in intellectual and artistic expression. It was a rebirth for romanticism and a reaction against the excessive philosophies of rationalism and skepticism. Clothing became freer and music exhibited a new dramatic style with a breakdown of classical form. The boundaries of European countries were re-defined as Napoleon's empire came to an end. The settlements brought 50 years of international peace to Europe. In the United States, sentiment toward antislavery gained momentum, eventually leading to a Civil War when planets moved toward their first 90° square aspect.

The significance of the 1992–1993 planetary pair cycle of Uranus and Neptune is apt to be extremely profound. It begins shortly after the solar eclipse on December 24, 1992 at 2° Capricorn, which is not only the degree of the previous Uranus/Neptune cycle, but also close to the degree of the solar apex and Winter Solstice point (i.e. I. C. symbology). It also occurs as the phenomenon known as the "Capricorn Climax" enters its last year (see chapter 21).

Like a rocket ship ready to launch a voyage into a vast, new dimension, humanity itself appears on the precipice of a major voyage. The journey ahead for the collective soul is no less significant than that of each individual's own journey through life. As this book is being written, humankind stands on the brink of a major shift in consciousness, a major shift in direction. The potential for an enlightened breakthrough is tremendous. The ideas and concepts that are now being conceived may serve as a foundation for the people of this planet for many generations to come. All the major planetary pair cycles of Uranus and beyond are just in their gestation phase as the twenteith century draws to a close. The Capricorn Climax itself symbolizes the conception of a new and long-lasting world order, an order that will not be fully birthed for several decades.

The souls now embodied upon Earth as the twenteith century comes to conclusion are faced with a major spiritual responsibility, as seen from the study of Evolutionary Astrology. They are responsible for the conception and the gestation phase of a major collective shift in consciousness. They are responsible for laying the foundation of a new collective awareness. This is the era in which darkness decreases (quadrant one). It is a time requiring meditation and reflection. It is a period in which intuition is at a height. The wealth of collective wisdom is coming from within (darkness, below horizon). Reality being imposed from without, or externally, may not be as relevant now as it was in decades past. The climate is very fertile for individual awakening, and as individuals become more and more receptive to the counsel of their inner voice (or soul), so too does the collective consciousness become more and more receptive to those who espouse wise counsel (i.e. the group soul, or inner voice).

It is a dynamic period, and one in which both individuals as well as large groups of individuals may make great strides in their evolutionary journey. Perhaps all that is left to complete the cosmic puzzle is the advent of a great comet, whose celestial sphere penetrates the egg-like path of the Earth's orbit around the Sun. The symbology of conception could then be no clearer as humankind truly enters the gestation phase that is already indicated by the movement of the furthest-out planets in the solar system.

CHAPTER TWENTY ONE

The Capricorn Climax

"By deep knowledge of principle, one can change disturbance into order, change danger into safety, change destruction into survival, change calamity into fortune. By strong action on the Way, one can bring the body to the realm of longitivity, bring the mind to the sphere of mystery, bring the world to great peace, and bring tasks to great fulfillment." [20]

Out in the deep, vast universe lies a small galaxy known as the Milky Way. There is nothing special about its location; as a matter of fact, it is not even close to the center of the universe.

But there is something special about the composition of this galaxy for within it are several orbiting bodies around a great star known as the Sun. And on one of the planets, known as Earth, human life exists. As far as the inhabitants of this planet know, no other life like theirs exists anywhere else in the entire universe. In a sense, this planet and its inhabitants are all alone in this great and vast universe.

For thousands of years (and perhaps millions) the inhabitants of this small planet in this small galaxy in this infinite universe used to look out to the heavens with awe. At first it was with appreciation and wonder. Then it was with reverence and respect, and even fear. Then at one point in their collective evolution, members of the human community began watching the heavens for **guidance**. They began to notice that rains and tides coincided with certain phases of the Moon. Before long they began to plant their grains by these lunar phases. In time

[20]Sun Tzu, *The Book of Balance and Harmony*, as in the introduction to *The Art of War* (Boston, Shambhala, 1988).

they noticed that certain celestial phenomena such as eclipses of the Sun correlated with famine and poor growing conditions, and when these would occur they would stock up on additional grains.

In time these inhabitants of Earth began to organize into communities. Each community had a leader, or ruler. Sometimes these small communities would come into contact with other small communities. Disputes would arise over such matters as growing or grazing areas. The leaders of the communities would lead their members into battle against those with whom they had disputes. Sometimes the leaders led their groups into battle because they were greedy; they would desire more land for their community and would aggressively "take it" from others. Oftentimes a community found a new leader during these battles. The one who was strongest or most brave would oftentimes emerge as the leader.

Before long, inhabitants upon Earth began noticing that the movement of the planets correlated not only with favorable and unfavorable times to plant grains, but also favorable and unfavorable times to enter battle. The planets, the Sun and Moon, were thus discovered to be important in the timing of affairs of the community.

It was during this period in the evolution of humankind that astrology truly came to be born. The planets and constellations were always "out there", but it wasn't until humanity evolved to the point of a communal society (organizational structures) that an awareness of the study of astrology came about. Man's relationship to the Infinite began with an understanding (or belief) that there was an orderliness to life, and this orderliness had its roots in the cosmos. Thus man (which includes woman) discovered astrology as the study of his/her connection to the universe, to a greater order.

Throughout the centuries astrologers have observed how the movement of the planets through the various constellations have affected the affairs of humanity. Astrology correlates planetary movements to conditions arising in the lives of individuals, and since leaders of communities or countries are individuals, it affects them and their nations as well. From these studies a branch of astrology developed known as Mundane Astrology, or the astrology of nations.

The title of this book is ***Evolutionary Astrology: The Journey Of The Soul Through States of Consciousness***. Throughout this book the approach has been that the individual soul being born has a karma, a destiny, which is the result of prior actions and choices. This karma and destiny (consequence and opportunity) are shown by the placement of planets at the moment of one's birth.

However, groups also have a karma and destiny as shown in the section on "The Karma of Identities." Not only do small groups have a karma and destiny, but so too does the entire community (group) of humanity. It is oftentimes said that the planet Earth has a karma, but in reality it is the inhabitants of Earth that collectively have a karma, and this karma is denoted by the movement of the planets. Just as an individual is confronted with specific challenges which require significant choices at specific times in his or her life, so too is humanity confronted with major crises at specific times in its evolution. The choices made at those times determine whether or not long-term cycles are altered, whether the human community evolves to the next level of collective awareness, or continues with a similar but more complicated script and pattern than before. Humanity, like individuals, is confronted with several opportunities to understand its collective needs, to make choices in alignment with its collective purpose. Humanity, like individuals, has the opportunity to learn through its experiences and thus "break through" to new levels of awareness and new scripts. These opportunities, through crisis, are most evident during periods of unusual planetary configurations.

These configurations may take many forms. They may take the form of a long-term planetary conjunction (planetary pair cycle, as discussed in the last chapter), or a combination of three or more planets in unusual multiple aspect formations, or the movement of major planets into solstice or equinox signs.

One such configuration is unfolding as this book is being written. It is known as the "Capricorn Climax". It is a long-term covergence (conjunctions) of Saturn, Uranus, Neptune and the Moon's North Node, all in the tropical constellation of Capricorn. The center of this configuration takes place in 1990–1991. However the intensity of this arrangement is likely to be quite pronounced from at least 1988–1993. The fact that it will take at least six years for this pattern to mostly unfold makes it perhaps the most unusual and potentially powerful configuration of the twentieth century. The fact that it is unfolding in the cardinal sign of Capricorn, the sign corresponding to beginning of the Winter Solstice, makes it potentially one of the most significant periods in the history of humankind. Nothing of this nature has happened astronomically since the early 14th century. Even that configuration in Scorpio was not as potentially powerful as this one will be in Capricorn. There have been conjunctions of three or more planets before, but not of Saturn and beyond in a solstice or equinox sign, and not during a period in which there was also a solar eclipse in the same sign (1991–92).

The importance of the sign of Capricorn was addressed in Chapter

19. When major planets cross into the sign of Capricorn, humanity has an opportunity to come to grips with its very essence, and with the needs of its communal soul. It represents a time when it can review its foundation, its basic collective principles. It has an opportunity to make choices which are in accordance with its deepest needs, and thereby modify or construct a long-term foundation that will be operative for many, many generations to come. This is as close as one comes to knowing what it is, to having an opportunity to behave in a manner that is in alignment with its purpose. Whatever choices are made at this time sets the tone, determines the karma or consequences it will undergo for a long, long time. It is the "darkest hour" of humanity, and within this experience is offered the gift of **faith**. Decisions made by world leaders at this time require a leap of faith. Without it the pattern cannot change. There is risk, but the risk is worth it if indeed the choices to be made are consistent with the needs of the community, and if the committment to adhere to its vows are honored. If not, the patterns and scripts become even more complex.

So what do we see happening during this period? Have any major decisions and changes taken place? Has there been any major crises that required an act of faith? Has something so significant arisen that the tide of history could be changed? The answer to these questions is yes.

Humanity has been faced with a gigantic challenge. For the most part it has chosen peace and cooperation over war and tyranny. In late 1989, the Union of the Soviet Socialist Republics granted independence to many of the Eastern Bloc countries which had been under Communist rulership for several decades. An era of repression had come to an end. Forty million people were granted the freedom of choice in their government structure.

That is not all. In August of 1990, Iraq invaded Kuwait. An unprecedented cooperative effort was launched by the majority of the world's countries, known as the "Allied Coalition" to liberate Kuwait. Never before had so many of the world's community come together in a cooperative venture for a common purpose which humanity valued: freedom of choice.

The task is not completed, and even as this is being written, many of those leaders who have made these choices (these leaps of faith) are being tested. Their committment to these decisions is being challenged. The choices being made under this Capricorn Climax are being questioned. Will Russia honor her committment toward freedom of choice for her people as well as for those to whom she granted independence? Will the Middle Eastern countries honor their promise to work cooperatively together for a peaceful world, particularly in that region, as well as their promise to respect human rights of one another? These are the questions. These are the vows made, in accordance with the needs of the evolving human community, at this time. To honor these needs, committments, and promises will break a debilitating script for humanity. It will allow humanity, as a collective consciousness, to "break through" to new levels of awareness, to new levels of creativity and productivity, to a new era of global understanding. To renege on these choices might result instead in a very long term and even more complex pattern of difficulty and stress for all humanity. It is indeed, a most critical time in humanity's evolution.

As humanity goes through this crisis, so too does every individual human being. As the collective is confronted with the consequences and choices of its relationship to one another on a group level, so too are individuals confronted with consequences and hence choices, in their relationships to one another. During this period many, many individuals are likely to experience a crisis in significant personal relationships. Close relationships will be threatened. Physical death, changes of location, threat of divorce, new mates, loss of jobs through "personality conflicts", new jobs with interesting "mentors" are all possibilities. Yet each relationship, and the conditions in these relationships, offers an opportunity. The opportunity is to more deeply understand one's self, the dynamics behind one's behavior. In a sense, it is an opportunity to understand the dynamics of one's karma, and in this understanding, to make conscious choices that are in alignment with the needs of one's soul. For many this requires a leap of faith, but for those with the courage to make such a leap, comes the reward of enlightenment, the experience of a blissful outpouring of compassion. For these souls comes a "break through."

As the Capricorn Climax, and other significant and unusual configurations unfold in the future, all members of the human community have an unusual opportunity to receive the gift of faith, a gift which comes with a new awareness of one's self, of one's soul, of one's Spirit. These are the moments when God returns upon Earth, when Christ consciousness is present to the collective mind. It is simply a matter of receiving, of not letting the ego dominate the conscious mind with its elaborate defenses of denial.

On an individual basis, it is significant to note where the Capricorn Climax unfolds in the natal chart. Is it in the first, second, third, or fourth quadrant? That will indicate the particular segment of reality the soul is evolving through. That will indicate the particular direction in which the soul may contribute understanding to the collective, or how the events of the collective affect the soul. If Capricorn is in the first quadrant, then the soul may discover a path of self-mastery. The intuitive faculties may be heightened, especially through meditative practice. It is also a time in which materialism may be greatly affected. In the second quadrant (houses 10–12), one may find great changes in work. One's level of productivity may be changed, and the committment to one's calling in life may be challenged. It is potentially a time of empowerment. In the third quadrant one may be given deep understanding of life. One may find a teacher, or become a teacher to others. There may be crisis in relationships, but it is a period of apprenticeship and preparation for something greater. In quadrant four, one's faith may be rigorously tested. It may be a period of great inspiration if one is receptive, a time of great spiritual awakening. One's deepest fears may be encountered, and a major risk may be undertaken as a result. Through faith and focus, this individual may come into an awareness of the soul, and experience a significant transformation.

The Capricorn Climax, 1988–1993, is very likely the most powerful astronomical set-up of the twentieth century. As a collective group, humanity has a chance to truly evolve into a new age. As individuals, one has an opportunity to evolve into new levels of awareness, and hence transform personal karmic scripts. Each individual has the opportunity, through periods like this, to commune with Spirit.

CHAPTER TWENTY TWO

The Challenge

"The mission of the artist is to elevate himself through study and insight to the highest attainable level and then to communicate with his peers, to seek them out, to exchange concepts with them, and to write or paint or compose so as to illuminate the problems that concern them." [21]

One of the most difficult challenges in life is to determine one's place in the grand scheme of things. Even more difficult is accepting this role.

The principles set forth in this book are based upon the premise that each person has a soul, that one's soul has existed before the birth moment and will continue after the moment of physical death, and that while in a physical embodiment, the soul has the opportunity to evolve beyond its present condition. There is an essence unique to each soul, and this essence has been molded by the circumstances this soul has experienced and the nature of its responses to those circumstances. As a responsive, physical entity, the embodied soul develops a multitude of personality variables. These personalities take on a temporal life of their own, and in the reality of the five-sensory world, decisions are made which are either in harmony, or incongruent, to the understanding of that soul. When these decisions are incongruent with one's spiritual understanding, the personality becomes fixed, and emotional patterns of a low frequency result. As the personality becomes more and more defined by these patterns of low frequency emotional responses, the scripts become more and more complex. Another way of stating this is to say that one gives birth to the ego, and the ego's primary function is

[21]James A. Michener, *The Novel* (New York, Random House, 1991.)

to protect the conscious mind from experiencing pain. The ego is amoral. The ego will do whatever is necessary to assure its survival, including lying, cheating, denying, avoiding or blaming. It will also rationalize and justify in order to convince the conscious mind to make a particular decision that is self-serving.

The ego is not the only voice the conscious mind is capable of hearing. There is also the voice of the soul, which expresses its own needs. The basic need of the soul is to evolve, to experience union with its own source, which has been referred to as Spirit. This journey toward wholeness with Spirit may take many lifetimes, for along the way one has likely made many decisions that gave rise to ego. In other words, one has made decisions that have set into motion various cycles which are not yet complete.

As an embodied being, one has a consciousness which interacts in the phenomenal, dualistic world. The conscious mind makes decisions. On the one hand, it must consider the immediate urges of seeking pleasure and avoiding pain, which is the role of the ego. On the other hand, the conscious mind receives counsel from the soul, whose purpose is to pursue evolution (union) with Spirit. The ego seeks to differentiate and separate, while the soul seeks to integrate and diffuse that which separates it from Spirit, which is formless.

By their very nature the soul and the ego are at odds with one another, yet within the same individual. Yet the dynamics of the one affect the quality of existance for the other. When the individual makes a decision that benefits the self at the expense of another, it is a victory for the ego, but ultimately an obstacle for the soul which now must overcome the consequences of the cycle initiated. In this case the ego goes to work and gains strength. Every time an issue arises which pertains to the dynamics of that self-centered decision, the ego directs the conscious mind to behave in a specific emotional manner that defends its decision. The individual may become angry, or hurt, or depressed whenever challenged on this issue. By responding in this manner, the individual sets into motion a pattern, a script, and this becomes a quality ascribed to that personality: "he is an angry young man", "he is weak and timid," "he is under alot of pressure and can't handle it." A cycle has been initiated, a personality characteristic has been created, an emotional response pattern has been developed, and as a result, a script for experience has been implemented. Throughout life, this individual will continue to experience the same results in relationships when this issue arises. Eventually he will develop a physical ailment whose cause relates to this issue. The script prevents him from experiencing fullness. It is as if he short-circuits himself.

The recipient of this decision is ultimately one's soul. It has to undergo the consequences of these cycles, from one lifetime to another. Like the ego, it too has purpose, but unlike the ego, its purpose continues from one lifetime to another. The ego on the other hand ceases to exist once the body ceases to exist.

The legacy the ego leaves behind is known as the karma of the soul. The karma colors the soul. It is this karma, or nature of cycles regarding each soul, that gives rise to the essence of each soul.

Before entering embodiment, the soul understands that it must undergo certain conditions (and encounter certain people) which are related to the cycles that its personality has set into motion, and which are not yet complete. It understands that these conditions and people are symbols for certain lessons it must guide the conscious mind into understanding in this lifetime. The soul understands what it must do in order to experience union with Spirit. It must serve as a guide, as a teacher, to the conscious mind this embodiment is taking on. The soul understands that individuals must undergo these experiences, and its role is to provide counsel, in the form of right thought, according to natural law. Unlike the ego, the soul is very moral insomuch as it understands the consequences or results of various choices of behavior. Some choices will "feel" right to the individual because they are in accordance with this natural law. Other choices may give one an apparent advantage over others, but do not "feel" right because they are separative in nature, and in violation of the principles of natural law. For each response, there is a cyclic result. In the former case, there is release and evolvement. In the latter case, there is impediment and complication upon one's journey.

The soul of an individual is part of a greater soul, or group. What an individual does reflects back upon this group soul, just as it reflects upon its own individual soul. This concept was alluded to in the chapter on "The Karma Of Identity." Decisions made on the basis of race reflect upon the cycle both the individual and his/her race are to experience. As an example, an assault by a White person upon a Black person, with the intent to do bodily harm, not only initiates a racial cycle for the White individual, but it may also initiate a cycle for the entire White community of which the individual was a member. All White people in that community may have to cope with the consequences of that single White individual's behavior.

There is a message in this example. The individual is not acting as just an independent variable in the grand scheme of things. Responsibility for one's actions is not just an individual matter. When an individual consciously commits an act, the consequences are not relegated to him or her alone. The act affects the groups with which he or she identifies. Ultimately they pertain to some extent to the whole body of humanity.

The soul understands this responsibility. That is why the destiny of every human being is to serve and teach others in some capacity. Every individual has a responsibility to elevate him or herself through study and insight to the highest level possible, then to share those insights with his or her peers. The soul knows this, but the ego finds it difficult to accept. The ego seeks to protect one from harm, whether physical, emotional, or psychical. It creates illusions that obstruct from this responsibility. It resists accepting its proper role in the grand scheme of things because it thrives on separativeness and duality. The possibility that all human beings share a common destiny threatens its very existence.

Yet while the ego persists in fostering the illusion of separativeness, it encourages the conscious mind of each individual to disregard the counsel of its own soul. In the process, acts are committed that are in the violation of natural law, and the entire collective of humanity enters into more and more complex group scripts.

Astrology is but one way of teaching and serving the soul of humanity. It is but one way of helping the entire collective elevate itself to a deeper level of insight and understanding, of illuminating the problems that are of mutual concern.

As described in the previous chapter a remarkable configuration known as the "Capricorn Climax" is unfolding in the heavens as this book is being written. It involves the planets Saturn, Uranus, and Neptune all coming together in the constellation of Capricorn. It involves the North Node moving through the sign of Capricorn, culminating in a solar eclipse on Christmas Eve, 1992, at 2° Capricorn, which just happens to be on the Solar Apex of the solar system, and near the Galactic Center. It preceeds the second longest planetary pair cycle known to humankind, the 1993 conjunction of Uranus and Neptune in 18–20° Capricorn. It is truly one of the most significant celestial configurations to unfold in the history of humankind.

The challenge is there. The astronomical configurations suggest a period of intense spiritual awakening. Individuals are experiencing a spiritual awakening. Groups are experiencing a spiritual awakening. The souls who have been chosen to return upon Earth at this time, who have earned the privilege of incarnating at this most critical time, share a beautiful and common purpose. It is no accident that you are born into this cosmic period.

If we don't save Her, we won't have Her. It all begins with you and me. . ."Lead us not into temptation, but deliver us from evil. . ."

Epilogue: The Trilogy of Evolutionary Astrology

It appears that I am on an 18–19 year cycle correlating to the Moon's North Node in Capricorn. It was 18 years ago, in late 1973–early 1974, when I sat down at the typewriter and channelled the first work on *Evolutionary Astrology: The Journey Of The Soul Through The Horoscope*. I use the term "channel" because I know of no other way to describe the process that happened. It was as if some strange and unknown inspiration energized my entire being. When the first book was completed, this stimulating and "friendly" energy seemed to disappear. It wasn't that I no longer experienced moments of intense inspiration, but rather it felt as if a special part of me had completed its task and left for parts unknown. Eighteen years later, as the Moon's North Node once again entered the constellation of Capricorn, it (I) returned. This same intense passion sought its vehicle for expression, and it was simply a matter of sitting down at the typewriter and letting thoughts take the form of written words in a particular order.

If there is validity to the ideas expressed throughout this book, then I believe a pattern, or cycle, may be unfolding here. The major concepts of Evolutionary Astrology center upon the importance of the angles of the horoscope, and cardinal points of the cosmos. In particular, the I. C. of the natal chart, 0° Capricorn in the tropical zodiac, and conjunction aspects all symbolize the principle of **conception**. They symbolize a point in time (and local space) when the individual and the collective seem most receptive to psychological or spiritual transformation. Shifts in consciousness and changes in the order of things may commence when these points are awakened by the passage of major planets.

The other angles of the natal chart, as well as the other equinoxes and solstices (0° Aries, Cancer and Libra) seem equally important in the evolutionary potentials of both the individual and the collective. To a great extent, so too are the midpoints of these natal angles and seasonal ingresses. When combinations of these astrological phenomena unfold simultaneously, a most fertile climate for meaningful change is presented for both the individual and the collective group (i.e. humankind). For example, when more than one major planet transits over any natal angle or angular midpoint in a short span of time, the potential for significant change in that individual's life is great. In the same manner, whenever two or more significant transits cross over into the seasonal ingress degrees (i.e. 0° Capricorn, Aries, Cancer or Libra) or their midpoints (i.e. 15° Aquarius, Taurus, Leo, or Scorpio), then significant changes are possible on a global level. This is also true when major planetary pair cycles reach any conjunction or 45° multiple aspect formation to one another, (i.e. conjunction, semi-square, square, sesquiquadrate, or opposition). **The most powerful periods for individual inspiration are likely to unfold when major transits either form one of these eighth harmonic aspects to one another, or cross over a seasonal ingress point or midpoint while, at the same time, a major transit crosses over a natal angle or angular midpoint.** At this time the individual is most receptive to a shift in consciousness, while at the same time, the entire body of humankind may also be undergoing an intense period of changing consciousness. The two together can be very powerful on an individual level.

In reviewing the recent past, one can note at least eight major periods of potential breakthroughs in the collective consciousness, according to the principles presented in this work. That is, there were at least eight distinct periods in the last 100 years when major planetary pair cycles of Uranus and beyond reached one of their conjunctions or 45° multiples, and/or major planets transited over one of the equinoxes, solstices, or their midpoints. They were:

1. **1892–1893:** Neptune and Pluto conjunct; Saturn 0° Libra; North Node of Moon 15° Taurus.

2. **1913–1915:** Saturn and Pluto conjunct 0° Cancer; Uranus and Moon's North Node conjunct 15° Aquarius.

3. **1928–1933:** Neptune 45° Pluto; Uranus 0° Aries; Saturn 0° Capricorn; Moon's North Node 15° Taurus.

4. **1942–1944:** Neptune 0° Libra; Saturn 0° Cancer; Moon's North Node 15° Aquarius.

5. **1950–1954:** Uranus 270° Neptune; Uranus 0° Cancer; Saturn 0° Libra; Moon's North Node 15° Aquarius and 0° Capricorn.

6. **1964–1966:** Uranus conjunct Pluto; Neptune 15° Scorpio; Moon's North Node 0° Cancer.

7. **1972–1974:** Uranus 315° Naptune; Pluto 0° Libra; Saturn 0° Cancer; Moon's North Node 0° Capricorn; Kohutek Comet.

8. **1987–1993:** Uranus 45° Pluto; "Capricorn Climax"; Uranus conjunct Neptune; Pluto 15° Scorpio; Uranus 0° Capricorn; Saturn 0° Capricorn; Moon's North Node 15°Aquarius and 0° Capricorn.

A cursory look at the world history will reveal the importance of these periods. Significant, life altering events which influenced the whole of humanity occured during each time frame.

In the early part of the twenty-first century, two periods stand out according to these principles. They are:

1. **2008–2009:** Pluto 0° Capricorn; Saturn 0° Libra; Moon's North Node 15° Aquarius.

2. **2011–2016:** Uranus 90° Pluto; Uranus 45° Neptune; Uranus 0° Aries; Moon's North Node 0° Capricorn; Saturn 15° Scorpio.

Of these two the latter appears the more significant since it contains a 90° aspect of a major planetary pair cycle: Uranus and Pluto. This is the "birthing phase" of the conjunction (conception) of these two planets which occured in 1964–1966. In other words, the ideas and concepts that were conceived in the late 1960's may take on real and lasting form between 2011–2016. In addition, Uranus enters 0° Aries, which is the "birthing phase" of a cycle which began in 1988–1989, when it entered 0° Capricorn (conception). It is also the first "crisis point", or moral dilemma, (45° aspect) of the Uranus/Neptune planetary pair cycle which began in 1992–1993 (conception or 0° aspect).

The first book on Evolutionary Astrology was written in 1973–1974, the seventh of the eight listed significant periods over the last 100 years. It was during the period in which the Moon's North Node was transiting over 0° Capricorn, and Uranus was forming its last 45° semi-square aspect to Neptune. The second book on Evolutionary Astrology is being written in 1991, and will probably come out in 1992, during the eighth and final period. Once again the Moon's North Node is transiting through the tropical constellation of Capricorn, while the powerful Uranus/Neptune planetary pair cycle moves toward its 171-year conjunction. Out of this time frame of intense celestial activity, new concepts in the model of Evolutionary Astrology were conceived, as presented in this book.

If the cycle follows the course of its previous pattern, then I suspect this period of stimulated channelling will soon draw to a close for me personally. A part of myself will feel as if it is leaving once again for parts unknown. Like a son bidding farewell to his father who is about to go to sea in times of old, not knowing if and when he will ever return, I stand on the shore of a personal spiritual frontier with tears in my eyes. The tears are of sadness that comes from the departure of one so dear and close, but also of a deep inner happiness of the memories that we shared together. I know my father must go, and I am stronger for the truth which he so generously handed down to me. Yet deep is my longing for the day when he will return and share new truths with me.

As Capricorn is my father, and Sagittarius the beginning of his long journey to far away lands, so it is that the Moon's North Node becomes my calendar, my hour glass, for understanding my own spiritual agenda. As the Moon's North Node enters Capricorn, my teacher returns; as it enters Sagittarius, he must go in quest of his innermost longings. My love shall not bind, nor shall my needs hold him.

In my heart, I know he is always with me. In my soul, I know his love gives me strength. In my mind, I know he shall return in about 18 years. If this indeed is the order of things, then the final part of the ***Evolutionary Astrology*** trilogy will unfold between 2011–2016, when the North Node once again returns to Capricorn, while the Uranus/Pluto and Uranus/Neptune planetary pair cycles enter important phases of their birthing process. Humankind may be on the verge of another significant awakening and, God willing, my father's ship shall return.